Instructional Design in the Real World: A View from the Trenches

Anne-Marie Armstrong
US Government Printing Office, USA

 Information Science Publishing

Hershey • London • Melbourne • Singapore

Acquisition Editor:	Mehdi Khosrow-Pour
Senior Managing Editor:	Jan Travers
Managing Editor:	Amanda Appicello
Development Editor:	Michele Rossi
Copy Editor:	Maria Boyer
Typesetter:	Jennifer Wetzel
Cover Design:	Lisa Tosheff
Printed at:	Integrated Book Technology

Published in the United States of America by
    Information Science Publishing (an imprint of Idea Group Inc.)
    701 E. Chocolate Avenue, Suite 200
    Hershey PA 17033
    Tel: 717-533-8845
    Fax: 717-533-8661
    E-mail: cust@idea-group.com
    Web site: http://www.idea-group.com

and in the United Kingdom by
    Information Science Publishing (an imprint of Idea Group Inc.)
    3 Henrietta Street
    Covent Garden
    London WC2E 8LU
    Tel: 44 20 7240 0856
    Fax: 44 20 7379 3313
    Web site: http://www.eurospan.co.uk

Library of Congress Cataloging-in-Publication Data

Instructional design in the real world : a view from the trenches /
[edited by] Anne-Marie Armstrong.
    p. cm.
Includes bibliographical references and index.
  ISBN 1-59140-150-X (hardcover) -- ISBN 1-59140-151-8 (ebook)
 1. Instructional systems--Design--Data processing. 2.
Computer-assisted instruction. I. Armstrong, Anne-Marie, 1942-
 LB1028.38.I562 2004
  371.33--dc21

                  2003008769

Paperback ISBN 1-59140-183-6

British Cataloguing in Publication Data
A Cataloguing in Publication record for this book is available from the British Library.

All work contributed to this book is new, previously-unpublished material. The views expressed in this book are those of the authors, but not necessarily of the publisher.

NEW Titles
from Information Science Publishing

Instructional Design in the Real World: A View from the Trenches

Table of Contents

Preface

WHY THIS BOOK, THIS TIME

The theme for this book came to me while I was doing my job — designing instruction. Of course I was multi-tasking. I was waiting for a subject matter expert to call me back about a question I had on an instructor-led course that I was updating and repurposing for the Web. So I read the latest release notes for the 8.1.1 version of another product that had been assigned to me. Its release had been pushed forward two more weeks, and I was hoping the release notes would help me to install this version on my computer. I could then design some hands-on exercises that would actually work. If I couldn't figure out what was happening from the release notes, I would have to call either the IT department or the actual developers. The developers were generally heavily into testing the final product at this stage, and I would have to leave messages on their voice mail.

It was 4:00 p.m. eastern time and I had three hours to kill before delivering the pilot of a blended course describing the new features of an invoice designer program that I had completed. The pilot would be delivered via teleconference to the Hong Kong sales office. I had already checked that the presentation material was on the internal server and available for the participants to download. The evaluations were also prepared and posted on a website to which I would refer when the pilot ended around 10:00 p.m. The phone rang and my boss, who is in Denver where it is two hours earlier, called to remind me that the biweekly instructional design meeting was about to start and I was the designated note taker.

Was this a typical slice of the work for an instructional designer in the real world of business and industry? Positively! Before this moment out of my typical day were the endless product and integration meetings that I attended either in person or via teleconferencing. Also, there had been an impromptu discussion with the document writers who are assigned to the same products for which I am designing the training. Things were a little behind because the day before I spent several hours going over the merits of the latest LMS and LCMS products that the company was interested in purchasing and wanted my feedback on its various merits versus its costs.

This was my tenth year in the instructional design world and I had worked for large and small companies, for contractors, for the government, educational institutions, business and industry. I had designed a computer-based course that provided needed information to Navy personnel whose ratings and jobs had been combined. I provided the architecture and the programming for a simulation of the newest air traffic control equipment. I spent hours studying the habits of airport baggage screeners in order to develop a "Decision Making with Machines" course. I also invested months of time for courses that were never even delivered because they were either superceded or because other means were found for the company to meet its goal. I put automated systems in place to collect data, assessment information, and to compare test results with actual job performance. So I knew that multi-tasking, long hours, endless meetings, constant learning of new things, frustration with products that needed fixes, and waiting for phone calls were pretty typical of an instructional designer.

After all these roles and responsibilities were met, I could return to the job for which my academic courses had prepared me, the challenge and fun of devising instructional strategies that would more efficiently and effectively present needed learning to course participants. I thought that someone has to capture these other parts of slices of time that instructional designers really have. Thus this book that would present real cases, problems, and advice for instructional designers in the real world was born.

THE PROCESS IN THE REAL WORLD

First I should make the reader aware of my general thoughts and biases on how instructional design takes place in the real world. How do I really design instruction? Well, I just get started. There usually isn't much time for thinking or planning. Some things you just have to learn while doing the design. Sure I start with the ADDIE process (Analyze, Design, Develop, Implement, Evaluate). In the first phase I set forth the types of learners for whom the instruction is being designed, the conditions under which it is presented, and the content and skill levels of the proposed outcomes of the instruction. I break the course content down into learning types, verbal information, intellectual skills, cognitive strategies, motor skills, and attitude. Then I send an outline of the course and the learning types to the potential audience and the Subject Matter Experts (SMEs). These people generally are already overworked. Also, administratively, there is no place on their timesheet where they can legitimately report the work they are doing on the analysis. So it is important that this process is streamlined. As it is I might be lucky to receive a 10 to 25% feedback.

While waiting for the learner feedback, I analyze the performance goals and the learning required to accomplish those goals by listing the specific skills needed and then differentiating them by learning type. This forms the basis for the learning analysis report and this is where cognitive strategies can be first mapped into the process. It is also common in my learning reports for objectives and enabling objectives to be written for each skill and for a testing or evaluation plan for each skill assessment to be included. The cognitive strategies are then incorporated at this point so that the objectives and the testing plan both reflect appropriate strategies.

The next step, after incorporating the feedback from the field, should be to produce the design plan. This plan can easily be used to produce storyboards, scripts, or the actual prototypes of the electronic instruction. But in the real world, there is rarely time for this step. Storyboards and scripts are constantly being rewritten as the product versions are completed. So it's jump in and start producing, and then test and try out. Once you can see what it is and what it does — then refine, tweak, and pilot.

Theory helps because it narrows the paths that you take to the result. Learning theory sets boundaries — some to be broken and re-evaluated. Sometimes you find a new path and that is exciting. For me, the design process has a certain amount of feel. It's feeling but it's definitely not groping in the dark. That is, you know what you're feeling because you are standing on the shoulders of the others in your field and that is how you make the needed quick judgments and design decisions. In the real world, that's how it's done.

Now that I have encapsulated the design process that I use, it's time to see how others have also adapted the traditional instructional design process for their own use and for adaptation to other systems. That is, how must ID be changed or how must it adapt to work within other systems?

The environments and systems that affect the ADDIE process and to which it must be adapted include corporations, industry, consulting organizations, health care facilities, church and charitable groups, the military, the government, educational institutions, and others. Its application must be filtered and altered by the environments and the systems where the learning or training takes place.

Most chapters in this book include a case study showing how the application of ID strategies, learning theories, systems theory, management theories and practices, and communication tools and practices are adapted and applied in various environments. Many chapters also contain lessons learned, tool tips, and suggestions for the future.

The chapters in this book are arranged so that they loosely follow the ADDIE process. That is, first the analysis phase is presented. Then, design, development, and implementation are grouped together because that is the real way they are done. Evaluation follows. The final section covers applying new ideas and technologies, and integrating instructional design projects into two systems, a university system and a military system.

ANALYSIS

The first chapter, "Concern Matrix: Analyzing Learners' Needs," by Dr. James A. Pershing and Hee Kap Lee, addresses the traditional learner analysis stage of the ADDIE system. Their approach to analysis emphasizes putting the learner first. Pershing and Lee are very much aware of the fact that in the real world, there are individual needs and organizational needs and that these needs can be either compatible or incompatible. They also point out the importance of differentiating between "felt" needs and "real" needs. Merely identifying the gap between present and desired performance is not enough. If the learners' felt needs are not met, the training will probably not stick. Learners will not accept that which does not fit their values and past experiences. Many Web-based courses suffer from a thorough learner analysis and are seldom used because the social benefits of classroom and group learning are not present.

Chapter II, "Responding to the Learner: Instructional Design of Custom-Built E-Learning," expands upon the learner needs theme presented by Drs. Pershing and Lee. Neil Carrick, an e-learning consultant in Dublin, Ireland, presents a case study that exemplifies the complexities of learner and organizational needs and how they can both be met through the instructional design process. Dr. Carrick's challenge was to produce an instructional solution for both expert and novice workers using non-standard information in a dynamic learning environment. The product also needed to be easily updated by the users themselves. His account of how that solution was designed and implemented shows exactly how an instructional designer must "represent the learner" during this phase. This case study also describes and gives the rationale for the environmental analyses. Frequently environmental analysis is skipped or forgotten because it is assumed that the learning will take place in some standard environment, i.e., the classroom or the worker's desk. But Dr. Carrick's "classroom" was a manufacturing clean room where technicians wore full body suits including headgear that restricted mobility, hearing, and vision.

DESIGN, DEVELOPMENT, AND IMPLEMENTATION

The case study written by Elizabeth Hanlis of the TELUS Centre for Professional Development in Edmonton, Alberta, Canada, is the substance of Chapter III. Her chapter, "Application of an Instructional Design Model for Industry Training: From Theory to Practice," examines, considers, and reflects on the "problems encountered when attempting to apply an instructional design model in the development of two different courses for industry training." Through her eyes, specific issues are addressed including "tight budgets, limited cooperation from subject matter experts, high expectations of clients, major changes to finalized designs," and more. Ms. Hanlis talks about her experiences while designing first a course for a large global health care company and then for a smaller international chemical company. She covers project team roles, needs analysis conducted by managers, designing without a budget, working within a team, and satisfying client desires while still living and working within the available resources. In her summary, Ms. Hanlis provides a great list of "dos and don'ts" from which all instructional designers, new or experienced, will profit.

Jillian Rickertt in Sydney, Australia, expands the view of the design-develop-implement process with a cross-cultural case study in Chapter IV. In "Cultural Wisdom and Hindsight: Instructional Design and Delivery on the Run," Ms. Rickertt takes the reader on a roller coaster ride that dramatizes an instructional designer's need to be quick thinking and flexible throughout the ADDIE process. Although promised preparation time and resources before leaving for India to put together a customized course, the author finds that she must use her entire toolkit of instructional design theories and strategies, designing and developing nightly during a two-week course She also must find new ways of communicating and listening in order to meet her company's goals while she is miles away from her home office. At the end of her saga,

Ms. Rickertt provides a list of lessons learned and suggestions for handling similar situations in the future. This chapter should be required reading for all instructional design students and novices.

A short case study follows. John Lew Cox and Terry R. Armstrong have taught business courses for many years in a traditional university setting. However, the environment suddenly changed and they found that delivering traditional management courses in a rural Finnish setting required instructional redesign. This case study describes that redesign, what happened during delivery, and provides advice to others who find themselves in similar situations.

In Chapter VI, "Applying Contextual Design to Educational Software Development," Mark Notess presents and justifies the need for a different instructional design methodology for those times when context and not content is the goal of the instruction. Contextual design, Mark argues, is suitable when delivery technology and the instruction must be designed simultaneously. "Contextual design," according to Notess, "emphasizes the need to base design decisions on a shared understanding of how real people do real work in real contexts." Much knowledge, he continues, "is embedded in the environment, including tools and processes." Readers can easily follow the step-by-step description of this process and its application to a course where music students need to both listen to and analyze their assignments. Professor Notess's approach is comparable to the user-centered approaches to design advocated by human factors gurus Donald Norman and Jacob Nielson.

EVALUATION

There are three chapters devoted to the evaluation phase of the ADDIE process. Evaluation is that part of the process that in the real world is most likely glossed over or in some cases actually skipped. But each of these chapters demonstrates why the evaluation phase remains an equal and powerful component in the instructional design process.

The case study in Chapter VIII resembles some of the more traditional evaluations of instructional design, such as one might find in academic research studies. A group from the Belgium Center for Instructional Psychology and Technology, Geraldine Clarebout, Jan Elen, Joost Lowyck, Jef Van den Ende, and Erwin Van den Enden, evaluated a computer-based, expert system training program called KABISA. This program was designed to help medical students develop their diagnostic reasoning skills. The evaluation used two approaches to answer its questions. To find out if students actually used the embedded help functions and which path the students used in order to reach their diagnoses, log files were examined and evaluators used think-aloud protocols. Experts were used to score the errors, deviations from criterion paths, and the seriousness of the students' diagnoses. The result of this study provided evidence that more attention should have been given during the analysis phase of this "expert system." They found, for example, that the difficulty level of the program was not adaptable to the students and that the feedback did not encourage them to adopt problem-solving processes.

The next chapter contrasts with the previous classical academic study from Belgium. "Guerilla Evaluation: Adapting to the Terrain and Situation," by Tad Waddington, Bruce Aaron, and Rachael Sheldrick, provides insight into the evaluation process within the unique world of training. The perceptiveness of this team provides practical advice for achieving effective evaluation within corporate systems where results are measured both by performance and return on investment (ROI). Their experiences have led to a set of tactics that are applicable to many situations and environments. They explain the value of each of those tactics and how they arrived at their "V-model" that bridges "local business context, best practices in evaluation, and the shift in emphasis from traditional training activity to performance improvement." Communication, timing, and information sharing are key to survival in an atmosphere where resources are scarce, budgets limited, and the stakeholders make decisions based on the data collected and reported. Dr. Waddington, Dr. Aaron, and Ms. Sheldrick present cases from their experiences to illustrate their four key strategies: leveraging statistics, leveraging available data, contracting for needed skills, and using technology to save time and money.

The final chapter in this evaluation section proposes various standards to be used for evaluating instruction. Noel Estabrook and Peter Arashiro from Michigan Virtual University have developed comprehensive standards that can be applied to online instruction in order to answer the important questions of what, if anything, was learned and how well it was learned. Their standards are based on their variety of experiences with educational, manufacturing, and government systems, and their goal is to "help identify, develop, and apply sound and appropriate instructional design standards" in order to "produce better courses" that are efficient and appealing. The result is over 100 e-learning standards in the areas of technology, usability, accessibility, and design. Drs. Estabrook and Arashiro remind us that instruction is both a science and an art, and emphasize the former. Additionally the chapter provides a case study in applying these standards to the development of an online course. Ultimately, they show how the standards can also be used in making decisions about building, fixing, using, keeping, and/or purchasing courses. This information is extremely useful to designers who find that their employers rely on them to be able to recommend or make informed decisions in these areas.

NEW METHODOLOGIES AND SYSTEM INTEGRATION

The final section of the book deals with new ideas and methodologies and system integration. The previous chapters have poignantly illustrated the need for instructional designers to be analytical, flexible, and creative within the ADDIE process. These last chapters provide additional resources, strategies, and lessons for the real world.

Reusable Learning Objects (RLOs) and Reusable Information Objects (RIOs) have the potential to update and enhance the ADDIE work process by using technology to flatten out "knowledge silos." Pam T. Northrup, Karen L. Rasmussen, and David B. Dawson address this issue in their chapter, "Designing and Reusing Learning Objects to Streamline WBI Development." Their project applies RLOs and RIOs to the design of an online teachers' professional development program for a local school district that could also be reused in other districts throughout their state. After investigating different models, they found that their program will allow learners to "customize their own knowledge paths by selecting RIOs and RLOs that most closely align to their immediate instructional needs." They explain how the RIO components of content, practice, and assessment are used, assigned to a cognitive level, and tagged. The RIOs can then be combined along with Overviews and Summaries to form RLOs. Their team included designers and subject matter experts who worked together to enter, review, revise, and approve the RIOs that became the basis for an educator's professional development Web-based system customizable for schools and school districts within the State of Florida.

Systems integration is addressed in the final two chapters.

The implications of integrating Internet-delivered courses into university systems is addressed by Vassilios Dagdilelis, who teaches at the University of Macedonia, Thessaloniki, in Greece. Dr. Dagdilelis speaks about the wide range of Information and Communications Technologies (ICTs) that must be integrated into university systems and of the problems thus far encountered. He describes the university ecosystem that is characterized by a history of rich learning environments, the necessity to conduct research, and the expectations of holding and creating new knowledge. He also recognizes the larger systems or tertiary institutions within which each university system is functioning. These tertiary institutions, although existing in different nations and states, tend to have homogeneous reactions. Globalization, instant communications, and academic drift ensure that as large, prestigious universities adopt certain aspects of ICTs, the less well-known institutions will adopt the same strategies without "necessarily passing through the intermediary trial stages." For this and other reasons, Dr. Dagdilelis believes that the ADDIE methodology needs some adjustments. He believes that ADDIE was originally intended for use when the audience was known and analyzable, and the interaction of the instruction with the learner was visible. He advocates the expansion of ADDIE so both of these constructs, the audience of the learning and the interaction of the instruction, can be approached by instructional designers in ways that are compatible with the new reality of the system.

Instructional design has many of its roots in the military, and it is fitting that this last chapter speaks to another type of integration, this one within the military training system. Mary F. Bratton-Jeffery, of the Naval Education and Training Command, and Arthur B. Jeffery, from the University of South Alabama, propose integrating business models with military instructional design and training. The business model that they propose for use with ADDIE is the Value Chain model. The result is a technique they call Quality Function Deployment (QFD). Stakeholder requirements and instructional imperatives or needs are identified and strengths of their relationships assessed. After this, some tradeoffs might have to be made or alternative designs proposed. A value analysis is completed and the no/go decision is made. The same QFD process can then be iterated using the instructional imperatives with instructional strategies and/or with instructional tools. They believe that combining the best practices of both worlds will improve the training because the stakeholders' needs and requirements drive the product. Again, they are not advocating losing the ADDIE system, but expanding it.

There is a tools section in the appendix. These are some of the tools that I have designed and used in my 10-plus years of designing instruction. They may prove helpful to students and new designers.

CONCLUSION

The works presented in this book are not comprehensive of instructional design as practiced in the real world, but are, I believe, representative. Some chapters that I reviewed were considered but could not be included because businesses and organizations have exclusive rights and consider the products of their designers to be proprietary. This is understandable but regrettable since it is my belief that information improves as it is shared. A friend and fellow instructional designer, who I met while editing this book, has developed her own theory about designing training. Luisa Cardenas, who works for a national non-profit organization, calls it the Penguin Theory:

> *How much about penguins would you like to learn?* the designer asked.
> *Excuse me?* was the reply.
> *There are volumes written about penguins. I need some parameters.*
> The designer smiled. *Well, what do you think? How much do you want to know?* the designer asked, still smiling.
> *Enough to know how to do my job,* was the answer.
> *Ah, now we're getting somewhere!* concluded the designer.

Hopefully the chapters in this book will provide the readers with what they need to do their jobs.

Acknowledgments

The editor would like to acknowledge the help of all involved in the review and preparation of the book, and a further special note of thanks goes to all the staff at Idea Group Publishing whose help throughout the whole process has been invaluable.

Special thanks to Louisa Cardenas of the American Red Cross of Greater Los Angeles for allowing me to use her "Penguin Theory," to Stacy Boyle and Rathna Patel of NETg, and to my husband Terry who has always served as my mentor.

Finally, I want to thank all the authors for their insights, patience, and excellent contributions to this book. Thank you all for believing in my idea and supporting this book to the end.

Anne-Marie Armstrong
US Government Printing Office, Washington, DC, USA

Chapter I

Concern Matrix: Analyzing Learners' Needs

James A. Pershing
Indiana University, USA

Hee Kap Lee
Indiana University, USA

ABSTRACT

Instructional development (ID) is a systematic and systemic process used in developing education and training programs. In the analysis phase, instructional developers need to account for the characteristics and particular needs of learners in order to design useful instructional interventions. It is very important to ascertain which learners' characteristics are most crucial in instructional decision making. However, current ID models seem to advocate a pedagogical approach that treats the learner submissively during the analysis phase of the ADDIE process (Knowles, 1984). There is no active communication between instructional developers and learners during the learner analysis process. In-depth analysis identifying learners' concerns and perceptions are usually not considered. In this chapter, we will introduce for use by instructional developers a learner analysis matrix that incorporates learners' levels of concerns and perceptions at the personal and organizational levels. The learner analysis matrix can be used to identify four areas of learner concern: (1) individual compatible, (2) individual incompatible, (3) organizational compatible, and (4) organizational incompatible.

THE IMPORTANCE OF LEARNERS

Instructional development (ID) is a systematic and systemic process used in designing and developing education and training programs. There are many ID models that have been created; however, most have as a main element a process consisting of five activities or stages called ADDIE: analysis, design, development, implementation, and evaluation. In the first phase, analysis, learners' learning needs and characteristics are analyzed (Kemp, 2000). In order to successfully implement a training intervention, instructional designers must know the specific characteristics of the target group of people. It is very important to ascertain which learners' characteristics are most crucial in instructional decision making (Molenda, Pershing, & Reigeluth, 1996).

Most ID models address the importance of learner analysis. For example, Molenda, Pershing, and Reigeluth (1996) recognize three areas of learner analysis in their business impact ID model: entry competencies, general characteristics, and learning styles. Kemp, Morrison, and Ross (1994) advocate in their model that learner analysis is the second procedure in developing an instructional program. Also, Heinich, Molenda, Russel, and Smaldino (1996) present their five-step linear ID model and emphasize that analyzing learners is the first task with three sub-areas: general characteristics, entry competencies, and learning styles. Rothwell and Kazanas (1992) identify three basic categories of learner characteristics in their 10 steps of the instructional design process: (1) situation-related characteristics, (2) decision-related characteristics, and (3) learner-related characteristics. Smith and Lagan's (1993) model locates analyzing the learning context as the first phase of ID. Kemp (2000) suggests learner analysis consists of the learners' emotional, physical, psychological characteristics, family and neighborhood relations, as well as detailed personal and academic information.

Hence, learner analysis among several ID models means reviewing the learners' characteristics before designing an education or training program. Usually, the models indicate that three types of information are gathered in learner analysis:

- general characteristics (e.g., grade level, gender, job or position, and cultural and socioeconomic factors);

- specific entry competencies (e.g., knowledge, technical vocabulary, attitudes, and misconception);
- learning style (e.g., anxiety, aptitude, visual and auditory preference, etc.).

NEW PERSPECTIVES OF LEARNER ANALYSIS

Current ID models advocate a pedagogical approach that treats the learner submissively during the analysis phase of the ADDIE process (Knowles, 1984). In fact, most ID models and practices were created and developed under the industrial age paradigm. In the industrial age, the economic system resembled a pyramid structure, in which a large number of people did the routine and simple work following rigid work rules and job classifications. Workers were guided on the job by standard procedures and their work performance was controlled by a pre-established sequence of steps (Reich, 1991). Training under this paradigm is much like the mass-production manufacturing system. Learners were considered identical, homogeneous raw materials in a standard process of educational production (Cameron, 1996). They were considered as an empty vessel that only needed filling. Hence, there was no active communication between instructional developers and learners during the learner analysis process.

Recently, however, several scholars have begun to advocate an approach to learner analysis that is different. First of all, many scholars agree that employees' knowledge, the information they are able to access, and creativity are crucial factors to add value in the information age. Therefore, it is crucial for an organization to discover how to tap people's commitment and capacity to learn at all levels (Senge, 1990). People in an organization, called 'knowledge workers' by Drucker (1993), are crucial assets who are collectively responsible for the performance of an organization. They need to know why they need to learn before attending an education or training program (Knowles, 1984; Knowles, Holton, & Swanson, 1998). They come to an educational activity with a greater volume and a different quality of experience. They are motivated to learn to the extent that they perceive that learning will help them perform tasks or deal with problems that they confront in their life situations. Therefore, a new paradigm of instruction has changed from standardization to customization, and from a focus on presenting material to a focus on making sure that learners' needs are met (Reigeluth & Nelson, 1997). Instructional designers have begun to recognize that the set of intrinsic needs held by the learners involve a change process that plays an important role in the proposed education or training intervention (Hall & Hord, 1978; Tofaya, 1983). If learners perceive that the value of a proposed intervention is incompatible with their values or past experiences, then it is difficult for them to accept the intervention. Hence, learners should be carefully analyzed in the beginning of the ID process. Unfortunately, there is no existing framework that analyzes learners' characteristics as well as learners' intrinsic needs such as concerns and perceptions.

COMPREHENSIVE LEARNER ANALYSIS

Need can be defined as the gap between desired and current status (Kaufman & English, 1975). It incorporates two sets of needs: felt and real need. The former is personal feelings and emotions toward a proposed change, while the latter tries to identify the gap between standard and current levels of performance in light of knowledge, skills, and competencies (Monett, 1977; Archambault, 1957). For a long time, real need has been emphasized by instructional designers. However, research indicates that the learners' subjective feelings, emotions, and attitudes, as well as their concerns and perceptions, are critically important for buy-in for the proposed intervention process (Hall & Hord, 1978; Ertmer, 1999; Lee, 2001). Disregarding the learners' felt needs results in learners' resistance to or delaying buy-in for the proposed intervention (Kotter, 1998).

Hence, it is necessary for instructional designers to identify learners' characteristics in a comprehensive way, identifying two sets of needs. The comprehensive needs analysis process consists of two dimensions that will help to assure the participation of learners in the design, development, and implementation of the proposed interventions. The two are:

1.   Is the proposed intervention compatible with the learner's personal values?
2.   Are concerns and needs addressed for both individuals in the target audience and the organization as a whole?

The first dimension refers to the learners' perceptions and concerns about the compatibility of the proposed intervention with learners' personal values. If the proposed intervention is not compatible with learners' current value system, then the change will be hard to implement (Rogers, 1995; Pershing, An, & Lee, 2000). However, the compatibility of an innovation with values will not guarantee adoption of the proposed intervention. Even when an intervention is compatible with current values, the adoption of an intervention usually takes quite a long time because of other barriers, for example, lack of organizational support or resources.

The second dimension refers to the level of the concerns. Concerns of individuals in the target audience are different from those of the organization, so they should be addressed separately. Based on the two dimensions, compatibility of intervention and levels of concerns, the following four areas of concerns are identified: (1) individual compatible, (2) individual incompatible, (3) organizational compatible, and (4) organizational incompatible (see Figure 1).

Individual-Compatible Area

Even when the value of an intervention is compatible with the target audience's values, the individuals of the target audience may not accept the intervention as planned for several reasons, including fear of the unknown and lack of information or knowledge required to implement the intervention.

The major strategy for addressing this area of concern involves preparing a detailed learning plan. These concerns can usually be overcome by providing well-organized training programs, job aids, and information sharing. Analysts have to identify the target audience's current level of knowledge necessary for implementing the proposed intervention, and thus set up suitable strategies for closing the gap between the current and desired level.

Figure 1: Two Dimensions of Learner Analysis

	Compatible	**Incompatible**
Individual	Individual-Compatible	Individual-Incompatible
Organization	Organization-Compatible	Organization-Incompatible

Individual-Incompatible Area

People are not usually willing to spend much time on a change they do not yet value (Dormant, 1986). If the values of an intervention are not compatible with the individual target audience's values or belief systems, then the intervention is difficult for them to adopt (Hall & Hord, 1978; Holloway, 1998). Also an innovation's inconsistency with past practices is a critical barrier to adoption (Dormant, 1986). Ertmer (1999) called these types of concerns second-order barriers. These concerns cause more difficulties because they are less tangible, more personal, and deeply ingrained (Kerr, 1989). Skepticism of the intervention, suspicion about the benefits of the intervention, and comfort with the traditional way rather than new or innovative ways are several examples of this kind of concern. If the resulting resistance is not addressed, then it can impact the audience negatively throughout the diffusion process.

Therefore, analysts have to identify the root cause of this area of concern by asking questions such as what are the target audiences' perceptions toward the intervention, and if they are negative, what is the main reason for the negativity and how it can be overcome? Several instructional designers mention that individual persuasion is a useful strategy to address this area of concern by providing counseling and consultation sessions. For example, Rogers (1995) indicated that person-to-person communication channels are important to address this area of concern. Dormant (1986) suggests that change agents should be counselors who draw out concerns, and listen to and clarify the target audiences' needs and interests.

Organizational-Compatible Area

Organizational-compatible area is extrinsic to the target audience. An intervention that is compatible with current organizational values is sometimes not accepted by the target audience as designed because of a lack of organizational support. Examples are a lack of organizational incentives and benefits, or inadequate technical and administrative support (Gilbert, 1996). Ertmer (1999) calls these types of concerns first-order barriers and concludes that they can be significant obstacles to achieving diffusion of the change.

This area of concern is relatively easy to ascertain and to eliminate if addressed carefully and in a timely fashion during the intervention implementation processes (Fisher, Wilmore, & Howell, 1994). Analysts should ask members of target audiences about the essential supporting strategies from the organization. Allocating money, assigning resources, and providing technical and administrative support, including incentives or motivational systems, are essential elements for ensuring the intervention is adopted (Foa, 1993; Ertmer, 1999).

Organizational-Incompatible Area

Education and training interventions sometimes produce conflicts with organizational values, cultures, or climates. Organizational context and cultural incompatibility are critical issues in an intervention implementation process (Hall & Hord, 1978; Ertmer, 1999). For example, Moore and Mizuba (1968) mention the concept of cultural incompatibility in their study, "Water Boiling in a Peruvian Town." They found that the training intervention was not adopted because it was incompatible with the experiences of the local villagers. The lesson of this story has to be remembered when one is introducing innovation into any type of institution.

The success of an intervention is influenced by the compatibility of the value of the intervention with the cultural values and assumptions of the organization. Analysts should work for incompatibility between the values associated with an intervention and the values of an organization. An organizational culture is a crucial reality that those seeking to introduce change must confront. For this, analysts must assess the culture before attempting any intervention. Then, they should adopt useful strategies for introducing and implementing the proposed change. Collaboration is the most useful strategy to address this area of concern. For example, creating a vision statement together and sharing intervention-related experiences with individuals in the target audience are helpful strategies. Another strategy is to arrange several sharing events in order to facilitate collaborative work among individuals of the target audiences. Through these events, individuals in an organization share their ideas with other people, which can facilitate change in an organizational culture.

CONCLUDING REMARKS

An educational or training intervention requires change. Change encounters difficulties when it disregards the target audiences' perception and concerns. To implement change successfully, two sets of needs, felt and real needs, on the part of learners should be ascertained before introducing an instructional intervention. Comprehensive needs analysis is a process of scanning the target audiences' reactions or attitudes toward the proposed intervention based on the two dimensions of the concerns: compatibility of an intervention with the target audiences' values, and two levels of concerns. Such an approach provides a systemic and systematic way of identifying the gap between the desired level and the current level in knowledge, skills, and attitudes in light of the four areas of the concern matrix.

REFERENCES

Archambault, R.D. (1957). The concept of need and its relation to certain aspects of educational theory. *Harvard Educational Review,* 27(1), 38-62.

Cameron, D. (1996). The role of teachers in establishing a quality-assurance system. *Phi Delta Kappa,* 78(3), 225-257.

Dormant, D. (1986). The ABCDs of managing change. *Introduction to Performance Technology* (pp. 238-256). Washington, DC: National Society for Performance and Instruction.

Drucker, P.F. (1993). *Post Capitalist Society.* New York: Harper Collins.

Ertmer, P.A. (1999). Addressing first and second order barriers to change: Strategies for technology integration. *Educational Technology Research & Development,* 47(4), 47-61.

Fisher, C., Wilmore, F., & Howell, R. (1994). Classroom technology and the new pedagogy. *Journal of Computing in Childhood Education,* 5, 119-129.

Foa, L.J. (1993). Technology and change: Composing a four-part harmony. *Educom Review,* 28(2), 27-30.

Gilbert, S.W. (1996). Making the most of a slow revolution. *Change,* 28(2), 10-23.

Hall, G.E. & Hord, S.M. (1978). *Change in Schools: Facilitating the Process.* Albany, NY: State University of New York Press.

Heinrich, R., Molenda, M., Russel, J., & Smaldino, S. (1996). *Instructional Media and Technologies for Learning (5th ed.).* New York: Macmillan.

Holloway, R.E. (1998). Diffusion and adoption of educational technology: A critique of research design. In Jonassen, D.J. (Ed.), *Handbook of Research in Educational Technology* (pp. 1107-1133). New York: Macmillan.

Kaufman, R.A. & English, F.W. (1975). *Needs Assessment: A Focus for Curriculum Development.* Washington, DC: Association for Supervision and Curriculum Development.

Kemp, J., Morrison, G.R., & Ross, S.M. (1994). *Designing Effective Instruction.* New York: Merrill.

Kemp, J.E. (2000). An interactive guidebook for designing education in the 21st century. *Techno Press of the Agency for Instructional Technology (AIT) and Association for Educational Communications and Technology (AECT).*

Kerr, S.T. (1989). Technology, teachers, and the search for school reform. *Educational Technology Research and Development,* 37(4), 5-17.

Knowles, M.S. (1984). *Andragogy in Action.* San Francisco, CA: Jossey-Bass.

Knowles, M.S., Holton III, E.F., & Swanson, R.A. (1998). *The Adult Learner (5ᵗʰ ed.).* Houston, TX: Gulf Publications.

Kotter, J.P. (1998). Leading change: Why transform effects fail. *Harvard Business Review on Change* (pp. 1-20). Boston, MA: Harvard Business School Publishing.

Lee, H. (2001). *A Comprehensive Innovation Diffusion Model in a Higher Educational Setting: Post Facto Formative Research.* Unpublished Doctoral Dissertation, Indiana University, Bloomington, Indiana.

Molenda, M., Pershing, J., & Reigeluth, C.M. (1996). Designing instructional systems. In Craig, R.L. (Ed.), *The ASTD Training and Development Handbook (4ᵗʰ ed.)* (pp. 266-293). New York: McGraw-Hill.

Monette, M.L. (1977). The concept of educational need: An analysis of selected literature. *Adult Education, 27*(2), 116-127.

Moore, S. & Mizuba, K. (1968, November). Innovation diffusion: A study in credibility. *The Educational Forum, 33*(1), 181-185.

Pershing, J. A., An, J. & Lee, H. (2000, June). Why do well-planned performance improvement innovations fall? The importance of perception analysis. Paper presented at the *International Society for Performance Improvement Culture & Change Management Conference*, Washington, D.C.

Reich, R.B. (1991). *The Work of Nations: Preparing Ourselves for 21st Century Capitalism.* New York: Alfred A. Knopf.

Reigeluth C.M. & Nelson, L.M. (1997). New paradigm of ISD. In Branch, R.M. & Minor, B.B. (Eds.), *Educational Media and Technology Yearbook* (pp. 24-35). Englewood, CO: Libraries Unlimited.

Rogers, E.M. (1995). *Diffusion of Innovations (4th ed.).* New York: The Free Press.

Rothwell, W.J. & Kazanas, H.C. (1992). *Mastering the Instructional Design Process: A Systematic Approach.* San Francisco, CA: Jossey-Bass.

Senge, P.M. (1990). *The Fifth Discipline: The Art and Practice of the Learning Organization.* New York: Doubleday.

Smith, P.L. & Lagan, T.J. (1993). *Instructional Design.* New York: Macmillan.

Tofaya, W.L. (1983). Needs assessment: Key to organizational change. *Journal of Police Science Administration,* 11(3), 303-310.

Chapter II

Responding to the Learner: Instructional Design of Custom-Built E-Learning

Neil Carrick

Instructional Design and E-Learning Consultant, Ireland

ABSTRACT

This chapter argues that the principal role of instructional design is to represent and advocate the needs of learners. It stresses the importance of needs analysis and requirements gathering in instructional design. As a case study to support these contentions, the chapter describes the instructional design of custom-built e-learning for adult learners working in the factory of a manufacturing plant. The case study reveals that the true value of instructional design lies in a learner-centered approach that prioritizes ease of use and facilitates learner control.

INTRODUCTION

The learner is the main beneficiary of sound instructional design. Understanding the link between the learner's needs and the design of instruction is vital to the effectiveness of that instruction. This chapter focuses on the importance of needs' analysis and requirements' gathering in meeting the needs of learners. It describes the design of custom-built e-learning for adult learners in a unique working environment. An analysis of that design demonstrates how to safeguard learners' needs and requirements. It reveals that the true value of instructional design lies in a learner-centered approach that prioritizes ease of use and facilitates learner control.

The chapter has three sections:

1. A brief discussion of the benefits and demands of creating custom-built learning
2. A case study based on the experience of designing job aids for use in a manufacturing environment illustrating those benefits and demands—the burden of the chapter
3. A summary of the lessons learned and the implications for instructional designers

The discussion raises questions and considerations for instructional designers including:

•   Whether to opt for custom-built versus off-the-shelf e-learning
•   How to place the learner at the center of instructional and technical design
•   How to allow the learner greater control (i.e., non-prescriptive learning)
•   The need to understand learner motivation
•   Why and how to determine the level of learner maturity (e.g., experienced versus novice learners)
•   How to provide a context in which to place new learning
•   The need to design an adaptable system that can be maintained by the user

When building customized e-learning as an instructional designer you do not have the luxury of imposing your ideal of a learner. You must consult, analyze a group of learners' needs, and build a solution that satisfies them. If you do not, the feedback will be immediate and negative. Designing a solution is not enough; a solution is only viable when it is used. Therefore, the fundamental requirement of any instructional design strategy is to concentrate on what learners need (to do their job). You cannot easily dictate to an adult learner. It is better to give guidance (where appropriate) and place him or her in a position of authority and control. If you do not, it is likely that the learner will, in any event, seize control and switch off. With e-learning it is especially hard to impose the discipline of the classroom. Moreover, it may not be desirable or necessary.

THE VALUE OF CUSTOM-BUILT LEARNING

Custom-built learning is instruction with specific learners and a specific learning environment in mind. To ensure that it meets the demands of both learners and the environment in which they learn, the instructional designer must perform a detailed needs analysis. Needs analysis involves talking to the learners who will use the instruction, as well as to the Subject Matter Experts (SMEs) who provide the core knowledge, and then assessing the best way to deliver learning to them. This is in sharp relief to off-the-shelf e-learning products that are mass produced for a mass audience. Off-the-shelf courseware presumes a standard audience and standard condition (workers at their desks working on computers linked by a local area network in a standard corporate environment, for example). The learning is designed and built for mass appeal and mass usage, usually according to an instructional design system and production process that suit above all the designer and producer. This is supply-side learning, driven by the lure of a mass market, with emphasis on reusability (for the producer as much as the learner). The producer of call center training, for example, hopes to have the product used not just in one call center, but potentially in all call centers. Naturally, the customers' concerns are evaluated, otherwise there would be no sales. However, the impetus is towards a generic, standard product that may contain some customizable features, but by and large operates in the same way irrespective of learning environment or learner. Once the sale is made (usually to a training manager), as far as the off-the-shelf courseware manufacturer is concerned the training can sit on the shelf. There is little need for follow-up evaluation, and the distance between learner and designer is so great that feedback is but a faint echo.

Nevertheless off-the-shelf products (with their economies of scale) do suit some areas of learning. If you are teaching someone a software application that is in wide usage and comes in standard versions, there is little need for a custom-built approach. Yet, not all organizations approach learning in the same way and many of them have distinctive practices which they want their e-learning to reflect. No wonder then that many organizations now want e-learning that suits their distinctive needs. Meeting those needs requires more in-depth analysis and ultimately places a greater burden on instructional design.

The real value of custom-built learning lies in finding a solution that matches the specific need of the client and that allows the client some control over the implementation and maintenance of that solution. It involves the creation of an intimate partnership between the supplier and the user. The process of design in such circumstances is more consultative than directive. A dialogue is established and the solution evolves from a series of suggestions and responses.

That process of needs analysis and requirements gathering brings the learning solution closer to learners, putting them first (rather than theory, technology, etc.). The aptness of custom-built learning replaces the expediency of off-the-shelf learning.

CASE STUDY: WHOM TO TRAIN AND WHY

The case study discussed here involves a specialized audience and environment where an off-the-shelf solution (even if there were one) would not work. It would just be too inflexible for an audience that requires non-standard information, a dynamic learning environment, and a product that can be easily updated by the users themselves. The only way to meet those demands is to make, rather than buy a solution. The account of how that solution was designed and implemented provides a useful insight into the process of customizing learning and the integral role of instructional design in that process.

The solution was devised for a large, multinational, semi-conductor manufacturer by an organization within the company that specializes in the design and implementation e-learning. The demand for new training or an information system was driven by the force of circumstances. The manufacturing plant is in the process of reorganization. Some experienced technicians are being moved to other processes and other plants to learn new skills. The concern was that their removal would lead to a marked reduction in expertise and hence job performance. The challenge was to ensure that the performance of tasks continued at a sufficiently high standard and that the loss of expertise would be minimized.

The manufacture of computer chips involves a high degree of automation but still requires the presence of technicians for two key areas: tool maintenance and trouble-shooting. Maintenance generally involves routine procedures. Nevertheless some of these procedures are infrequent, occurring only three or six months, and some of them are irregular, occurring only when a problem is discovered with the machine. Trouble-shooting is by definition an irregular activity and requires the ability to diagnose as well as resolve problems.

The tasks performed by the technicians are highly practical. Technicians acquire skills through constant, supervised work on the tools in question. This hands-on, working experience is not easily taught in a classroom. As a result on-the-job training forms a significant part of the instruction of new and experienced technicians. A so-called 'buddy system' teams inexperienced techs with more experienced counterparts in a relationship that resembles an apprenticeship.[1] Once technicians are able to perform a task to the satisfaction of their seniors and peers, they receive certification confirming that they have reached a desired and measurable level of competence.

That is where the formal training ceases. It is not, however, where learning stops. Informal and *ad hoc* training continue to ensure the technician gains experience and performance levels increase. It is here where experience counts most. Frequently a newly qualified technician will turn to a more experienced colleague for advice and instruction. This interaction is critical, but informal. It is not documented, for much of the information imparted by the experienced tech resides only in the head of the tech. The information may be subtle and verge on the intangible. While all work processes are documented, certain approaches (ways of doing a specific task) are not. These are acquired over time, with practice and with increased confidence in one's own ability. Judgment is learned, not taught.

Let's look at the role of the expert here. Expertise is not simply about attaining a high level of knowledge and performance for oneself. Expertise also plays a role in the delivery of information. An expert can judge what a non-expert needs to know and how much he or she needs to know. The delivery of such informal knowledge is different from the provision of formal knowledge. Experts provide quick and ready access to information (sometimes called 'just enough, just in time'). Contrast this approach with the reams of official, standard documentation which details processes and correct procedures. It often runs to hundreds of pages with minimal indexing through which technicians might have to trawl to find what they are looking for. The expert provides the short cut which is missing from the documentation. Experts obviate the need for searching and discrimination. They not only know what you need to know, but they also know how to find what you need to know.

Both paper and electronic copies of mechanical and process documents exist, but the electronic copies are read-only for security and operational reasons and cannot be easily customized or otherwise manipulated for individual use. The documents are mostly text with occasional, highly detailed, and complex line drawings. The diagrams do not show the tool *in situ*, because they are specific to the tool and not to the plant or to the specific processes that run on the tool. They are largely descriptive; they are not specifically designed for the instruction of technicians. Although available in electronic format, the illustrations are flat and non-dynamic. Moreover, technicians are actively encouraged to consult documentation rather than attempt to memorize or develop mnemonics for long and complex lists of tasks. The tasks themselves may be easy to perform in isolation, but what is critical and more complex is the prescribed order in which tasks are to be attempted. Failure to repeat the order can result in the faulty completion of a procedure which, in turn, renders a tool non-operational.

The difference between standard, approved, and documented practice and actual performance techniques is worth emphasizing. The tasks carried even by experienced technicians are generally routine and follow set procedures. To ensure maximum efficiency and standard practice, little room is left in the procedures for alternative methods or innovation. Nevertheless, certain tacit discrepancies exist in the day-to-day performance of set tasks. These tacit practices result from the experience of knowing what will work (well) and what will not in a given set of circumstances.

Furthermore, experience extends not only to a technician's own performance but also to his or her evaluation of the performance and skills of other technicians. Experienced technicians are able to judge where skills are wanting and where gaps in training lie. There are forums set up in which they can share their experiences with other technicians from different shifts within a plant and with technicians working on the same processes in other plants. Sometimes changes are made to procedures based on their recommendations. Frequently they provide new information in the form of documents which are available on shared drives on computers or in Xeroxed hard-copies. This information needs to be assimilated by colleagues, quickly.

That information, although piecemeal, is vital in the successful operation of a machine or in reducing the time that a tool spends out of commission. Nevertheless, although often documented, the information cannot be easily accessed. It is not detailed systematically. To introduce it into the system requires a thorough knowledge of existing procedures to ensure technicians know where it belongs. This informal, additional information demands both context and organization. If experienced technicians leave an area, there is a risk that they not only take away their knowledge of how to do a particular job, but that they also take away the knowledge of where and how their less experienced colleagues can acquire the knowledge they require to do the job. Hence there is a potential gap in both information and metadata (that is, the context for that information) that has to be bridged.

For both provision and design of training, experience is thus at a premium. Reliance on experienced technicians is likewise at a premium, not only in the performance of their own jobs but also in ensuring the performance of other technicians. So the decision to reduce the number of technicians in a given area results consequently not only in the loss of actual expertise, but also in the loss of potential learning. Moreover, the removal of experienced technicians places a greater burden on those who stay. The experienced technicians who remain will be required to answer more queries as well as trying to ensure that less experienced colleagues enjoyed the attention required to gain experience quickly. So access to the remaining expertise may be compromised.

The challenge to our e-learning group was to find a way in which the loss of that expertise could be minimized. This involves not only detailing and organizing the knowledge that would leave with the technicians, but also providing a way in which those experienced technicians who remain can share their knowledge more widely and effectively, thus allowing them more time to do their own critical work.

Time is also a factor. To minimize the effect of loss of experience leading to serious loss of performance, experience needs to be acquired swiftly and effectively. As most of this experience is job related, it can only be replaced on the job and at the tool. Classroom and even desktop training are too inflexible to meet that demand. They require techs to leave the factory at a critical period in performance. Information needs to be available at the point of work, which in this case means at the tool within the factory, in a clean room environment. And that environment presents a whole host of different e-learning challenges.

CASE STUDY: WHERE TO LEARN

If you are to provide effective on-the-job training, it needs to be on or near the job. For many instructional designers and learners, that is not a problem. Many office workers have a computer on their desk, connected to a local area network or the Internet, which can provide them with information and indeed training at the press of a button or the click of a mouse. In this particular case, however, those conditions do not exist. Indeed conditions in the manufacturing environment actively hinder (e-)learning. As a result the instructional designer has to take into account a very special set of learning circumstances.

The tools that produce the microchips are housed in a factory, but it is a factory unlike most. The chips produced are so small (invisible to the naked eye) that even the smallest amount of dust particles in the process can ruin them. Hence the tools have to operate in a clean-room environment, which is cleaner even than an operating theatre. Technicians have to work in this clean room, but to avoid creating particles and contaminating production, they are required to wear special full-body suits and glasses. The suits naturally restrict mobility and involve some discomfort. The suits can make them hot. The headgear and extraneous noise mean that hearing is not optimal. Bear in mind also that technicians work 12-hour shifts and can easily spend the majority of that time in the clean room.

It is not only the working conditions, but the physical infrastructure itself that also presents an impediment to learning. The manufacturing area is designed primarily to house tools to ensure their smooth and effective operation. It is not designed for communication or learning. The floor space is devoted to the business of manufacture, allowing room for machinery and the necessary movement of people, but not the establishment of desks, chairs, let alone a classroom. Some of the areas run processes that are light sensitive, so subdued and colored lighting is used, which can make reading difficult.

If and when technicians need to leave the clean area, they must remove and discard the suits and then don another suit when they return. It makes retrieval, of information outside the factory, time consuming and onerous. Moreover ordinary paper-based materials cannot not be admitted into the clean environment unless they have been specially treated or laminated.

Nevertheless, the factory does contain computers that are linked to a network. The obvious solution is therefore to use this network to deliver information and training electronically. But even this is not straightforward. Some terminals are low specification and do not support the latest versions of applications that are standard in many other work areas. It is costly and difficult to replace the network or even to upgrade individual machines. Bandwidth is low because of the infrastructure and the volume of use. The network arrangements do not map exclusively to a specific tool. So part of one area may share network resources with its neighbor. Consideration must therefore be paid to the type and size of information that this network can be expected to deliver if we are to achieve a workable, cost-effective e-learning solution. Moreover, the computers that are available are not necessarily adjacent to the tools, meaning that technicians may have difficulty reading a computer screen while working.

CASE STUDY: THE SOLUTION

The peculiar working environment played a critical role in determining the design. Lengthy and detailed consultation with supervisors and experienced technicians were required to understand fully the particularities of the working and learning environment into which an e-learning solution would be introduced. But there were other equally important factors to take into consideration. Technicians required quick and timely access to complex, changing information within the factory working environment. If a change is agreed via the established consultative process, it needs to be implemented immediately and across the board. Any learning solution would need to accommodate change easily and with minimum disruption to existing information and proce-dures.

The instructional design analysis concluded that the best option was to design and establish an online reference base of job aids, accessible at the point of work, besides the manufacturing tool and which can be added to, amended, and deleted as required. Job aids would thus directly support work, activity, and performance.

But why job aids and not a more formalized set of lessons?[2] It is helpful here to introduce some working definitions of job aids. Alison Rossett and Jeanette Gautier-Downes characterize job aids as follows:

- They specifically aid performance, rather than learning.
- They provide job support, rather than job training.
- They are not, *per se* or intentionally, instructional.
- They are generally technical in nature.
- They assist in the performance of a task.
- They provide just-enough, just-in-time information.
- They are always available for consultation.

Note the contrast drawn between job aids and learning or training. I have deliberately amended the absolute distinction in the original classification of the first two criteria (e.g., in the original 'performance NOT learning') to the milder distinction of 'rather than,' because usage by the technicians showed that they regarded job aids as a part of training. One can argue that learning from job aids is incidental, i.e., not intentional, and that therefore it is difficult to assess the degree of learning transferred by job aids. Nevertheless, it is worth recognizing that some learning does occur in the provision of job aids.

Job aids ease the burden on long-term memory where retention and transfer of knowledge are not a priority. For example, you do not need to know or memorize all (or indeed any) phone numbers; all you need to know is that you can find a number in a phone book.[3] Manuals, phonebooks, and cooking recipes can all be seen as examples of job aids. You can rely on job aids so all you need to know is not so much the answer to a question itself, but where you might find that answer — the source and its location. To use another example, if you are looking for a recipe, you consult the cookbook which is conveniently located on a shelf in the kitchen where you will do your cooking.

Job aids are particularly effective for jobs where speed, complexity, infrequency, and time and effort are issues. Job aids work well in the following circumstances[4]:

- When performance is infrequent
- When the situation is complex
- When the consequences for error are high
- When it becomes necessary to access vast or changing bodies of knowledge
- Where there is high turnover or task simplicity

Let us see how those criteria correspond to the case in hand.

The performance of preventative maintenance may be infrequent depending on the degree of maintenance required. It some cases it will be weeks, in others months before the task is performed again. In the meantime, technicians may have forgotten aspects of the procedure, or indeed new technicians may be performing the procedure for the first time. The availability of job aids means technicians need not memorize procedures. They replace the potentially faulty memory of the operators.

While preventative maintenance involves tasks that are often quite straightforward, some factory tasks involve complex manipulation of equipment or data. Robot calibration, for example, is not an exact science and technicians who perform the calibrations need expert guidance and detailed information accessible while they calibrate. Given the complexity of the task, it follows that the possibility for error is high. The consequences for error are equally high because failure to calibrate a robot correctly can result in broken wafers and the need for recalibration, whose cost in purely financial, as well as time, terms is hugely expensive running to thousands, even hundreds of thousands of dollars. Job aids provide expert guidance at the place it is most needed — by the tool, at work.

Although not every procedure performed is as complex (or indeed as critical) as robot calibration — many tasks are indeed technically straightforward and routine — the number of tasks, the density of the specifications, and the varying frequency with which they are performed could overwhelm a technician. Moreover, in a constant drive to improve efficiency and performance as well as solve long-standing or newly occurring problems, different practices and techniques are continually introduced. This means that information is subject to change and technicians need to be apprised quickly of these changes. The changes in themselves may be quite small (creating an additional step or the reordering of steps, for example), but the cost of failing to be aware of them or adopt them is relatively high. The existing documentation, which is cumbersome and inflexible, would not adapt swiftly enough to account for these changes. However, online job aids can be amended immediately and the changes readily highlighted.

Job aids address the problem of the removal from the environment of experienced technicians and their replacement (if at all) by less experienced, even trainee, techs. Job aids provide easily accessible information required to bring these technicians quickly to a working knowledge of the environment. Moreover, they provide a fail-safe system so that technicians can know that simple tasks are covered and do not need to be memorized.

CASE STUDY: HOW JOB AIDS ARE CREATED

The instructional design strategy recommended creating a series of job aids containing high-level, expert information at the point of work, taking into account the peculiar environment in which the work is performed. Job aids thus build on existing classroom and other training; they do not replace classroom training. Job aids are based on existing procedures detailed in tool and work practice specification and other approved documentation. They also include any gaps in detail. The instructional designer gathered information from Subject Matter Experts in a series of interviews. Some of this information was already documented, but some was not. The idea was to build into job aids any implicit knowledge residing with expert technicians and make it explicit. The SMEs who created the job aid content also took the opportunity to review existing documentation to ensure it reflected current practice and vice versa to ensure current working practices concurred with documented best practice.

However, while still following existing practices, online job aids do offer advantages over existing documentation. The electronic format facilitates graphical (still and dynamic) illustrations. Illustrations can be more descriptive than plain text, and we exploited the power of graphic representation. So job aids extend training by providing better access to information and enhancing its presentation. This is of particular benefit to new or inexperienced technicians who may not have had sufficient time to internalize the information provided and are not so familiar with the tool.

Individual job aids cannot, however, exist in isolation. They have to be grouped in a meaningful way so that access to them is easy and logical. Again we can draw an analogy with phonebooks where information is ordered alphabetically, by area or some other fixed criterion or convention. Secondly, job aids needed to appear within a work context: by tool area, focus area, procedure, task, even down to individual step. This hierarchy was devised to match, as far as possible, the way technicians worked on tasks and procedures. The intention was to make job aids intuitive to use. The cataloging and numbering within that system were vital to ensure that changes made to the ordering of job aids would not necessitate the complete reordering of the system, especially when amendments were made by a designated administrator.

The critical need here was to provide a context in which job aids could reside and, more importantly, function. The usefulness of job aids can only ultimately be measured by the use made of them by the audience for which they were designed — manufacturing technicians. But even the most useful job aid will be rendered useless if a technician does not know where to find it. To return to the phonebook analogy, the successful retrieval of a phone number is dependent on the ability to locate and then use the phonebook. Fortunately standard structures and formats are used, so that users know that once they can use one phonebook, they can use any. However, for job aids none of these familiar structures existed, so we had to also create the environment, the 'book,' that contains job aids, the index and navigation that allow access to them, and the practice by which they were regarded as *the* standard repository of useful information. The individual job aid could not and cannot be divorced from the framework of all job aids. Content is inseparable from form.

The attention paid to the context in which the job aids are used extends also to the system devised to ensure they could be maintained and even extended by the users themselves. Currently in each of the factory teams when information needs to be updated, there exists a process whereby approval is sought and given. A forum is empowered to make decisions on what information needs to be changed and when it should be changed. The system is designed to ensure that information is regularly assessed and that a standard corpus of information is maintained.

The existence of this infrastructure enabled us to embed the solution into the current working environment. Job aids are designed to be flexible and to respond quickly and effectively to changes in information and practices. To make this happen, the responsibility for maintaining and updating them needs to rest with the users themselves. If users needed the help of instructional designers and editors whenever they wanted to make even the smallest change, the system could become inflexible and thus unusable. Therefore job aids should require minimal editing and should be in a format that would enable technicians themselves to put further information online. To make this possible a special sustaining application — essentially an editing tool — was designed to accompany the job aids. It has a user-friendly interface that allows technicians with only minimal acquaintance with standard computer operating systems to add, amend, and delete information in individual job aids and even to add new ones.

However, in its very flexibility, this application gives considerable freedom of action to users and raises the prospects of misuse. A technician could, for example, delete all existing material or add erroneous new material. To ensure standard practice and to give some degree of security, the system was limited to administrators or super-users who alone had the right to change the information contained in job aids. This person would be chosen by the existing forum. His or her actions would be mandated by peers or supervisors according to the current practices for implementing change. Hence the job aid editing tool works within the existing infrastructure and follows accepted practice. Again the logic behind the introduction of job aids was to make them fit the environment, to become an organic part of the existing infrastructure, rather than provide a radical departure — less brave new world than an updated version of the old one.

CASE STUDY: WHAT DO ONLINE JOB AIDS LOOK LIKE

The job aids themselves are essentially lists of simply phrased steps that comprise a task. The task in question could be the calibration of a tool via a computer screen interface or the steps (in correct order) required in a troubleshooting procedure to determine the cause of machine failure.

Language and Text Formatting

The tasks are phrased as a series of instructions using action verbs: turn off, remove, replace, adjust, and so on. What seem like bald and uninformative statements to the uninitiated, provide sufficient information for the trained technician. The idiosyncratic language and technical terminology are no barrier to the technicians' comprehension of the task in hand.

However, while the language and the content are readily intelligible to technicians, the formatting of that content for online job aids requires care and attention. The text is in a large font to enable technicians to read it from a computer screen that may be several feet away from the task they are performing. The layout of the factory means that technicians cannot always be in ideal distance from the screen.

Graphics

In addition to the text, there are visual illustrations that enhance comprehension of the task in hand. These illustrations can be line drawings, still photos, or animated graphics — features not available in existing paper-based or even online material currently used in the factory. The illustrations are placed entirely in context. A small icon beside the description of the task indicates that there is some visual aid for the technician. It is up to technicians whether they click on the icon to access the illustration. Nevertheless when they do they will find illustrations that reflect the exact configuration of the tool they are working on and may find explanations with animations unavailable elsewhere in the factory.

In this case job aids are at the low end of e-learning. They comprise only text and graphics to minimize demands on the limited bandwidth in the factory. There is no audio because it would be virtually impossible to ensure that you could hear anything in the factory where there is considerable background noise. The use of headphones is impractical, as they impede mobility and are of limited value when the wearers have to have hoods covering their ears. Other high-media solutions, such as simulations, are unnecessary when the learner is already working on the tool itself.

Interactivity

Interactivity too is minimal. Job aids focus on performance rather than learning, hence there is no need to ensure complete identification with Gagné's nine instructional events.[5] There is no standard assessment component, as the application of knowledge derived from job aids is measured in actual performance and the application of the information contained in the job aids on the tool during calibrations and PMs. Assessment is accomplished instead through the comparison of various time, accident, error, computer logs, or other job performance records over time, since the introduction of job aids. In other words, assessment like job aids in general becomes integrated into the job environment. Rote learning can indeed be harmful to performance, because failure to consult job aids or the equivalent can result in the omission of a critical step. The hardware issues also meant interactivity was a secondary consideration.

Flexibility

Job aids may not be technologically sophisticated or high media, but they are designed to minimize the inconvenience of accessing information in the difficult factory environment. The steps themselves are by and large straightforward and require minimal explanation. Moreover, the simplicity of the job aids' structure and formatting allows technicians the opportunity to create their own job aids themselves, as and when they require and without recourse to an external learning provider and the lengthy production process that would entail.

Integration

Job aids are further integrated into the working environment by following the hierarchy and (where possible) the nomenclature of the factory. Job aids should be accessed via toolset, then the relevant focus area, then the procedures within that focus area, and finally the tasks within that procedure. Each task contains a number of steps. This imitation of the existing hierarchy and nomenclature is essential for the successful contextualization of the information. Context in turn makes orientation easier for the learner and facilitates navigation and use. In short, learners know what they are looking for and where to find it. They also know where to add or amend information as that becomes necessary.

Navigation

Navigation within a particular task is by means of forward and back buttons. Information within each job aid page is grouped by the logic of the task. That is to say, if a step belongs with two others, it will appear with those related steps on a single screen and not at the foot of another screen containing unrelated steps. Again what is important here is what suits the user and not what pleases the aesthetics of the designer.

When learners reach the end of the steps in a job aid, they are informed they have reached the end of the task and the next button returns them to the task list. Navigation between tasks, procedures, and focus areas is also possible by a hyper-linking bread crumb. The bread crumb system also allows learners to see where they currently are and where they have come from. However, for users who want a more direct route to particular information or want similar information grouped together, a search function has been included that allows the user to call up all relevant job aids via a keyword or phrase.

The navigation is designed to allow learners to proceed at their own pace. This is in keeping with the spirit of job aids' design: to place the learner or user in control. Similarly, any animations are fitted with a replay button so that the user can replay them as many times as necessary to understand what is being illustrated.[6]

The navigation devised for job aids meant that information currently to be found (often after laborious searching) on shared drives was accessible in one place via a standard system. The idea was to make job aids *the* repository of information, so that it would be the place a technician looked first for information. The hierarchy and nomenclature are standard so that the search can be conducted in a logical way and remain familiar to those working in the factory environment. The navigation reflects the way information is currently ordered in the workplace and so minimizes the confusion a new system is apt to cause its users.

LESSONS LEARNED

The design of navigation to allow the learner to move at his or her own pace is at the heart of the key lesson to be learned from this job aids case study. The technicians working in the clean room are independent learners. They are independent in two ways: first, they are not in a classroom where information is controlled by an instructor, and second, they use information only when and if they need it. Job aids are not part of some institutional curriculum, but are an aid to working practices. The motivation to use them comes from the technicians themselves. The solution we devised does not contain traditional assessment or tracking, because it presupposes that the users will decide for themselves how and when to use it best. In essence, we designed an expert system and relied on experts to use it.

Trust Learners

The culmination of the trust we placed in learners can be seen in the development of an application to sustain and augment the solution. We built a customized but extendable solution. Unlike an off-the-shelf product or indeed many customized products, job aids allow their users to determine their usefulness and, critically, remove and add job aids to meet new needs and new requirements. That design ensures a longer life and better usage over time by building in flexibility and sustainability.

Design for Flexibility and Adaptability

The shelf-life of any learning material must be a critical consideration of instructional design. We know that some information remains the same, but other information changes. What we also need to consider is how often does information change. If you need to build a new e-learning solution every six months, you will barely have finished one before the next one is needed. In environments where information dates rapidly, you require a solution that can adapt to new information. Thus jobs aids are not just about content, but also about the system that contains that content. The content can and will change and the users can change it themselves, but the solution is robust enough to support those changes and flexible enough to allow them.

As an instructional designer it is not sufficient to design a solution and then wash your hands of it. You have to think about how it will be used, by whom, and in what setting. You also need to consider how usage will change the solution. Instructional design is not a one-way process, but rather a dialogue with the learner. Unfortunately, especially with forms of distance learning (and that includes e-learning), the learner's response can be so distant as to be barely audible.

Build In Performance-Based Evaluation

Instructional design systems always stress the importance of evaluation (take, for example, Dick and Carey's system[7]), yet in practice evaluation is piecemeal, if conducted at all. It happens late in the instructional design cycle by which stage the hard-pressed designer is being asked to concentrate on the initial stages of another project. Although they stress evaluation, few instructional design strategies indicate how long that evaluation should last. How do you know when the evaluation is sufficient? And that question leads to another: when does the instructional design of a project stop? The view from the trenches suggests the answer to the second question is, when your manager tells you to stop!

Include an Exit Strategy

An e-learning instructional designer may not be part of a training department. That instructional designer's duty of care to a group of learners may not extend beyond a single project. In such circumstances, what is the relationship between designer and learner once the e-learning product has been implemented?

Any instructional design requires an exit strategy, but ideally it should be one that leaves the learner in control. Job aids do this by providing the system and the context in which learners themselves can develop and maintain learning without the guidance of instructional design. The design is now there in the system and works by default. The systematic design of instruction has therefore another aspect: the design of an instructional system.

SUMMARY

The case study I have described emphasizes the range and scope of instructional design. Effective instructional design requires detailed needs analysis and requirements gathering at the outset. This is a critical phase where the instructional designer must listen as well as recommend. In custom-built e-learning, the instructional designer cannot always rely on past experience or existing templates or indeed on existing mechanisms for delivery of content. The instructional designer not only needs to understand the learner's needs and requirements, the designer must also represent the learner in any solution he or she designs. In e-learning in particular, the instructional designer must treat the learner as a social individual (as one would in a classroom environment or broader school setting) and not simply as a computer user. The effectiveness of any learning depends on the response of the learner, and that is why one must place the learner first and why one must make sure that the instruction designed suits the learner and the context in which he or she learns.

Furthermore, one must trust the learner. As an instructional designer, it is important to recognize how learners learn and not simply determine how learner should learn. The theory behind job aids suggests that they are not primarily instructional. Indeed the job aids we designed presumed a familiarity with the material and prior instruction on job tasks. Nevertheless when job aids came online, we found that technicians used them not just to perform their jobs, but also to refresh their own knowledge and even to train others.

Questions for the Future

Do these actions suggest a gap in current training? Have job aids, presented in small, manageable gobbets of information at the place of work, made it more attractive to learn? Has the job aid system allowed better access to information previously buried, un-catalogued, and un-indexed, on a shared drive? Are job aids a better way of learning these tasks? It is too early to say. The answers to these questions will require more analysis and, critically, the attention of an instructional designer. In providing those answers, the designer underscores the continuing value of instructional design.

ENDNOTES

[1]   The relationship described here between apprentice and expert resembles Vygotsky's 'zone of proximal development.' See Vygotsky, L.S. (1978). *Mind in Society*.

2   The following discussion of job aids is based on Rossett, A. & Gautier-Downes, J. (1991). *A Handbook of Job Aids*.

3   An ex-directory number will, of course, not appear in the phonebook, so the phonebook is not exhaustive. But the vast majority of phone numbers appear in the phonebook, so it is still the place where one looks first. Hence one refers to numbers not found as 'ex-directory.' To be an effective resource, therefore, any job aid system must contain a majority, a 'critical mass,' of job aids to ensure it is regarded as the standard. An aid not found in the system is therefore an 'omission.'

4   See the job aids homepage at: http://edweb.sdsu.edu/courses/edtec540/540WWW/home.html#TOC.

5   The nine instructional events identified by Robert Gagné can be found in his seminal *The Conditions of Learning* (1965).

6   Note animations do require specialist design and technological knowledge, so while the editing system allows technicians to add any kind of illustration as well as text, technicians are less likely to be able to develop additional animations and will probably require specialist help to do so. Nevertheless, most of the information in job aids can be created, formatted, and added by technicians will minimal or no specialist training.

7   Dick, W., Carey, L., & Carey, J.O. (2001). *The Systematic Design of Instruction*.

Chapter III

Application of an Instructional Design Model for Industry Training: From Theory to Practice

Elizabeth Hanlis
University of Alberta, Canada

ABSTRACT

This chapter examines reflections, considerations, and the problems encountered when attempting to apply an instructional design model in the design and development of two online courses for industry training. Recommendations are included for instructional designers to avoid and handle many of the issues that arise in the real world. Specific issues addressed include: tight budgets, limited cooperation from SMEs, high expectations of clients, major changes to 'finalized designs,' and the importance of dealing with such matters promptly and effectively. The significance of both formative and summative evaluation and the role of project management are also discussed.

INTRODUCTION

I took my first course in instructional design as a grad student. This introductory course presented structured step-by-step instructional design models, which, initially, I strictly followed and adhered to. I found these models, especially the Kemp, Morrison, and Ross (1998) one, very useful when I completed my first instructional design plan for a class project. While I found the application of an instructional design model very straightforward when applying it to an imaginary project, it did not seem as simple when I tried to use this same model for the design of online courses for business training a couple of years later. This chapter will discuss my reflections, considerations, and the problems that I experienced when attempting to apply an instructional design model in the design and development of two courses for industry training.

DEFINITIONS

While there are several definitions in the literature for Web-based training and instructional design models, the following two will be used for the purposes of this chapter.

Instructional design "is the process of designing the environment, methods, and resources for effective learning of specified goals and objectives" (Boettcher & Conrad, 1999, p. 49).

According to Hall (1997), Web-based training is instruction that is delivered over the Internet or over a company's intranet. This instruction is accessed using a Web browser, and is characterized by the readily available, interactive, multimedia nature of the Web and its associated plug-ins.

BACKGROUND

Among the many possibilities for growth that have stemmed from the World Wide Web, the most promising is its use for distance education (Swan, Shea, Fredridcksen, Pickett, & Pelz, 2000). Unfortunately, in our rush to create these online courses, the emphasis has often been on technological issues (Swan et al., 2000), instead of the instructional design process (Downs, Carlson, Repman, & Clark, 1999). Ritchie and Hoffman (1997) advocate that the Web's potential for instruction, combined with our knowledge of instructional design principles, can create a distributed instructional medium that is unlike previous methods of distance learning.

According to the literature, the application of instructional design in business training has several benefits. Following an instructional design model can reduce the time it takes to complete a course (Boettcher & Conrad, 1999) and solve "a performance problem by designing effective instruction that increases worker productivity" (Kemp, Morrison, & Ross, 1998, p. 11).

Course designers/developers should therefore refer to instructional design models and techniques and follow step-by-step procedures to ensure that high-quality instruction is created (Dick & Carey, 1990; Gagne, Briggs, & Wager, 1992; Smith & Ragan, 1999). Although instructional development models and processes may differ to some extent, the majority of them follow the same basic stages of: analysis, design, development, and evaluation (Willis, 1992).

Several studies have been published that advise course designers on how to use such instructional design principles and models for the development of Web-based courses (Canning-Wilson, 2000; Dewald, Downs et al., 1999; Hsu, Marques, Hamza, & Alhalabli, 1999; Miltiadou & McIssac, 2000; Saba, 1999; Scholz-Crane, Booth, & Levine, 2000; Smaldino, 1999). Specifically, Hirumi and Bermudez (1996) and Nalley (1995) illustrate how the use of Dick and Carey's (1990) instructional design model can guide the creation of innovative, interactive online courses. Similarly, Sabine and Gilley (1999) discuss the instructional design process followed to create an online course for a college, which consists of the following stages: planning, design, production/trial, evaluation, and implementation. This article listed many of the problems that the instructional designers faced, including simulating classroom interaction, communication, testing, and administrative issues, and how these issues were resolved (Sabine & Gilley 1999).

While so much literature has been written on the application of instructional design models and principles for the development of online material, most of the focus has been on secondary and post-secondary institutions. As noted earlier, this chapter examines the application of instructional design for the development of online courses for business training. Issues and problems encountered, as well as suggestions for future instructional designers in industry, will be made.

DESCRIPTION OF COMPANIES AND BACKGROUND INFORMATION

A brief description of the companies for which the online courses were built will help you better understand many of the instructional design decisions that were made and the problems encountered while developing the courses.

The first online course was built for a health care company, situated in Chicago, Illinois, that has more than 70,000 employees and offices in 130 countries around the world. The pharmaceutical division of this company requested that our team build an online course on the topic of Release Specifications. It would be used to train managers internationally. Previously the course was taught via traditional classroom instruction; however the instructors were involved in so many projects that they no longer had time to teach the course.

The second online course was built for a chemical company of 4,700 employees that produces energy and chemical co-products. Its main offices are located in Calgary, Alberta, Canada, and it has facilities strategically situated in 18 locations around Canada, the United States, and Europe. This company had recently implemented a customized business system to more effectively meet business demands. To build awareness of the system among its employees, and to educate managers on how to plan and implement the system, the company requested that our team develop instruction that was user friendly and easily accessible at all their petrochemical locations.

PROJECT TEAM ROLES

The project team for the development of these two courses consisted of a project manager, two instructional designers/programmers, a graphic designer, and a network specialist. The instructional designers worked on the projects for almost a month full time, while the remaining team members worked on the project on a part-time basis or whenever their expertise was required. Work on this project was completed in a collaborative manner.

As an instructional designer/programmer, I was expected to apply instructional design principles for the development of the two courses and complete the authoring of the course. These two responsibilities where shared with the other instructional designer.

DESCRIPTION OF COURSES

A brief description of both online courses, including the instructional and navigational components, is provided below to enhance the readers' understanding of the instructional design process followed to build them.

The main page for the Release Specifications course contains a tutorial for new users demonstrating the function of all the navigation and utility buttons of the course. This main page also includes an orientation link demonstrating to users how to navigate through the course, a link to the course site map, and a link to contact information for the two instructors at the health care company. From this main page the user can select a module to complete from a pull-down menu.

Within the module, a frame on the left contains the instructional components of the course, while a frame on the top contains the utility buttons. The navigational buttons on the left include a rationale, a pretest button that links to multiple-choice questions, and an objectives button, from which the learner can access all the learning resources (including text, images, practice activities, and self-assessment exercises). Exercises buttons, where the learner can access dynamic spreadsheet exercises, a visuals button with links to all the important images of the module, and a resources button are constantly visible on the left frame.

From the top frame the learners can go to the homepage, search the site, view a glossary with all the key concepts covered in the course, participate in a threaded discussion board, or even print the current page.

The Business Systems course is composed of the following four modules: Overview, Plan, Execute, and Review. Within each module a navigational menu appears on the top right-hand corner of the page. From here the learner can access the main page for the course, the module objectives, the module content, fill-in-the-blank/matching exercises, multiple-choice evaluation questions, a summary of the main points of the module, and a link to the homepage.

APPLICATION OF AN INSTRUCTIONAL DESIGN MODEL

A combination of two instructional design models where utilized for this project. The first is the Dick and Carey model (1990), which comprises five phases: analyze, design, develop, implement, and evaluate. This is the model that we used when communicating with the clients, because it is straightforward and easy to understand.

However for identifying in detail the tasks under each of these phases, the Kemp, Morrison, and Ross (1998) model was utilized. According to Kemp, Morrison, and Ross (1998), a comprehensive instructional design plan consists of the following tasks: (1) identify instructional problems, (2) examine learner characteristics, (3) identify subject content and analyze task components, (4) state instructional objectives, (5) sequence content, (6) design instructional strategies, (7) plan the instructional message, (8) develop evaluation instruments, and (9) select resources to support instruction and learning.

ANALYSIS

During the analysis phase, the instructional designer defines the instructional problem, identifies possible solutions, and examines learner characteristics (Kemp, Morrison, & Ross, 1998). To collect this information a formal needs assessment is usually conducted (Kemp, Morrison, & Ross, 1998). However, for the design of the Release Specifications course for the pharmaceutical division, the main problem and solution were outlined by the training manager from the start.

Specifically, the pharmaceutical division had an existing Release Specifications course that was delivered to managers via classroom instruction. Managers were forced to leave their offices and travel to their central offices in Chicago to take this three-day course. The training manager, with the encouragement of senior management, was asked to transform this course for online delivery, to reduce both training and travel costs.

Therefore a two-day needs assessment was completed on the client's site, during which two instructional designers, the training manager, and SMEs participated in working sessions to collect as much information as possible about the organization's structure, environment, and attitude. The main purpose of this session was to examine learner characteristics, the existing training processes, and learning resources. The learners for this course were managers who were in the Release Specifications, marketing, or applied research department. Most of the learners were well educated with a minimum of a master's degree. The content of the course already existed in Power Point slides.

Unfortunately, for the Business Systems course, the client was not willing to allocate the time or budget to conduct a formal needs assessment. Thus the instructional designer was forced to conduct informal working sessions via the telephone and drive to the client's site for an afternoon to identify the instructional goal, determine the possible solutions, and examine the learner characteristics. The client requested that a binder full of processes and information be transformed into instructional units that could be accessed online by plant employees at any time, enabling just-in-time learning. Limited information was obtained about learner characteristics. However, the company's SMEs informed the instructional designers that the instruction was intended for adult learners that on average had an eighth-grade-level education, a minimum employment requirement to work at the chemical plant.

From this experience it is possible to conclude that even if a budget is not allocated for the analysis phase, the instructional designer must attempt to verify at a bare minimum:

- the skills that need to be taught (if any),
- the learning resources already in place,
- the intended audience, and
- the client's expectations and requirements.

As seen from this example verifying the above information is not always easily accomplished.

DESIGN

During the design phase, information obtained from the needs assessment, whether formal or informal, is used to plan a strategy to develop effective instruction (Kemp, Morrison, & Ross, 1998).

Content for Instruction

A first step towards developing effective instruction is to identify and outline the content (Kemp, Morrison, & Ross, 1998). However, finalizing the content for the two online courses that we developed was far more complicated and time consuming than expected. The content for the Release Specifications pharmaceutical course already existed in Power Point slides; however, this format was not appropriate for online course delivery. In the face-to-face course, these slides were supplemented by the instructor's lecture. Senior administration from the company designing the course decided that the instructional designer would attend a course taught by the instructor, to capture the information required to supplement the Power Point slides with notes. The instructional designer attended a personalized three-day course from the instructor/SME. This session was recorded and at the same time the instructional designer took detailed notes. This first step of the content analysis was completed on the same business trip that the needs assessment took place, thus saving on travel expenses and time. This observation emphasizes the importance of managing the project effectively, a responsibility that is primarily the project manager's and to some extent the instructional designer's. The recorded tapes were transcribed and the instructional designer grouped the content into digestible chunks of information with learning objectives that were suitable for online delivery. This information was then sent to the SME for validation.

This was a time-consuming process that delayed the production of the course and prolonged the timeline of the project. A more efficient use of time might have been for the SME to supplement the PowerPoint slides with notes, during a three-day working session, rather than teach the course to the instructional designer. This process would have taken full advantage of the three days that the SME had scheduled for this work. After that time it was extremely difficult to arrange further meetings with the SME due to his unavailability. Unfortunately, supplementing the slides with notes might not have been the most effective way to conduct this content analysis either, as the instructor could have overlooked important information that the instructional designer could have retrieved by listening to the instructor teach the course.

The content for the Business Systems course was provided in print format. However, what the client considered to be instructional content was simply a list of processes and references that were not suitable for online delivery. The instructional designer chunked this content into instructional modules with learning objectives. This content needed to be validated by both the project manager and the SME. Unfortunately, the SME changed his mind several times on how he wanted the information organized, extending the content analysis by almost a month.

The prolonged content analysis could have been avoided if the SME was expected to sign off on the content analysis, forcing him to reflect on his decisions and take his responsibility more seriously. Unfortunately, because the contract did not include a clause outlining the responsibilities of the SME or a sign-off expectation, there was nothing that the instructional designer could do, apart from redo the organization of the content three times. As a result the project timeline was extended.

Instructional Objectives

Instructional objectives define what the learner will know or be able to perform, under specific conditions, upon completion of instruction (Kemp, Morrison, & Ross, 1998). For both courses, each learning module had several learning objectives that were validated by the SME, along with the content validation. The difficult task for the instructional designer was to decide on how the content and course would be structured around these objectives. The most effective approach seemed to be for the learning objectives to be associated with specific content and evaluation components, and sequenced in the order in which the knowledge is required and performed on the job. Consequently, when a learning objective was selected within the course, hyperlinks to the appropriate content and evaluation components appeared.

Sequencing of Instruction

Once the instructional objectives are written, the instructional designer, normally with the help of the SME, will sequence the content for instruction (Kemp, Morrison, & Ross, 1998). In reality when designing the two courses for industry, the SMEs for both courses did not assist in sequencing the instruction. Instead they expected the instructional designer to perform this task, while they would validate the work.

The Release Specifications course modules could be completed in any sequence, as each module taught a specific concept. Even so, the modules were numbered to suggest a recommended sequence. This was the sequence that was followed during the classroom training, and starts with basic concepts and gradually introduces more complex ones.

For the Business Systems course, the content was sequenced starting with a general overview module of all the processes. The remaining modules followed the sequence that the tasks were performed to implement the system (Plan, Execute, and Review). Within the modules the content was sequenced in the order that each procedure was performed on the job; even so the learners were still given the freedom to complete them in a different order if they preferred, skipping any information that they were already familiar with. Learners could, therefore, complete a module when the information was required on the job (just-in-time learning), serving the purpose of an electronic performance system.

For both courses a suggested sequence was provided. Even so learners could come in at any time and reference material from a specific module, or complete only the modules that they were not familiar with. This type of self-directed learning seems to be effective with adult learners according to studies conducted by Knowles and Tough (cited in DeMartino, 1999).

Instructional Strategies

The instructional designer determines how to present the content related to each individual learning objective in a manner that helps the learner master that objective (Kemp, Morrison, & Ross, 1998). Ideally instructional strategies are selected for each individual objective separately. However, this would be a very time-consuming process, which was not feasible for the development of a course with hundreds of objectives. Instead the instructional designer reviewed the objectives and decided on instructional strategies that would be appropriate for the majority of objectives, and applied these strategies to all of them, for reasons of efficiency.

For both courses the following instructional strategies were selected:

- overview of what will be learned (objectives);
- presentation of information through the use of visuals, texts, and animations (knowledge/learning);
- opportunities for practice and feedback (in the form of matching exercises and dynamic spreadsheets); and
- self-assessment/evaluation questions (in the form of fill-in-the-blank/short answer).

In addition the Release Specifications course provided pre-instructional activities to ensure that the learners are not already familiar with the information presented. Links to related resources were also available for further enrichment.

These instructional strategies (represented in the course with hyperlinks and buttons) are consistent with the strategies identified by Ritchie and Hoffman (1997). According to Ritchie and Hoffman (1997), instruction on the Internet should motivate the learner, identify what is to be learned, require active involvement, provide guidance and feedback, test, provide enrichment and remediation, and summarize.

Instructional Message

Once the instructional strategies have been identified for the learning objectives, the instructional message can be designed. Certain considerations that need to be made at this point include: selecting specific pre-instructional and instructional activities, deciding how to structure text, and when and where to use visuals (Kemp, Morrison, & Ross, 1998).

The first pre-instructional activity for the Release Specifications course was a rationale, which had a sentence stating why the information is important for the employee and a few points on the purpose of the module. This information ensures that the material is relevant and meaningful for the learner. The pretest was the second pre-instructional activity, which was a set of multiple-choice questions used as a diagnostic to determine whether the content of the module is already familiar to the learner. The final pre-instructional activity was a listing of instructional objectives for each module. A button was created for each of these activities.

No pre-instructional activities were created for the Business Systems course, as the client did not want any. In many instances, the desires of the client will override the knowledge and experience of the instructional designer. While you can make suggestions and make a case about incorporating certain elements in the course, ultimately it will be up to the client to decide if they will include these specific elements or not. However, a good suggestion would be to document such instances and sign off on the treatment and content at a regular interval to avoid problems later on.

There were several instances where a video or animation would have effectively demonstrated a process or concept; unfortunately, due to budget constraints the designer could not justify the cost of producing video or animation, especially since we did not have in-house expertise. Instead the instructional designer had to compromise and use static graphics which would take less time for the graphic designer to build. This decision was very difficult, especially when the client had been promised multimedia elements, like animation and sound files. Such false expectations could have been avoided if the marketing employees and executives, who produced the proposals and signed off on the contracts, clearly understood the in-house capabilities, as well as the cost and time involved in creating videos and animations for instruction. Such unfortunate instances could have been avoided if the marketing staff and managers had consulted with the multimedia experts regarding the cost, time commitment, and in-house capabilities around media production, prior to talking with the client, estimating costs, or writing the proposal. Instead the clients were told after the project had been initiated that an additional cost would be charged for any multimedia they requested. Unfortunately, as project problems such as the above mounted, client expectations were not resolved; this proved to be detrimental for the success of the project later on.

Deciding on how to evaluate the learner's knowledge after instruction is also decided during this phase. The course was intended for professional development and the development of higher order thinking skills, rather than mastery of specific competencies. Therefore self-assessment activities, with long-answer questions that the user could complete and receive feedback on, seemed to be more appropriate than multiple-choice questions for evaluation, especially considering that most of these learners had a graduate degree and were accustomed to this type of evaluation.

The downside of using long-answer questions is the time and subsequent cost required for grading the evaluation. The cost of grading long-answer questions is considerably higher than marking multiple-choice questions, which is normally completed and tracked automatically by the computer. Therefore, in many instances, the instructional designer is forced to use multiple-choice questions, due to large class sizes or budget constraints, even when long-answer questions are more appropriate for the specific learning needs and learners. Fortunately for the Release Specifications course, the class size was expected to be fewer than 10 learners and the instructor was willing to spend the time to provide feedback to long-answer questions.

Flowchart

Flowcharts are graphical presentations of how the HTML pages are mapped out and connected to form the online course. Such flowcharts were used for both courses and seemed to enable effective communication among the project team when they were building the online courses. Flowcharts were also used extensively as a communication tool with the clients, when explaining the structure of the course. Seeing how the pages were connected allowed both the project team and clients to better visualize how all the components of the course were connected, while ensuring that the clients and instructional designers were envisioning the same layout. Therefore the use of flowcharts is highly recommended during the design phase.

Storyboards and Style Guides

Ideally when designing instruction, storyboards should be drawn on paper to visually illustrate how the text and graphics will be presented on each page. Also style guides can be created to provide an outline of how a document should be structured, including elements like corporate logos, screen design, methods of interaction, links graphics, and animations (Lemiski, 2000). For both the Release Specifications course and the Business Systems course, no storyboards or style guides were created, because there was a very tight timeline. The pages for the online modules were immediately built in HTML. Unfortunately so many major changes were made afterwards that using a storyboard and style guide initially would have saved time and been a more cost-efficient approach in the long run. This substantiates the findings of Lemiski (2000) that not having a style guide has proved to increase the development time of projects. Even if there is no time to create a storyboard, at the least cascading style sheets and templates should be used to allow the instructional design team to quickly make mass changes.

DEVELOPMENT

Once the storyboards and design specifications have been decided on, the next steps involve the production of the final product. In reality this phase starts almost at the same time as the previous phases, to shorten the project timeline. Thus the activities in these two phases tend to overlap, saving both time and money.

For both the Release Specifications and the Business Systems courses, the instructional design team built a prototype module, based on specifications outlined in the design phase. This sample of the whole course was provided to the client early on to identify any problems or concerns, and to resolve these prior to finishing the whole course. The production team and the client collaboratively reviewed the prototype modules for the courses. Once the requested changes were made, the production team was given the go-ahead to continue building the remaining modules. This process took longer than expected, as the SMEs (from the client side) seemed to find it difficult to schedule time to collaboratively review the prototype module.

The review of the prototype module revealed that the static images were quite large in file size, as were the navigational buttons for the Release Specifications course. To reduce the download time for employees that were on a 56.6K modem connection, the images were reduced in size by reducing the number of colors from 256 to 128. Changing the navigational buttons from having 4-states to 2-states also seemed to reduce the file size considerably. Therefore the buttons only had an inactive state and a rollover state, sacrificing the active and visited states in exchange for smaller file sizes. Learning to use graphics wisely was a major challenge during the development phase, which was also noted by Thrush and Young (1999) who developed online courses for university-level English courses.

Once the client is satisfied with the prototype module, templates, cascading style sheets, and library items should be created. This was learned the hard way. When the clients indicated that they were pleased with the design and layout of the prototype module, the production team simply replicated this module using the "Save As" feature and adding the new content. Unfortunately, throughout the production of the remaining modules, many changes where made to the layout and interface design that affected all the modules already built. Hundreds of files already created needed to be opened and changed. These changes could have been made globally, if templates, cascading style sheets, and library items were used from the start, decreasing the time needed to produce the course and increasing profitability for the company.

In addition, the client should have been asked to complete a sign-off sheet to validate that they are satisfied with the prototype module. The sign-off sheet signifies that the work for a particular phase or task has been completed and that the client is satisfied with this work. The client could have been expected to incur additional charges for any modifications made to the layout or structure of the module after the sign-off sheet was signed. This process might have forced the client to review the prototype module more carefully and not make as many changes later on in the development process.

As a final step within the development phase, technical testing — otherwise known as quality assurance testing — was conducted for the Release Specifications course. This involved checking every link from within each module to ensure that the links were working as intended (Hall, 1997). This quality assurance testing was originally conducted by the instructional designer, who developed the course, by clicking through the links on every page. However, some mistakes were not detected, as was revealed when a second person reviewed the work. To avoid this, a checklist was developed, which listed all the components that should be examined on every page. This type of testing seemed to be even more effective when employees that were not directly involved in building the module did the quality assurance testing. It seemed that their evaluation was more objective, as they would offer a "fresh set" of eyes and detect mistakes that the course developer often overlooked.

During quality assurance testing the modules should be uploaded on the server and tested on several machines, using different types of browsers. If this had been done, the Release Specification course would have run smoothly when we were presenting our work to the senior managers of the health care company during an update meeting. Unfortunately, the senior manager seemed very disappointed with the work when the dynamic spreadsheet did not seem to work on their machines and several screens appeared distorted (as their browsers did not support layers). To make matters worse, several practice and self-assessment exercises were not completed, as the SMEs had not validated and returned them to the instructional designer in the timeframe that had been promised. This incident was quite devastating and, along with poor communication between senior management of the health care company and their SMEs, contributed to the company terminating the project. Thus the Release Specification course that was nearly complete was put on hold and never completed. As a result, further related projects with this health care company were not initiated.

IMPLEMENTATION

Since the Release Specification course was terminated prior to completion, only the Business Systems course was implemented. This involved burning all the files on a CD-ROM and delivering it to the chemical company. The final product was delivered to the client, after the final payment had been deposited. The chemical company uploaded the course on their intranet, to validate the product on the client system. Fortunately, no problems were encountered and the course ran smoothly on the client's server and system browsers. Employees were then given an address to access the course from their computers.

Learners were expected to complete the Business Systems awareness course at their own pace, when they had time. While there was no formal instructor, an individual from the company was assigned to maintain and update the course. Therefore a session was arranged to provide coaching and advice to this individual on maintaining and updating the learning modules using Dreamweaver.

EVALUATION

Formative testing and revision are conducted throughout the design and development of the online courses, to identify and eliminate weaknesses before full-scale implementation, contributing to the success of the project (Kemp, Morrison, & Ross, 1998). Apart from critically examining the suitability of the instructional design objectives, subject content, learning methods, and materials, formative evaluation should examine every factor that affects the performance of the instruction (Kemp, Morrison, & Ross, 1998).

For both the Business Systems and Release Specifications courses, formative evaluation was conducted when the instructional content was examined and revised, when storyboards were examined and modified, when the prototype module was reviewed, and when the modules that were completed were tested. Unfortunately more efficient formative evaluation should have been conducted, examining issues like communication, expectations, and technical specifications for the Release Specifications course. Closely examining such issues early on might have prevented the termination of the project.

Summative evaluation is conducted at the end of a project to measure the degree to which the major project objectives are attained (Kemp, Morrison, & Ross, 1998). This type of summative evaluation, examining the final product, was not conducted for either of the two courses, since the Release Specifications course was not completed, and there was no budget allocated for summative evaluation of the Business Systems course. In fact, most clients do not want to pay the added cost to complete a summative evaluation and examine the return on investment, the effectiveness of the course, or even the long-term benefits of instruction. Designers may want to consider completing summative evaluation for a few selected clients at no cost, because the results from such studies could be used as a marketing tool with future/potential clients if they are positive, or as learning tool to enhance the development of future online courses. If a business does not have the expertise internally to complete a summative evaluation or would like a 'fresh' perspective and outlook on the project, an uninvolved external evaluator can be hired to complete a summative evaluation.

ADDITIONAL OVERALL REFLECTIONS

Throughout the chapter I have attempted to outline the instructional design process that was applied for the development of Web-based training, describing the problems/issues that were encountered and adding my personal reflections. At this point I would like to discuss two additional reflections regarding project management responsibilities of the instructional designer and the overall approach to the courses.

Project Management and Instructional Design

While my main responsibility as an instructional designer was the design and development of Web-based training, in many instances I was also expected to take on project management responsibilities. Since the project manager was busy with several projects, I was tasked with writing the initial proposal for the project, managing the work of the graphic designer, and ensuring that he met deadlines, as well as tracking and reporting the hours and resources utilized for the development of the course. I was also expected, along with the other team members, to complete the project within the estimated timeline and budget, and ensure that the client's expectations were met, which according to Kerzner (2000) indicates that a project is successful. For this reason, I blame myself to some extent for the termination of the Release Specification course.

There were many issues or problems that I identified; however, since these were the first two projects I was assigned as an instructional designer, I did not feel confident enough to express my concerns. For example, the SMEs/

instructors of the Release Specification course communicated that they felt uneasy about converting their traditional classroom course into an online course, despite the eagerness of senior management to go ahead with the project. According to McCallie and McKinzie (1999), if industry people do not feel comfortable and at ease with the online course, the project will be terminated. Therefore, I could have suggested to the project manager that the instructors were given mentoring sessions on how to teach an online course, making them feel at ease with this new delivery format. This might have led to more cooperation on their part, and ultimately the completion of the online courses. While one might consider such concerns to be solely the project manager's responsibility, I have realized that the line between the instructional designer and project manager role is starting to fade. In fact, it seems that you need to develop project management skills, if you are going to be a successful instructional designer in industry. As I have gained more experience building Web-based training and acquired experience and education in project management, I hope to prevent the termination of projects in the future, by detecting and resolving detrimental issues early on in the process.

Constructivism Versus Behaviorism

Both Web-based training courses were developed to teach specific concrete facts and procedures, and employees were paid to take this training. Therefore instruction needed to be completed in the least time possible, and at a time and pace that was suitable for each employee. Under such conditions, it was difficult to incorporate constructivist type of activities like collaboration, communication, exploration, and reflection (Lebow, 1993), which require a fair amount of instructional time and to some extent need to be done in a time-based course.

Even so, the Release Specifications course included a threaded discussion board for students to ask each other questions and discuss any concerns, establishing some form of communication among learners. The Release Specifications course also included the opportunity for reflection, through the completion of long-answer questions. Exploration was evident when learners completed the dynamic spreadsheet exercises, from which they could change certain values and explore the results.

Constructivist values such as collaboration, personal autonomy, reflectivity, active engagement, personal relevance, and pluralism (Lebow, 1993) were overlooked to a great extent in the Business Systems courses. The client advocated that these types of activities would take too much time to complete, and that they would not appeal to learners who are used to being "fed with information." Nevertheless, communication between students and instructor and among students would have made the course more interesting and meaningful, allowing learners to effectively share their knowledge and enhance their learning experience (Swan et al., 2000). As an instructional designer in industry, my role was to listen to what the client wanted, rather than prove them wrong.

In fact, constructivism does not seem to fit with the traditional training culture where organizations and employees are held directly accountable for their performance. When skills such as operating dangerous equipment are concerned or the life of a patient is at stake, it is important that employees have mastered all the skills required to successfully perform their job, in the least time possible. Learning by using collaboration and reflectivity takes too long and does not guarantee that specific skills are mastered. It is simply not sufficient or acceptable for the employee to learn only 50% or 60% of the material or to spend time building analytical thinking skills through collaboration and reflections, because the lack of required knowledge may result in a fatal accident or a detrimental lawsuit for the company. Under these circumstances behavioristic approaches to learning, such as competency-based learning, may be more appropriate than constructivism. Through self-paced modularized learning, immediate feedback, and remedial instruction, employees are expected to achieve 100% mastery of skills. Even so, a combination of the two approaches, as was seen in the Release Specifications course, may be the most effective approach, where elements from both are utilized, allowing mastery of specific skills, while spending some time reinforcing learning through collaboration and communication (i.e., threaded discussion board).

CONCLUSION

Attempting to apply an instructional design model for the development of two online courses for business training was not as straightforward as I had originally expected. While the use of an instructional model was useful for identifying the tasks that needed to be completed, it did not prepare me for several issues that I encountered.

Specifically, there was no budget allocated for a needs assessment for one of the courses, therefore informal interviews needed to be conducted to gain the required information about the project and audience; ultimately this may have affected the quality of the course in a negative way. The SMEs for both courses were either too busy to cooperate or were indecisive about how they wanted the content to be organized, extending the timeline of the project. Even though the client had been promised multimedia elements such as video and animation, these elements could not be included when the instructional message was being designed, due to the limited budget and the lack of in-house expertise to produce them. During the development phase many changes were made to the "finalized" design layout of the course, after most of the modules had been built, which extended the timeline of the project dramatically, because templates and cascading style sheets were not originally used. During a progress meeting, finalized modules were presented to the client with technical problems and features that were not working properly. As a result the client was disappointed and unsatisfied with the project outcome; as these and other problems were not addressed promptly, eventually the project was terminated. Once again due to budget and time constraints, evaluation — a critical phase in the instructional design model — was not completed extensively, if conducted at all. Efficient formative evaluation would have detected problems early on in the process, and possibly resolved critical issues before the project was terminated.

Finally, while I was not a project manager for either of the courses, in many instances I was expected to take on this role. However, due to my limited experience with designing and building online courses, I did not feel confident enough to voice my concerns, or have the experience to effectively and aggressively resolve theses problems. By dealing with these issues throughout the development of two Web-based training courses, I have realized that the instructional designer is at the mercy of the existing budget and resources, technical infrastructure, and the timeline of the project. Other determining factors include the expectations of the client, the decisions the project manager makes, and the experience of the instructional designer. The above factors determined most of the choices that I made as an instructional designer, rather than the instructional objectives and content, or the steps outlined in the instructional design model. Due to these constraints and factors, the type of instruction that was developed was not of superior quality. In an ideal world, the time and resources and experience would be available to design and develop leading-edge Web-based training that is instructionally sound and impressive. Unfortunately, that is usually not the case.

Table 1

Problem Encountered	Suggestions for Future
Lack of budget for needs/job/task analysis	1. Conduct informal working sessions via the telephone or schedule a brief face-to-face meeting to identify the instructional goal, determine the possible solutions and examine the learner characteristics. 2. At a bare minimum, interview company SMEs regarding typical learners and typical job performances 3. Complete the needs assessment at the same time as observing the face-to-face being taught 4. Review any existing instructional resources and instruction with experienced trainer
Prolonged content analysis	1. Include milestones in proposal, where client is expected to sign-off on content 2. Ask the SME to supplement existing Power Point slides with notes during a three-day working session, rather than teach the course to the instructional designer
Lack of assistance from SMEs in sequencing instruction	The instructional designer could attempt to sequence the course and give it to the SME to validate, ensuring that the project moves forward
A large number of learning objectives, and a limited budget	Review the objectives and decide on instructional strategies that would be appropriate for the majority of objectives, and apply these strategies to all of them, for reasons of efficiency
The desires of the client will override the knowledge and experience of the instructional designer	1. Document such instances 2. Complete sign offs at regular intervals
False promises made to client and false expectations were created around multimedia production possibilities	The marketing staff or managers should consult with the multimedia experts regarding the cost, time commitment and in-house expertise around media production, prior to talking with the client, estimating costs, or writing proposals
Limited time and budget for marking assignments and evaluations, coupled with a large class size	Use multiple choice questions, even if long answer questions are more appropriate for the specific learning needs and learners

Guidelines

Table 1 outlines many of the problems encountered when attempting to apply an instructional design model for the design and development of two courses for industry training. Based on my experience, I have outlined some suggestions for dealing with similar problems in the future.

Table 1 (continued)

Problem Encountered	Suggestions for Future
Uncertain of the final structure and layout of the online course/Website, including elements like corporate logos, screen design, methods of interaction, links graphics, and animations	1. Use flowcharts extensively as a communication tool with clients 2. Develop storyboards and style guides initially, as this is a more time and cost efficient approach in the long run 3. Use cascading style sheets and templates to make large scale changes later on in an efficient manner 4. Ask for client sign off at several different stages of development
Overlooked errors during quality assurance testing	1. Ask individuals that are not directly involved in building the online coures to do the quality assurance testing, as they will offer a "fresh set" and more objective evaluation 2. Test the online course on several different browsers and machines
Termination of project	Efficient formative evaluation should be conducted examining issues like communication, expectations, and technical specifications through out the duration of the project
Unwillingness of client to pay for summative evaluation	1. Consider completing summative evaluation for a few selected clients at no cost, because the results from such studies could be used as a marketing tool with future/ potential clients if they are positive, or as learning tool, to enhance the development of future online courses 2. Consider hiring an external evaluator to complete a summative evaluation, if there is no in-house expertise

REFERENCES

Beard, M.W. (1999). Evolution of the ID process at Sprint: A practitioner's perspective. *Performance Improvement, 38*(8), 21-25.

Bi, X. (2000). Instructional design attributes of Web-based courses (Report No. IR 020 507). *Proceedings of the WebNet 2000 World Conference on the WWW and Internet* (Eric Document Reproduction Service No. ED 448 746). San Antonio, Texas.

Boettcher, J. & Conrad, R. (1999). *Faculty Guide for Moving Teaching and Learning on the Web* (Eric Document Reproduction Service No. ED 437985). Laguna Hills, CA: League for Innovation in the Community College.

Canning-Wilson, C. (2000). *E-Learning, E-Teaching, E-Assessment: Aspects of Course Design for Online Web-Based Courses Used with*

EFL/ESL Learners (Eric Document Reproduction Service No. ED 449 788).

DeMartino, D.J. (1999). Employing adult education principles in instructional design (Report No. IR 019 584). *Proceedings of the Society for Information Technology & Teacher Education International Conference SITE 99* (Eric Document Reproduction Service No. ED 432 255). San Antonio, Texas.

Dewald, N., Scholz-Crane, A., Booth, A., & Levine, C. (2000). Information literacy at a distance: Instructional design issues. *Journal of Academic Librarianship, 26*(1), 33-45.

Dick, W. & Carey, L. (1990). *The Systematic Design of Instruction* (3rd ed.). New York: Scott Foresman.

Downs, E., Carlson, R.D., Repman, J., & Clark, K. (1999). Web-based instruction: Focus on learning (Report No. IR 019 584). *Proceedings of the Society for Information Technology & Teacher Education International Conference SITE 99* (Eric Document Reproduction Service No. ED 432 254). San Antonio, Texas.

Gagne, R.M., Briggs, L.J., & Wager W.W. (1992). *Principles of Instructional Design* (4th ed.). Fort Worth, TX: Harcourt, Brace.

Hall, B. (1997). *Web-Based Training Cookbook: Everything You Need to Know for Online Training.* New York: John Wiley & Sons.

Hirumi, A. & Bermundez, A. (1996). Interactivity, distance education, and instructional systems design converge on the information superhighway. *Journal of Research on Computing in Education, 29*(1), 1-16.

Hsu, S., Marques, O., Hamza, M.K., & Alhalabi, B. (1999). *How to Design a Virtual Classroom: 10 Easy Steps to Follow* (Eric Document Reproduction Service No. ED 437 027).

Kemp, J.E., Morrison, G.R., & Ross, S.M. (1998). *Designing Effective Instruction* (2nd ed.). NJ: Merrill-Prentice Hall.

Kerzner, H. (2000). *Project Management — A Systems Approach to Planning, Scheduling, and Controlling* (7th ed.). Toronto, Canada: John Wiley & Sons.

Lebow, D. (1993). Constructivist value for instructional systems design: Five principles toward a new mindset. *Educational Technology Research and Development, 41*(3), 4-16.

Lemiski, D. (2000). *An Examination of the Importance and Use of a Style Guide in the Development of Online Documentation and Computer-*

Based Training. Unpublished Capping Project, Requirement for Master's Degree, University of Alberta, Edmonton, Alberta, Canada.

McCallie, T. & McKinzie, L. (1999). Teaching online: A professional development model (Report No. IR 019 584). *Proceedings of the Society for Information Technology & Teacher Education International Conference SITE 99* (Eric Document Reproduction Service No. ED 432 247). San Antonio, Texas.

Miltiadou, M. & McIssac, M.S. (2000). Problems and practical solutions of Web-based courses. Lessons learned from three educational institutions (Report No. IR 020 112). *Proceedings of the Society for Information Technology & Teacher Education International Conference 2000* (Eric Document Reproduction Service No. ED 444 471). San Diego, California.

Nalley, R. (1995). Designing computer-mediated conferencing into instruction. In Zane, L.B. & Mauri, P.C. (Eds.), *Computer-Mediated Communication and the Online Classroom: Volume 2*. Cresskill, NJ: Hampton Press.

Ritchie, D.C. & Hoffman, B. (1997). *Using Instructional Design Principles to Amplify Learning on the World Wide Web* (Eric Document Reproduction Service No. ED 415 835).

Saba, F. (1999). Designing instruction for the distant learner. *Distance Education Report, 3*(4), 1-7.

Sabine, G. & Gilley, D. (1999). Taking it online: A bootstraps approach (Report No. IR 019 734). *Proceedings of the Mid-South Instructional Technology Conference* (Eric Document Reproduction Service No. ED 436 126). Murfreesboro, Tennessee.

Smaldino, S. (1999). Instructional design for distance education. *Techtrends, 43*(5), 9-13.

Smith, P.J. & Ragan, T.J. (1999). *Instructional Design* (2nd ed.). Upper Saddle River, NJ: Merrill-Prentice Hall.

Swan, K., Shea, P, Fredridcksen, E.E., Pickett, A.M., & Pelz, W.E (2000). Course design factors influencing the success of online learning (Report No. IR 020 507). *Proceedings of the WebNet 2000 Conference on the WWW and Internet* (Eric Document Reproduction Service No. ED 448 760). San Antonio, Texas.

Thrush, E.A. & Young, N.E. (1999). Hither, thither, and yon: Process in putting courses on the Web. *Technical Communication Quarterly, 8*(1), 49-59.

Willis, B. (1992). *Instructional Development for Distance Education* (Eric Document Reproduction Service No. ED 351 007). Syracuse, NY: Eric Clearinghouse on Information Resources.

Chapter IV

Cultural Wisdom and Hindsight: Instructional Design and Delivery on the Run

Jillian Rickertt
Technical Trainer/Instructional Designer, Australia

ABSTRACT

This chapter describes a real situation in Asia where an instructional designer encounters numerous unexpected challenges and cultural experiences. The experiences are described, along with advice for anyone intending to take a similar path. It is expected that many of the experiences could make interesting case studies for students studying instructional design.

INTRODUCTION

If you have ever phoned your telecommunications provider to connect a new phone or to query a phone bill, you may be able to relate to the nature of the software package used for such tasks. Thousands of telecommunications customer service representatives (CSRs) worldwide use such software to provide products and services to telecommunications customers (corporate, business, and residential) and to resolve associated queries that customers may have. The software system described in this passage is widely used for these tasks. It is a highly flexible system, and each telecommunications organization using the software has different products and services and different interfaces into the system; therefore, customized on-site CSR training is necessary for each implementation.

The organizational benefits of a well-trained CSR can perhaps best be judged by considering the consequences of a poorly trained CSR. If products and services are not provisioned correctly, then the number of internal and external queries will multiply exponentially, thus increasing the workload of the CSR.

The vendor who provides the system primarily delivers core IT training for new implementations. CSR training is a new opportunity which is performed on the customers' site, rather than in traditional classrooms on vendor premises. Setting up a training room in a normal vendor classroom is a complex operation involving computer communication, databases, and operating systems. There are usually good support processes in place for vendor classroom training. Many resources are available whose combined expertise ensures a smooth set up and ongoing support for the duration of the training. This is not so for customized CSR on-site training, There are many technical challenges — servers must be set up, communication between the servers and the students' PCs must be established, a myriad of software must be loaded, training databases must be set up so that implementation databases are not impacted, backups must be taken so that the training databases can be refreshed — this list is indicative rather than exhaustive as each site is entirely different, with different interfaces and modules implemented. There is little support available from the implementation team, as the timing of training usually coincides with tight implementation deadlines — i.e., training is delivered "just in time," and the implementation team is excessively busy at this phase of the project ensuring "on time" live implementation. For all of these reasons, on-site trainers need good lines of communication (email, phone, intranet) back to the office.

Customized training naturally necessitates customized instructional design. Many of us who have studied instructional design formally have learned of the different phases involved — Analysis, Design, Development, Implementation, and Evaluation (ADDIE). There is an ADDIE process in use by the vendor organization. It has been devised over a period of time for the core IT training traditionally offered. The analysis phase focuses solely on task and content analysis. The output of the task analysis is used at the design phase to formulate course aims, learning objectives, and delivery strategies, all of which are designed and developed around the task analysis. Training is then implemented and evaluated. For core training, initial evaluation is usually performed through dry runs and pilot courses with internal team members. The application of the ADDIE process by this organization is shown in Figure 1 as a Concept Map.

I would like to relate a recent experience in Asia, which touches on the commercial and logistical arrangements that often accompany and impact this methodology when it is applied on site.

The project was almost complete, the customer almost due to go live; however, none of the training team members had yet been involved in the project. I received an email asking whether I could design and deliver a Train the Trainer course for customer service representatives which would be delivered to approximately 60 trainers, who would then train approximately 2,000 CSRs. I was given a timeframe of two weeks for analysis and design, and would perform this on-the-job, where all of the SMEs (Subject Matter Experts) and process analysis would be available. I would also have two weeks lead time before traveling to the on-site location to get across as much as the project documentation as possible. A team of people experienced in curriculum design would be assembled to assist in the compilation of the training material. My immediate reaction was that this was tight, but not impossible if the CSR processes had already been documented and tested. I was assured that they

Figure 1: Current ADDIE Model

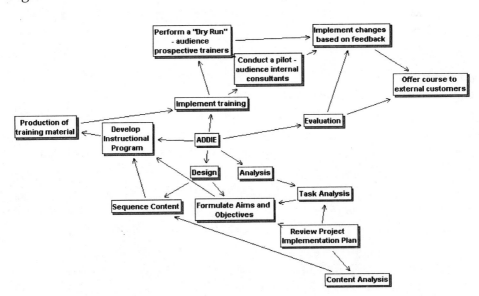

were almost complete, and were being prepared by a team comprising the Customer and the Systems Integrator. I agreed to undertake the project.

ANALYSIS

On the day before I was due to leave, facts began to emerge:

Fact 1: The first three days that had been allocated to Instructional Analysis and Design would be spent training the team in the application. "The team" was the System Integrator and the Customer, who were preparing the business processes. *How could the processes be almost complete if the people preparing them had not been trained in the application?*

Fact 2: In the two weeks lead time that I had as I read through the documentation, I could see "gaps" in the solutions proposed. Inquiries revealed that for many solutions, the reply was, "We are still working on the solution; we don't know quite yet how this will work." *How could complete processes and training material be compiled if the solutions were not yet defined?*

Fact 3: On arrival, I inquired as to how I would connect to the training environment, or to the latest environment available in order to begin. Perhaps I should explain that in this context, an environment is a copy of a customized computer database, configured specifically for an implementation. Access to this database is necessary in order to complete a task analysis and to incorporate one of the attributes of constructivism into the design — namely activities that are "either replicas of or analogous to the kinds of real-world problems faced by citizens, consumers, or professionals in the field" (Jonasson et al., 1995). I was advised that there was not an available environment at this stage. The integrators were having difficulty creating one — maybe by the end of the week. *So far I have lost three days where I have had to perform unexpected training, and it looked like I would lose another two days waiting for an authentic environment.*

Fact 4: On arrival I have no email, Internet, or intranet access to anywhere. It can take up to two weeks to process a request for Internet/email access. The only way I can communicate electronically with my office is from my hotel room, which is very slow, very expensive, and will cause time delays, as email queries and responses can only be sent or received early morning and late evening. *How can I be effective in my role if I cannot easily communicate with my wider team of trainers/colleagues and SMEs?*

I am almost ready to go home, but the best is yet to come. Immediately after integration team training, a meeting is called where I get to meet the rest of the team, and we begin to plan our project.

The first thing that I learned is that my colleague, the only other person who knows anything about this project, will be away for one week — returning on the day that the project is expected to be complete. I am told that other resources are available. They are administrative staff who have no experience in instructional design or delivery. *How can we achieve production of the material in the time given — which is now down to 12 days including weekends?*

I decide to task my colleague who is going on leave to spend one day with me getting across as many details about the local responsibilities and skills as possible. This "handover" being completed, she would also work with me to ensure that an authentic environment is available and would arrange urgent email access for me.

A handover is achieved — it is worse than I imagined. There are **two** applications involved in the solution, and the training material needs to integrate both of them. The person developing the training material for the other application has no training experience whatsoever, and is looking for direction from me. I need to stress that when I requested a handover, I really did not feel that I had time for this step, but without it I would not have had any direction at all, and would not have known where to begin in putting together a project plan. Imagine if I had not known up front that the training material would need to integrate both applications. I could have spent precious time (by now even hours are precious) developing something completely unusable. The handover brought me up to date with what the expected deliverables would be, what resources were available to achieve this, and at what stage the project currently is. It also identified the associated issues and risks. None of this would have been achieved by reading any of the project material before arriving on site.

DESIGN

Now that I know the full status of the project, I am very ready to go home. I peruse the business processes that have been defined by one of the senior administrative resources. They are very good — missing the "how," but certainly showing promise. I immediately befriend the person writing them. I also befriend the person responsible for developing the training material in the other application. I find that I have two very keen people who are receptive to suggestions, and have many good suggestions of their own. We develop a plan, shown as a Ghantt chart in Figure 2, and begin to apply it with enthusiasm. It is very ambitious, but so are we.

Figure 2: Gantt Chart — Proposed Activities

Activity / DAY	1	2	3	4	5	6	7	8	9	10	11	12
Combine objectives for both applications -- all modules	■											
Design instructional integration for both applications		■										
Complete and review first module			■									
Complete day 1 overview module		■										
Complete modules 2 to 4			■									
Review modules 2 to 4				■								
Complete modules 5 to 7					■							
Review modules 5 to 7					■							
Complete modules 8 to 11						■						
Review modules 8 to 11						■						
Complete modules 12 to 14							■					
Review modules 12 to 14							■					
Test combined modules in integrated environment								■				
Confirm processes are correct									■			
Review instructional strategies/content									■			
Pass training material to printing department										■		
Prepare training database and take backup											■	
Test a sample of the training material											■	
Restore the database from backup												■

Days are long, many issues are discovered and resolved, weekends are non-existent, but we are making progress! The implementation team (those who are installing and integrating the new software with the company's system) are extremely stressed in meeting deadlines, but provide invaluable assistance by explaining functionality whenever they can. The task analysis is not prepared as a separate document; it is embedded immediately into the training material. We are able to do this because the content outline (business process document) has provided a usable template for sequencing of content and for the generation of aims and objectives. There are problems with development of the other application that is needed for this particular solution. The problems are similar to those identified in my application and are directly related to the fact that the solution is not yet fully developed. This is not uncommon in commercial software integration, but we need to make some decisions:

1.   Remove the training for the areas which do not yet have solutions — this leaves large gaps in the training material and the logical end-to-end processes.
2.   Provide "workaround" interim training and re-train the impacted areas when final solutions are available from the implementation teams. The number of areas impacted is significant, resulting in approximately two days more training when final solutions are defined. It is an expensive exercise, as the training is to be delivered to 60 trainers in different geographical circles in face-to-face mode.
3.   Wait for advice on the final solution — the software implementation team is under pressure to resolve all identified issues before going live.

I should add that many of the issues being worked out by the software team (both software bugs and gaps in processes) had been discovered while my team was developing the training material.

We review our project plan in consultation with the implementation teams in order to establish where the bugs and gaps are and when solutions are expected. It is quite complex, as we are working with two systems, two implementation teams, a system integrator and of course the customer. We conclude that if we slip training by one week, approximately 90% of the gaps/faults will be resolved, leaving a handful of issues requiring workarounds that will need to be trained as an interim process. We are able to design and document much of the missing content, including the workarounds, flagging it as needing to be confirmed for accuracy as the solutions are implemented. There is still a lot to be done, however everyone is relieved that we now have an extra week and an opportunity to deliver a more complete and comprehensive training course.

DEVELOPMENT

My colleague returned from leave and is amazed at what we have achieved. Project commercials rear their head — nobody has signed an approval for the development of the training material. My colleague and I are advised by the Project Manager to stop work until the approval is forthcoming. I take my first day off in two weeks, but it is difficult to relax, as we cannot afford to lose a day. We spend the day catching up on non-project-related administrative tasks that have been sorely neglected. In the evening I cannot stop myself from developing a little more of the content, hopeful that the financial issues will be resolved quickly. The team member who has defined the business processes phones. She is very upset, and justifiably so. She is ultimately responsible for this delivery and understands the impact of losing a day or possibly more depending on how quickly the wheels of finance turn. Approval is gained late that evening — we are back on site with a day to make up.

We have also been allocated more resources for the assessment phase. However, they have no experience whatsoever in education and training, and we did not request these resources. They strip all of the hands-on exercises from my training material and ask me to replace them with "quizzes." I am mortified. I explain that the exercises they have stripped out form part of the assessment. They are not listening. I talk to my good friend with the business processes and she gets the exercises put back in. The new team hounds me every day — more quizzes, more quizzes. I appease them by creating some multiple-choice/true-false questions. They love it! They want more! I show them my assessment plan and explain patiently how each objective is to be assessed. They do not really understand, but they seem to get the message and stop pestering me for more "quizzes."

It is Friday and training is to commence on the following Monday. We are urgently completing last-minute modifications. There is something going on around us — we get the feeling that all is not well with the training room. We ask to take a look. At 5:00 p.m. they invite us to view the training room.

It is difficult to find the right words to describe the "training room." There are wobbly wooden benches that are higher than most normal desks, with very low chairs that have a fold out arm on which the students will place their training material and their mouse. It is cramped. Each student will need to remain quite still. There is simply not room for them to move their body too far without colliding with another student. The benches are in lines, with just enough room for each student to file in and take a seat. If the person in the far left corner of the room needs to leave the room, then almost every other student in the room will need to move. There is a myriad of cables — more than normal — due to the multiple systems required. They are scattered all over the floor, making it extremely difficult and dangerous to navigate the room. It is going to be impossible for a trainer to stand behind any student to see what is on their screen. The overhead screen is covered in black stains — there will be absolutely no point whatsoever in trying to project onto it, and we are relying heavily on the data projector for this training. In many countries, Occupational Health & Safety rules would eliminate this environment immediately. Our hearts cannot sink any lower. I inquire as to whether there is a bigger room — there is not. I ask that the overhead projector screen be replaced, explaining that this is absolutely essential. They say they will "do their best," but cannot promise. I point out the danger with all of the wires over the floor — they assure me that this will be fixed. I wonder how. I turn on one of the computers — it doesn't work. I am assured they will all be working by Monday morning. I ask that two of them are operational by tomorrow, as we need to enter some training data into the system. I am very ready to go home.

We arrive early on Saturday morning and examine the room again. We are alone, so we can talk freely — we establish that with a few changes, we can commence training. We are not excited at all at the prospect, but determine that as we have come this far, we should at least give this our best effort. We test the computers — three out of 20 are operational. We populate the database with what we need, and go on our way. We take Sunday off — we are both quiet, apprehensive, wondering how on earth this is going to work! Many activities that should have occurred have not occurred — the database has not yet been backed up, and we still have not seen both systems operating together.

IMPLEMENTATION

We arrive Monday morning, two hours early, thinking we will be first. Approximately 10 people are there already — the HR Manager, the Project Sponsor, the Training Manager (where has he been up until now?), my good friend who owns the business processes, my good friend who has developed his application in conjunction with me, and an army of engineers, who are rapidly testing/fixing each computer. The wooden benches have been covered in festive coverings — they look quite good. I test one to see if it is still wobbly. It does not wobble. The HR manager is laughing at me. There is a carpet on the floor, covering the myriad of wires — sure there are still some protruding, but it is workable. *The overhead screen is pearly white, with just a faint sign of a stain in the middle — it will be OK.* Our spirits are lifting. The students begin to arrive — they are very enthusiastic — they don't seem to notice how cramped they are, they simply file in and take a seat. They begin to flick through our training material. This is a proud moment.

An agenda is passed around — we have not seen it before, we have focused on our training program. We discover that for the first two hours, key speakers will address the trainees. Looks like we just lost two hours…no, upon further reading, it looks like we will not finish until 7.30 p.m. We go through the rest of the agenda — every day is scheduled from 8:00 a.m. to 7:30 p.m. — surprise!

The key speakers are excellent — very motivated and motivational. The students are wound up, so are we! The speakers have described the trainees as "the chosen ones" — key people within the organization who will train hundreds of CSRs. They praise our instructional design and delivery team highly. One of the aspects of motivational systems theory (MST; Rouse et al., 2000) is based on the living system framework (LSF; Ford, 1992). This theory describes motivation as the patterning of goals, emotions, and self-concept. The theory considers a person to be "an open, living system that interacts with his or her environment." We can almost provide an analogy for this MST theory in our context:

Goal: Trainees become proficient enough to on train hundreds of CSRs. This is a shared goal between trainees and trainers.

Emotions: Being described as "the chosen ones" will most likely promote emotive pride in the trainees. Our emotions are also running high; we realize that other people in the organization value our work, and we too relish some emotive pride.

Self Concept: It is likely that the description of "the chosen ones" to provide training to hundreds of CSRs will result in a very positive self-concept. It could be debated that the culmination of the goals and emotions will result in positive self-esteem.

Interaction with the Environment: We have an environment that is far from perfect, yet we are all ready (in fact eager) to interact with that environment.

We commence training delivery. We get to see whether the two systems operate together as documented — they work!

EVALUATION

Now the assessment surprise. Training finishes at 7:00 p.m. The assessment team begins distributing "assignments," which students must take home and complete. I take a look — the assignment is ill written and has nothing to do with the content covered today. Besides that, students are exhausted. It will take most of them at least an hour to travel home. I gently suggest that perhaps students could read over today's material. The students look at me thankfully. We suggest they read through today's material with a view to making a presentation on the content. The students depart, and I ask the assessment team if I can please see the rest of their work. I explain that assessment must measure specific objectives. The customer stakeholders (including my good friend with the business processes) are adamant that students must be given assignments every night. I disagree, but it is late and we are tired, so we agree to take it up tomorrow. I obtain a copy of all of the assignments that have been prepared by the "assessment team" and examine them that night. They are not appropriate. I have to admit that the assessment I had designed was not that good either, due to time constraints.

We compromise. I create some more true/false, multiple-choice, and short answer questions that are administered at the end of each day, before students go home. This is still not perfect, but in hindsight was actually quite effective. It was not uncommon for us to be printing the assessment 15 minutes before the end of the class. Marking keys were made up on the fly, and this culture was extremely interested in their results — if they got a question wrong, they wanted to know why and would debate vehemently if they disagreed with the answer. They worked extremely long and hard — perhaps more so than most of us in a Western culture would be prepared to do.

Their final assessment was a presentation on a selected topic. The topic was not allocated to them until 30 minutes before they were to present it. I had designed a specific criteria which we would use to mark them — a panel consisting of myself, my colleague, my process friend, and my other application colleague performed the assessment and agreed on marks for each student.

At the end of the presentations, we reviewed all marks, including the daily quizzes, to determine whether each student was competent enough to train CSRs. This is where I had the biggest cultural surprise of all! Although we had methodically marked according to specific criteria, my two colleagues tended to ignore that criteria for certain people, and to evaluate their competence on personality alone. We discussed and debated well into the night, and eventually agreed on all gradings except for one. We called in another person the following day to get their opinion and it was similar to that of my colleagues — based on personality rather than fact. I have to say I found this quite fascinating! They agreed that this person would need to do another presentation that they would re-evaluate. The person in question had rated quite highly in all of the quizzes and the presentation criteria. Unfortunately, the presentation was performed after I had left. I heard that he passed it easily, so I can only assume some cultural reason for forcing that particular person to present twice.

Hinkle (1994) presents some interesting opinions on cross-cultural assessment. He discusses the need to provide in-service training in assessment in order to remove bias and also recommends that practitioners scrutinize the content of tests in cross-cultural situations. These opinions are certainly confirmed in this context. We had a situation where unqualified people were writing and administering assessment with no in-service training, and where I was fortunately on the spot to rectify this and perform the necessary scrutinizing and modification.

Formative Evaluation

Throughout the first iteration of training, we reviewed the design continuously. Every evening we would meet to discuss what had worked well and what had not worked well. We would toss around new ideas and incorporate them where possible. The evaluation team consisted of myself, my colleague, the trainer for the other system, and the business process author. We also distributed daily evaluations to the trainees, asking them to rate the content, the training strategies, the trainers, and the equipment. Trainees were also given the opportunity to comment on any aspect of the day's training. Feedback from these evaluations was also incorporated into the design review. Trainees generally rated the course very highly and provided candid feedback when necessary.

I have since been back to this site and could not resist doing informal evaluation of the training. (There is no budgetary allowance to do this formally.) It seems that the project is considered very successful, and that the CSRs are managing the system very competently — this is indeed a miracle!

Upon reflection, many lessons were learned during this project, which I have summarized below:

- *When training on-site, all of the ANALYSIS steps in the ADDIE process should be addressed.* Clark (1997) describes an analysis step of choosing an instructional setting, part of which requires a decision on how and where the training will take place. While this step is taken care of in normal classroom delivery, the on-site requirements need to be clearly communicated, and must be followed up and monitored. Had we followed up on this point earlier, we may have been able to secure a larger classroom with more ergonomic desks and chairs. Readings linked to the Graduate School of Education-George Mason University website on instructional design discuss air quality, lighting, decoration and tidiness, noise, furniture, and ergonomics in some detail — I can state with utmost confidence that none of the requirements listed were present in our training environment. We were extremely fortunate to be able to claim success under these conditions.

- *Another of the steps which forms part of the ANALYSIS phase is learner analysis* (Clark, 1997). This analysis was performed on the run and did not include some major areas — e.g., motivation of learners, and specific interests and biases of learners. For example, the handling of assessment could have been significantly improved if we had known that the use of "quizzes" was a motivating factor for this culture.

- *Double check on external and internal communication.* The fact that we had no knowledge of the agenda prepared by the HR department could have had major repercussions. We should have presented our agenda to HR as soon as it was known so that a merging of the two agendas could have been agreed to earlier. We should also have had much more interaction with the Training Manager who would most likely been able to provide valuable input regarding the learner analysis.

- *Ensure everybody understands their roles and responsibilities and follow up on these,* e.g., the team tasked with preparing the PCs in the training room, testing the integration of the two applications, and for installation and back up of the databases had many responsibilities. We were extremely lucky that everything worked together on the day and that the integration of the two systems was successful. This risk should have been mitigated much earlier than it was.

- *Most projects of this magnitude have an overall Project Manager who will most likely handle work orders for all aspects of the project.* The project commercials or resource needs of the project are handled differently in each company's environment. A work order or a commercial agreement — usually stating deliverables, number of resources for a specified period, and a daily rate for each resource — will more than likely be required. Communicate with the project manager regarding the commercials; ensure that the necessary paperwork has been completed, preferably before you arrive on site. Being put in a position where you have to walk off the job does not present a professional image. Ensure you check this aspect with the person directly responsible (see above on roles and responsibilities). In this situation we had been advised that the commercials were in place, but the advice was incorrect.

- *Ensure there are communication channels open.* This is vitally important when you are away from your usual environment. You need access to your colleagues and access to key people on site within the project. You cannot operate effectively if you cannot communicate. My strategy of ensuring that my colleague arranged email access for me before going on leave may seem an unusual task when there was so much else to be done; however, it proved to be extremely valuable in keeping me connected with everyone I needed to be connected with. Be prepared for this to take some time in a large organization, and try to start the process even before you depart.

- *Be prepared to be flexible, probably to put in many additional hours, but also be realistic.* Ensure that the scope of work is reasonable for the time allowed.

- *Allow for system downtime when estimating duration.* When the system is available, use it wisely. Dump screens in advance if possible, and make brief notes on "how to" areas which may be expanded when the system is down.

- *Find out quickly who the key players are and get to know them.* Communicate with them daily. Even though you are most likely pushed for time, try to do some social activities such as lunch or dinner whenever possible. Good relationship building will assist everyone in the team.

- *Verify functionality with the implementation team, and verify business processes with the client.* Many technical trainers come from a technical background and can unwittingly move to solution mode rather than instructional mode. If you find gaps in functionality, don't try to solve it; rather, discuss it with the implementation team. In my experience the development of training material often uncovers bugs which were not detected at testing phase. Be prepared for this, and if possible allow time for it when scheduling.

The point of this story is that in the real world, very often time and resources are sacrificed for the sake of the project, both logistically and commercially. In many developing countries, be prepared for the type of classroom environment described in this passage. Since this experience, I have learned that the circumstances I have described are not uncommon. A colleague has suggested that perhaps one should "expect" this situation — not necessarily like it, but do expect it, and prepare accordingly. This appears to be an extremely practical approach when designing instruction "from the trenches."

REFERENCES

Clark, D. (1997). *Big Dog ISD Page.* Accessed September 12, 2002: http://www.nwlink.com/~donclark/hrd/sat.html.

Graduate School of Education-George Mason University. *Doing an Instructional Design Project.* Accessed September 12, 2002: http://classweb.gmu.edu/ndabbagh/Resources/Resources2/Environment.htm.

Hinkle, J.S. (1994). Practitioners and cross cultural assessment: A practical guide to information and training, 27(2), 103-15.

Jonassen, D., Davidson, M., Collins, M., Campbell, J., & Bannan Haag, B. (1995). Constructivism and computer-mediated communication in distance education. *The American Journal of Distance Education,* 9(2), 7-26.

Rouse, G., Kimberly, A., & Cashin, S.E. (2000). Assessment of academic self-concept and motivation: Results from three ethnic groups, 33(2), 91-105.

Chapter V

Combining Technology, Theory and Practice: A Finnish Experience

John Lew Cox
University of West Florida, USA

Terry R. Armstrong
Armstrong Consulting, USA

ABSTRACT

Offering a valid educational experience at remote locations having few academic resources has always been a problem, financially and logistically. Yet, previous models and attempts at distance learning came up short in a number of areas. Now the Internet has opened up new possibilities. The authors were given the task of teaching an undergraduate course in Strategic Management in a remote Finnish location without many needed library resources. Their experiences led serendipitously to an approach combining a few strategic models, the Internet, and student presentations to allay fears the authors had about academic soundness in previous models. This chapter gives details of how the design of the course, which could not have been taught adequately without the Internet, has led to a fascinating approach for using the Internet in a traditional classroom as well as in remote areas.

INTRODUCTION AND BACKGROUND

In most countries in the world, higher education has been hit with a quadruple threat. These are:

1.   a lack of what many see as adequate funding for faculty and ancillary support people;
2.   a lack of adequate funding to keep the information technology infrastructure up to date (or even close) to that available to business organizations;
3.   a lack of adequate funding and knowledge of the capabilities of the omnipresent Internet, as concerns the educational process; and
4.   the inexorable encroachment of "distance education" (however defined) along with the concomitant questions on quality of offerings.

While higher-level policymakers are trying to address the four threats above, the educational process must go on, with the participants making the best use of the tools available at the time. This is a practical and personal example of preserving a quality educational experience, utilizing tools from ancient (the Socratic method) to contemporary (the Internet).

Not long ago, one of the authors was asked to teach a basic management course in a rural Finnish location. The course was based on traditional readings and experiential exercises as may be found in many Fundamentals of Management courses. It went well. The students learned but there was no involvement and the professor was exhausted at the end of the day. It was extremely difficult to keep the students attentive. While teaching this very traditional course, the professor discovered that the school had several computer labs with Internet access. Partly because this was an extremely rural environment, many of the school's students spent hours on the Internet and several had already adventured into e-commerce. The professor was asked if he could return in July to teach a capstone course in Strategic Management. While initially hesitant, because he did not feel the school had the resources for teaching a capstone strategy course, he reluctantly agreed.

Upon his return to the U.S., the two authors worked together to develop a course utilizing the Internet that would achieve results similar in rigor and outcome to U.S. strategy courses and would at the same time keep the students involved and attentive. This case study describes that course and its outcomes, and provides suggestions on using and improving upon it.

OVERVIEW OF THE REDESIGN

The course began with lectures concerning the strategic aspects of management. The lecture topics covered theories of strategy, internal and external pressures for change, competition, cultural influences on business strategy, and organizational leadership. Lectures also covered a number of well-known strategic models, and several class experiential exercises and short case studies were used to reinforce the lecture materials. The strategic models the students were taught and used included:

- SWOT Analysis (Strengths, Weaknesses, Opportunities, and Threats)
- PETS Environmental Analysis (Political, Economical, Technical, and Social)
- The Boston Consulting Group's Growth/Share Matrix
- Collis and Mongomery's Market Force Model
- Michael Porter's Strategic Wheel

The students were then tested to see how well they understood those models.

In the next part of the redesign, Internet usage was incorporated. The students were given assigned readings, some of which they could get from the Internet and some from journal articles put on reserve in the library.

Then the class was divided into study groups and given a list of 40 global companies, from which they selected one to investigate. The companies/industries from which they could choose included:

- LVMH Moët Hennessy Louis Vuitton, Fashion Industry
- Chrysler/Daimler-Benz, Automobiles
- Merc, Pharmaceutical
- Nokia, Telecommunications
- Disney, Entertainment
- Sony, Electronic
- McDonald's, Fast Food
- British Petroleum, Oil
- Compaq, PCs
- Fuji, Film
- Raytheon, Radar
- Nordstrom, Department Store

- Telekom Malaysia, Telecommunications
- DHL Worldwide Express, Express-Transportation Market
- Swiss Air, Airlines

Each group was to study its selected company, then prepare a detailed report for presentation to the entire class, to include an identification of the strategy used by their company, along with a comparative analysis of their company's competitors' strategies. Since the location was remote, there was no budget for long-distance telephone charges or for travel, and timing precluded the receipt of information by mail; the only tool the groups had for conducting the corporate study was the Internet.

The first week of class the students were given three hours of lecture in the morning and then went to the computer lab to search the Web. They were shown numerous sites that deal with news, economics, demographics, politics, technology, finance, and social trends, all of which have an effect on corporate strategy. The instructor assisted groups and individuals as they searched the Internet sites of their selected companies, as well as of their companies' competitors. Thus, the instructor was discovering with the students the kinds of problems they were encountering in their search. Whenever a particular generic problem was encountered and a solution discovered, the information was shared with the entire class. Teaching by example, this sharing of search techniques quickly became a norm in the class and students readily shared search strategies, although they did not share information about their specific companies. Company-specific information was saved until they gave their oral presentation to the class. Quickly the students differentiated between strategies for finding information on the Internet and strategic information about the companies under study.

The students' experience with the Internet was similar to what the authors have found in other courses utilizing it. The students obtained such a volume of information that they would have been overwhelmed without the models to act as filters. Their instruction in strategy and the various strategic models given at the beginning of the course, however, gave the students the structure they needed to analyze their companies from a strategic point of view. Thus, they were able to determine the various strategies their selected corporations were using and compare them with the strategies of competitive companies.

The last week of class, each group prepared a lengthy report and gave a 20-minute classroom presentation using PowerPoint. After the presentations were completed, the class discussed what they had learned. All the students were surprised at the specific strategies their global companies were using, and were impressed with their own abilities to identify these corporate strategies. In addition, the students commented on how helpful the models had been for organizing the material in a manner that allowed them to carry out useful strategic analysis.

RESULTS

The methods used in the course were different from the usual "lecture and reporting" expected by Finnish students in their typical course. In his first experience teaching Fundamentals of Management to the Finnish students, the instructor had found it difficult to engage them using experiential techniques, the Socratic method, and traditional cases. By contrast, he found they became totally involved in the learning process in this "Web-facilitated discovery learning approach." Class evaluations showed that students appreciated and enjoyed the clarity of the models and were surprised at how useful the models were for analyzing the information they had retrieved from the Internet. Students also reported they felt they had developed practical Internet skills as well as their power of analysis, skills that should stand them in good stead in later courses or industrial positions.

IMPROVING THE COURSE

The course was a textbook case of "Much has been done; yet, much still remains to be done." Though the authors consider the course to have been a success, as well as a great learning experience for themselves, it still has room for improvement. Possibilities include the development of a website which provides a tutorial on how to do a Web search, and which also gives hints on good starting points. In addition, examples of graded reports could be posted to such a site so students could benchmark their work with previous classes. A template aiding them in the organization of their reports might also be posted. Further, students could do content analysis of websites using packages like MS Word, EXCEL, and ACCESS, thus becoming even more sophisticated in using these available tools for research.

CONCLUSIONS

While higher education may be under attack from many different directions, that does not connote a lesser learning experience for students. What has become rudimentary use of technology, such as the Web and basic MS Office tools, can be very effectively used for teaching business strategy (and likely a wide variety of other courses). As an example of lagniappe, the students also greatly improved their abilities to conduct Web searches, and to use models as a way to structure and organize the results of their searches. Thus, it appears this experiment with using the Web and rudimentary computer package technology as an auxiliary tool for teaching business strategy is an effective way to engage students while teaching the importance of models for analyzing large amounts of information.

Chapter VI

Applying Contextual Design to Educational Software Development

Mark Notess
Indiana University, USA

ABSTRACT

Contextual Design is a methodology for developing information systems from a rich understanding of customer work practice. This chapter considers how Contextual Design can be applied to educational software development and how Contextual Design might interact with Instructional Systems Design (ISD). Following a brief overview of ISD, I describe Contextual Design and provide a detailed case study of its application to educational software development — to the design of an online tool for music listening and analysis in undergraduate and graduate music education. I conclude with some reflections on the relevance of Contextual Design to instructional designers.

INTRODUCTION

Contextual Design is a methodology for designing information systems from a rich understanding of customer work practice (Beyer & Holtzblatt, 1998). This chapter considers how the Contextual Design methodology can be applied to the development of educational software and how Contextual Design might interact with Instructional Systems Design (ISD). I begin with a brief overview of ISD, brief because I assume readers of this chapter will already have some acquaintance with ISD. I then describe Contextual Design and provide a detailed case study of its application to educational software development—to the design of an online tool for music listening and analysis in undergraduate and graduate music education. I conclude with some reflections on the relevance of Contextual Design to instructional designers.

INSTRUCTIONAL SYSTEMS DESIGN

The ADDIE (Analysis, Design, Development, Implementation, Evaluation) model of Instructional Systems Design provides a general framework for designing instruction. The model seems to have emerged anonymously during the 1960s (Michael Molenda, personal communication, August 1, 2002) but has since become broadly known. In a 1988 booklet from ASTD, ADDIE is described as one of a variety of models for Instructional Systems Design (ASTD, 1988, p. 2). A Web search of "addie" and "instructional systems" yields hundreds of hits. ADDIE is widely known and is sometimes even described as *the* instructional systems design model (e.g., Fardouly, 1998).

However, ADDIE is not the only model for instructional systems design. Over the years, more refined, comprehensive, flexible models have evolved; it is these more recent models that structure the textbooks in the field (e.g., Dick & Carey, 1996; Kemp, Morrison, & Ross, 1998). For example, the Kemp, Morrison, and Ross model contains nine *elements* (their preferred term) instead of five (pp. 5-7):

1. Instructional problems
2. Learner characteristics
3. Task analysis
4. Instructional objectives
5. Content sequencing
6. Instructional strategies
7. Designing the message

8.   Instructional delivery
9.   Evaluation instruments

Kemp, Morrison, and Ross add some additional overarching topics such as project management, planning, and support services, and state that not all steps need be included in every situation, nor do the steps need to be strictly linear (pp. 5-7). They also emphasize the need for formative evaluation and revision during design (pp. 162-163).

CONTEXTUAL DESIGN

Contextual Design and ISD have different backgrounds. ISD models are process models for the development of instruction or instructional *systems*. In this context, "systems" refers to the interrelatedness of all the parts of an instructional program and the attempt of the development process to account for the many parts and their interdependencies. ISD primarily targets instructional *content* (objectives, material, sequencing, testing). Contextual Design grew out of very different soil — a soil in which "systems" means "information systems," i.e., computers, software, and related technology. As a (computer) system design method, Contextual Design focuses on how best to design systems (hardware, software) to meet customers' needs. While these needs may include learning or training, the concern is less with learning how to do something than with actually doing it — quickly, cheaply, effectively. With instructional design, *content* is nearly always critical. With Contextual Design, as will be seen below, *work practice* is critical.

Though they sprang from different soil, Contextual Design and ISD have some occasion to become acquainted. One reason is that learning must be taken into account if work performance is to excel. A second reason — and the one motivating this case study — is that learning itself is a variety of "work." Moreover, with the growth of online learning environments, designing instruction (or learning) is not always easily separable from the design of the technology used in delivery. This linkage is not new. Instructional designers have had to concern themselves with the design of delivery technology for decades. But the capability and malleability of computer-based and especially Web-based delivery technologies has heightened the need for instructional designers to attend to technology design. I will return to this distinction at the end of the chapter.

While some instructional designers may have the luxury — or the curse — of designing instruction within a predetermined technical framework, others must concern themselves with the simultaneous design of instruction and its delivery technology. Still others design delivery technologies without designing instruction at the same time, hoping (or naively assuming) that the technology will suit the educational needs it purports to address. Such is the case I will introduce later, after first describing Contextual Design.

Overview

Contextual Design is a user-centered design methodology created by Karen Holtzblatt and Hugh Beyer to address the needs of commercial software and information system development (Beyer & Holtzblatt, 1998). Contextual Design emphasizes the need to base design decisions on a shared understanding of how real people do real work in real contexts. Contextual Design has been applied to such varied design problems as enterprise portals, system administration tools, and library systems (Holtzblatt, 2001; Rockwell, 1999; Curtis et al., 1999; Normore, 1999). My own experience with Contextual Design goes back to the early 1990s, when I introduced Contextual Design into one of Hewlett-Packard's development groups (Rockwell, 1999; Curtis et al., 1999). Subsequently, I have been exploring the applicability of Contextual Design (and other methods from the field of human-computer interaction) to instructional contexts (Notess, 2001).

Because Contextual Design is described in great detail in Beyer and Holtzblatt (1998), this chapter will provide only a brief overview of the pieces of the process, yet with enough detail to render the case study comprehensible. Contextual Design consists of six steps:
1.   Contextual Inquiry
2.   Work Modeling
3.   Consolidation
4.   Work Redesign
5.   User Environment Design
6.   Paper Prototyping

In describing each of the six steps, I will make connections, chiefly through examples, to instructional settings.

Contextual Inquiry

Designers identify real users (or potential real users) and go visit them in their places of work. The inquiry is a combination of observation and interviewing. The interviewing focuses on understanding the users, their work, and the context of their work. A key assumption behind contextual inquiry is that if you take people away from their work tasks and context, they cannot give you an adequate explanation of their work (what they do, why they do it, how they do it). Their decontextualized explanations are less detailed and less accurate than what you learn if you observe and discuss *in situ*. The reason for this difference is that skilled workers are skilled and productive because they do not rely exclusively on what is in their conscious awareness. Much of one's work knowledge is either internalized to the point where it is subconscious, or the knowledge is embedded in the environment, including tools and processes.

In contextual inquiry, the interviewer asks the users to continue doing their work while the interviewer observes and plies them with questions about what is happening and why. Contextual inquiry is typically done in one to three hour sessions, and in some situations the session may be recorded, although often this is not necessary. The interviewer takes notes, makes sketches, and asks clarifying questions in order to form a detailed picture of the work. An important function of the inquiry is to arrive at an accurate understanding of the activity being observed. As the interviewer watches, he or she will form hypotheses about the work — e.g., why something is being done. The interviewer then articulates the hypotheses to see if they are accurate. Beyer and Holtzblatt (1998, p. 56) call this validation process "interpretation."

Although we use the term "work" to describe what we are interested in understanding, the word should be taken in its broadest sense of purposeful activity. In an educational environment, "work" could include reading, doing assignments, preparing a lesson, lecturing, answering student email, meeting in a study group, browsing the Web, etc. Any of these tasks are potentially relevant targets for contextual inquiry.

Work Modeling

The contextual interview is followed by the interpretation session. In the interpretation session, the design team (or a subset) meets to hear the interviewer "replay" the interview — to talk through the entire interview, describing what was seen and heard.

During the replay, design team members ask clarifying questions and capture data in the following types of models:

- The *flow model* identifies the key people/roles involved in the work and what moves between them (communication, work products). For example, in a classroom setting, the key people are the teacher and the student. Some of the work products that move between them are assignments (teacher-to-student) and completed homework (student-to-teacher). However, the goal of contextual inquiry is to capture realistic detail, not just idealized descriptions. So a flow model might well include seemingly peripheral people such as departmental secretary or roommate — anyone with whom the user interacted in the course of doing the work of interest. Another important type of data to capture on flow models are *work breakdowns*. Breakdowns on the model indicate problem areas in the work. For example, if a student is doing homework and is confused about one of the requirements but cannot find his or her assignment sheet, that is a work breakdown. Breakdowns are important because they indicate opportunities for new systems to make improvements.

- The *sequence model* captures the actual sequence of steps the user followed, along with what triggered each activity and what the motivating goals and intents were. If work is purposeful activity, it then becomes crucial to understand the intents that drive the work. Nevertheless, much of what people do is the result of certain triggering events in their environment. For example, I may be working on writing a paper — my intent is to finish it and hand it in. But while I'm writing, I notice that my email icon appears, and so I stop what I'm doing and open my email. Reacting or replying to my email may lead to another work sequence and set of intents, which may or may not be relevant to my original intent. But regardless of their relevancy, an interruption is an important aspect of my work environment, one which needs to be taken account of in design (can I find my place in my initial task quickly after I'm diverted into a secondary task?). As with flow models, sequence models also capture work breakdowns. A work sequence breakdown is seen when a user goal is thwarted because the action doesn't accomplish its purpose, either because it was the wrong action or because it didn't work properly.

- A *cultural model* shows the power, influences, pressures, and emotions that operate in the user's environment, impacting the work. For example, in a group project, students may feel a certain amount of pressure from the teacher's expectations and attitudes, but they also respond to expectations within the group. In addition, students' actions may be influenced by their friends, their parents, or by their attitudes towards current events. Instructional technology needs to account for the cultural realities where it is deployed. If you are designing a discussion board for an online class, for example, key decisions need to be made about privacy, protection, and monitoring. These design decisions need to be driven not only by official policy but also by the informal culture. Breakdowns in a culture also occur, manifesting themselves as interpersonal conflict, resentment, anger, cheating, etc.

- *Physical models* depict workplace layout, network topologies, the organization of windows on a computer screen, or anything else in the physical environment relevant to the work. Physical models of a student using a home computer to do homework might include such data as the layout of the home computer work area, what windows or icons the students has on the screen, and how the computer is connected to other computers. Breakdowns noted on physical models might include ergonomic issues or inefficiencies in how the environment is organized. Often people find ways to "work around" problems in their environment. Technology redesign has the opportunity to remove these obstacles.

- *Artifact models* describe key "things" — artifacts created or used in the course of work, e.g., notebook, bulletin board, cheat-sheet. In an educational context, examples of artifacts include assignment books/planners, grade books, syllabi, course Web pages, and assignment sheets. Since a common role of technology is to move paper-based artifacts online, it becomes particularly important to examine all such artifacts and understand their role in the work. Artifacts are not always used as intended by their designers. Again, breakdowns can be associated with artifacts as well — the student writes the assignment on a slip of paper that gets lost, or the course website is out of date, has broken links, etc.

Each of these models represents important information about the user's work. Having the design team work together to construct these models enables everyone to design from a common base of understanding. Ideally, the design team is not just instructional designers or technology people. Sharing data in a cross-functional team can help align people with differing motivations and backgrounds around a single purpose (Holtzblatt, 1994).

Consolidation

Contextual Design typically involves multiple observations. A two-hour observation only reveals slice of the work, and an individual may be idiosyncratic. To broaden their understanding of the work, Contextual Design teams observe a wide variety of user (or context) types and then consolidate their learnings across users.

Taking the results from multiple contextual inquiry modeling sessions, the design team consolidates each type of model across the different users. For example, all the flow models are consolidated into a single consolidated workflow model. Consolidated models are detailed rather than generalized so that important variations in the data are not lost. The work modeling sessions also generate a large number of short notes from the interview that may not fit into any of the models. These notes — sometimes hundreds of them — are consolidated using an affinity diagram process. Consolidated models are used for communicating the work of the design team to a broader audience of stakeholders.

Consolidation has a dual emphasis on similarity and difference. Similar work patterns are combined, but differences are not ignored. In an educational setting, there is often a wide variance of practice, as a result of individual differences, comfort levels with technology, departmental history and culture, etc. Consolidated models can capture common elements (e.g., instructors produce syllabi or grade assignments) while not losing the variety of details (e.g., syllabi may be online or on paper).

Work Redesign

The design team, often with help from the broader audience, creates a vision for how the work could be improved. This vision is developed in some detail with storyboards, which show how the original work story (represented in the consolidated models) is transformed and improved by the new design. The redesign is not just a design of technology (a program or a user interface). It is a redesign of the work practice, the larger system within which the technology operates.

This stage of the process is what many people mean by "design" — coming up with new or improved ideas. But in Contextual Design, the generation and refinement of new ideas emerges from a wealth of shared understanding — of users, their work, and the context of their work. This yields solutions more likely to succeed. Traditionally, many educational systems designs are technology driven: people see new technology and then think of ways to deploy it in educational settings. But without a detailed awareness of how people are learning, teaching, or training without the new technology, people throw technology at problems and achieve random results. For example, there have been numerous reports of "a computer in every classroom" efforts resulting in lots of underused computers. Grounding design in real work data helps avoid this tendency, even on highly technical teams.

User Environment Design

This is the phase where the system's functions and structures are defined in a way that supports the new work process as envisioned in the redesign and specified in the storyboards. Beyer and Holtzblatt (1998, p. 306) liken the user environment design (UED) to an architectural model or "floor plan" for the new system. A floor plan for a house shows rooms. The UED shows "focus areas," which are places in the system where users perform an activity. Often, focus areas become distinct windows or Web pages in the resulting system.

Focus areas, and the connections between them, are built by walking through the storyboards and making the focus areas that the storyboards suggest or require. If one were building a learning management system for a corporate environment, focus areas might include Browse Course Calendar, Register for a Course, Review Personal Development Plan, or Perform Gap Analysis Against a New Job Classification. If I am browsing the course calendar and see a class that interests me, I should have a direct link to Register for a Course. The storyboards help determine the directness (or salience) of the links between focus areas and the data and functions required by each focus area. A "Register for a Course" focus area, for instance, may need a function for obtaining supervisor approval if the target environment requires such approval. That requirement would have been captured in a sequence and/or flow model and would have been included in the storyboard about signing up for a course.

Paper Prototyping

Paper-based user interface prototypes are generated directly from the user environment design and are taken back to users (in their real contexts) to see how well they address users' needs. Feedback from prototype interviews is incorporated back into the work models, user environment design, and user interface design. Paper prototype iterations continue as new ideas need to be tested during actual system development.

Why use paper prototypes when online prototypes are often so easy to create? The answer to this question lies in the intended use of the prototypes. The prototypes are not intended as exact replicas of the final project, to be given to developers so they know what to build. The purpose of the prototypes is to allow validation of the design with users. Finished-looking online prototypes tend to intimidate users, who are often polite and reluctant to criticize something that looks as if it took a long time to create. Paper prototypes look provisional and can be modified by anyone with a pencil, scissors, or tape. Paper prototypes level the playing field between designer and user so that users can feel comfortable criticizing, reorganizing, changing, and improving.

The feedback users give on the prototype has to be sorted into appropriate categories by the design team. One level of feedback is superficial, having only to do with the representation in the user interface. For instance, a button may need to be relabeled "class" instead of "course" if the former term is the familiar one in the target environment. A deeper level of feedback occurs when users identify problems in the system structure. If a user says, "How would I get my supervisor's permission first?," the problem may be that the UED provides no function for getting permission from the course registration focus area. However, if the design team never considered the possibility of employees needing permission to take a course, the problem is even deeper — an incomplete understanding of workflow, and so the work models need to be corrected and the changes propagated through all levels of the design.

Principles of Contextual Design

Contextual Design coheres, in part because it is guided by some underlying principles. Beyer and Holtzblatt identify three principles in their book (1998, pp. 416-421):

- *Data.* "Ground all design action in an explicit, trustworthy understanding of your customers and how they work." (p. 416)
- *The Team.* "Design is done by people, and managing people is an important part of any design." (p. 417)
- *Design Thinking.* "Support the needs of design thinking itself. A design process naturally alternates between working out a piece of design sequentially, then stepping back and considering the whole design as a structure." (p. 420)

To this list I would add several more distinguishing characteristics,[1] even though they are perhaps implicit in the first three.

- *Context.* Work data is largely embedded in its context — to get the data you have to examine the context. Apart from this examination, the data are not "trustworthy" (as required above).
- *Partnership.* Too much technology is foisted on people. The contextual inquiry and paper prototyping steps of Contextual Design provide a way for users to participate in the design process as expert partners. This yields a better design and facilitates acceptance.
- *Visualization.* A key strength of Contextual Design is the diagrammatic representation of data and design throughout the process. From the initial individual work models to consolidated models and the affinity, to visioning, storyboarding, the UED, and ultimately the paper prototypes, these graphical representations of data and design help the team pay attention to all the various faces of work and manage the design process.

- *Iteration.* Contextual Design is not strictly linear. Paper prototyping assumes design iteration is necessary (cf., Beyer & Holtzblatt, 1998, pp. 409-411) and leads to iterative refinement of the work products from the earlier phases of the process (consolidated models, affinity, UED). The need for iterative refinement through prototyping is well known in instructional design (e.g., Tripp & Bichelmeyer, 1990).

Many of the elements of Contextual Design are not unique. Observing users doing real work, examining artifacts, creating diagrams to represent task flow, using paper prototypes — these and other techniques are widely described and, one hopes, widely used. But Contextual Design is more than just an assortment of techniques to be used as needed; it is a systematic process where each step builds on the preceding ones.

THE CASE STUDY

Variations2 is Indiana University's NSF-funded Digital Music Library project (Variations2, 2002). One of the main goals for the project is to integrate digital music content (audio, video, and scores) into undergraduate and graduate music education. Thus in addition to creating a body of digitized content, the project is developing software that students will use for music listening and analysis assignments. This case study describes how Contextual Design has been applied to the development of this educational software. When this study was carried out, the first version of Variations2 had already been designed and was being developed. The researchers in this study, apart from myself, were not part of the Variations2 software team, but were students in a graduate course in human-computer interaction. One benefit of this arrangement was that most of the researchers were unaware of design work that had already been done for Variations2, so the Contextual Design process was expected to provide new data to assist with future versions of Variations2, and to confirm or challenge our earlier design decisions.

This case study illustrates the Contextual Design process. It describes the activities undertaken and exhibits some of the resultant diagrams and data. It shows the initial contextual inquiry, modeling and consolidation, redesign, and paper prototyping phases. But it omits the system design (user environment design) phase because of the time constraints of the academic semester.

Contextual Inquiry

When designing something new, you cannot observe people using that new thing because it does not yet exist. Typically, however, the work that the new tool will support is work that is done today, but with different tools. In this case, music students are of course already going to the music library, listening to music, following along with a score in hand, and performing various kinds of analysis. Researchers therefore conducted contextual inquiry into this current work practice.

Five researchers observed undergraduate music students who were completing listening and/or analysis assignments in the Cook Music Library on the IU Bloomington campus.

During the observations students were doing real work (class assignments, studying for a test, preparing for a recital) using today's production system called Variations (Variations, 2002). Researchers then created Contextual Design work models during interpretation sessions.

Flow Model

Figure 1 shows one of the individual flow models created after conducting contextual inquiry with a music student preparing for a recital. U1 is the code name for the student. During the interpretation session, the models are drawn on flipchart paper with markers. Subsequently, they may be redrawn or put online.

In the model, the bubbles represent roles and the responsibilities those roles demonstrate. The arcs between bubbles show the communication or flow

Figure 1: Flow Model

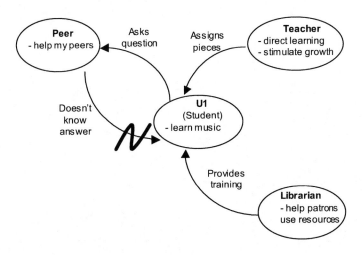

between the roles. A dark, squiggly line (usually drawn in red) indicates a work breakdown. Work breakdowns represent occasions when the student had a difficulty. In this case the student attempted to get an answer to a question but was unable to.

This is a fairly simple flow model as studying tends to be a solitary activity. The activities performed by the teacher and the librarian were not actually observed during the inquiry session. However, in response to questions by the researcher, the events were reported by the student. Asking about previous events can yield valuable data. Beyer and Holtzblatt call this "retrospective accounting" (1998, p. 49). Retrospective accounts of real events should not be confused with generalizations about behavior (e.g., "I usually do things this way"), which do not describe actual events and are less accurate guides to understanding.

Figure 2: Sequence Model

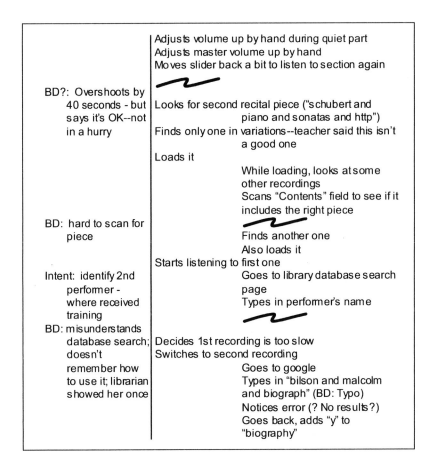

Sequence Model

Figure 2 shows the second page of a sequence model. The sequence model shows four work breakdowns (abbreviated BD on the left-hand side and shown by a dark squiggle on the right-hand side)—occasions when the student had difficulties. The left-hand side of the sequence model captures the researcher's meta-level notes about what is going on. The right-hand side captures the user's actions and the system's response.

Typical annotations on the left-hand side capture "intents"—the specific objective the student was trying to accomplish—as well as work breakdowns or other explanatory notes.

Cultural Model

The cultural model (Figure 3) shows the person being observed at the center of the surrounding cultural influences. Arrows represent pressures (e.g., a teacher telling the student to play a piece in a particular way) and push back (e.g., the student insisting on following her own interpretive instincts). Most of the cultural model data were gathered through clarifying discussion with the student about why she was doing certain things (retrospective accounting). She reported conversations with her teacher and explained why she was looking for a variety of recordings. She also expressed frustration at how little she knew about how to use the technology. In fact, the library had provided training, but she couldn't remember what she'd learned.

Figure 3: Cultural Model

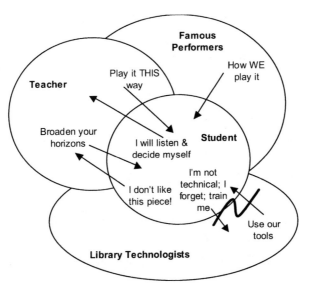

Figure 4: Physical Model of the Workspace

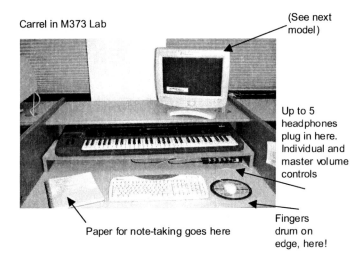

Carrel in M373 Lab

(See next model)

Up to 5 headphones plug in here. Individual and master volume controls

Paper for note-taking goes here

Fingers drum on edge, here!

Physical Model

In this study, we captured two aspects of the physical work environment in models: the workspace (Figure 4) and the computer display (Figure 5). Again, the models are annotated to show the relevant pieces and observed behavior, even as trivial as noting that the student drummed her fingers on the edge of the desk. While not all of these details (or indeed details from the other models) may be useful in subsequent design, they help imprint a memorable image of the user's experience into the minds of the designers.

Figure 5: Physical Model of the Computer Display

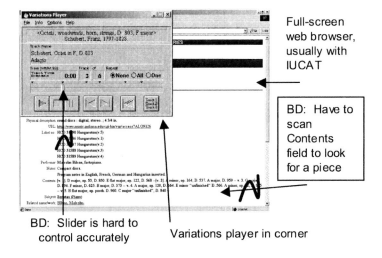

Full-screen web browser, usually with IUCAT

BD: Have to scan Contents field to look for a piece

BD: Slider is hard to control accurately

Variations player in corner

Figure 6: Artifact Model

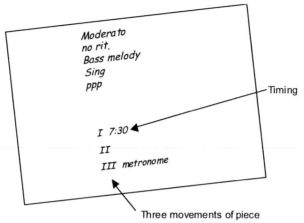

Notes to self as reminder on a half-sheet of paper.

Artifact Model

The artifact model (Figure 4) shows a diagram of the work artifact, annotated with explanations. In this example, the artifact was a half-sheet of paper upon which the student wrote notes to herself while listening.

Insights

At the end of each interpretation session, participants created a list of insights — what we'd learned about the work. Insights from the U1 interpretation session are shown in Figure 7. The "DI" abbreviation after the last insight

Figure 7: Interpretation Session Insights

- Lack of Mac support w/ Variations is a problem
- "High-level" listening tasks are different from detailed listening
- High-level listening can be multi-tasking
- Finding resources on the Web is easier/more familiar than using library resources
- Need user education
- Didn't use any non-visible features (hidden behind button or menu)
- Need a way to see all performances of the same <u>piece</u>.

    DI: do this in Variations.

in the list was a "design idea" offered by one of the researchers. Design ideas are flagged so that we do not confuse them with user data, and so that we can go back and look at our design ideas before we do redesign. While not all of the insights are profound, the seeds of nearly all of our significant work redesigns were captured in one or more insight lists.

Table 1: Work Notes

U1	1	Profile: performance student prep. for recital; pieces memorized; listening to interpretations to compare to teacher's.
U1	2	Realizes (too late) that Variations doesn't work on a Mac.
U1	3	Moves to another computer with a different monitor, but it is also a Mac.
U1	4	In Var., moved back 40s too far using slider bar.
U1	5	She does not use a score b/c it distracts her; pieces already memorized.
U1	6	Her teacher is very opinionated but compromise on interpretations is possible.
U1	7	Teacher comments have influence on her choice of recital pieces.
U1	8	Hard to scan 'contents' field for a piece on a CD.
U1	9	Asks interviewer how to search a library database.
U1	10	No results for search for performer name in library DB.
U1	11	Misspelling error in Google search query: 'biograph' instead of 'biography'.
U1	12	Goes to "bad" results page; not clear which results pages are best.
U1	13	Wanted the bio. info. purely for her own knowledge.
U1	14	Domain 'experts'/larger community standards influence her perception of appropriate performance time, interpretation, etc.
U1	15	Listens to music on CDNow/Borders instead of using available library recordings; possible professor influence.
U1	16	Q: Is she going to go back and do detailed listening? Is high level all she needs?
U1	17	Frequent IE browser error messages; public access computers have to be 'retrained' for profiles.
U1	18	Q: Why didn't she use Var. track buttons or Options menu?
U1	19	Has never been instructed on how to use Var.; would like a "Clippie" feature to assist her.
U1	20	DI: Include a link to info. about the performer.

Work Notes

During the interpretation session, a running list is kept of any data that is mentioned but doesn't fit into one of the other work models. Figure 8 shows the work notes from the U1 interpretation session.

Consolidation

After all of the interpretation sessions were complete and all the individual models were built, we consolidated the models. Table 2 shows one of our consolidated models — the consolidated sequence model. (Space does not

Table 2: Consolidated Sequence Model

Activity	Intent	Abstract Step
Figure out what to do	• Focus activity • Prepare for correct assignment or test	• Read paper syllabus copy **or** • Go to course website
Gather/locate resources	• Find the piece needed for assignment • Locate multiple versions of pieces to prepare for performance	Go to course syllabus site **or** • Go to IU Cat o Course reserve lists **-or-** o Search **or** • Go to CDNow.com or other commercial site 1. Search 2. Listen to clips • Determine if appropriate music has been found
Listen (overview)	1. Get a sense for the piece 2. Determine appropriateness of the piece for intended need	1. Click play on variations 2. Listen 3. Make notations on paper score
Listen (detailed/analytical)	1. Analyze chord changes 2. Find transitions in the music 3. Prepare for transcription	1. Click play on variations player 2. Listen 3. Stop 4. Restart from beginning **-or-** pause 1. Move slider back to try to find beginning of section 2. Click play • Make notations on score • Repeat

permit the inclusion of all of the consolidated models.) Reading down the left-hand column yields a sense of the main kinds of work in which Variations use was involved. The center column lists the users' intents for each of the activities. The right-hand column shows alternative steps users took to accomplish their intents, at a higher level of abstraction than the individual models.

In addition to consolidating work models, we also consolidated the work notes, using an affinity diagram process. In all, the interpretation sessions generated 99 work notes. Table 3 shows data from one of the five major sections of the resultant affinity diagram. Work breakdowns (BDs) and design ideas (DIs) also find their way into the affinity.

Table 3: Affinity Section for "I figure out or find what to work on"

I figure out or find what to work on
- How I figure out the assignment
  - Reads description in syllabus + underlines two sentences to "keep straight what I should be listening for…"
  - Looks in day planner for assignment notes. Planner is a detailed artifact with many course notes.
  - She says that she still hasn't obtained a binder for her paper scores and class notes. "I really need" one, she says.
  - Found piece in Variations from class syllabus [explained this after interview started].
  - Checked e-mail using Webmail interface for message and link to class webpage from instructor.
  - Working Section F of syllabus.
  - BD: "Transcription looks wrong compared to example and what I am hearing…"
- How I find what I need to listen to
  - Listens to music on CDNow/Borders instead of using available library recordings; possible professor influence.
  - Hard to scan 'contents' field for a piece on a CD.
  - Always tries to use listening list in course reserve page to find correct version.
  - Retrospective: got to Variations from class listening list.
  - BD: Locating correct version of piece difficult in IUCAT.
  - BD: Initially played the wrong piece in the Variations player. Says "it doesn't seem right."
- How I find what I need to look at
  - BD: Hard to specify score or recording in IUCAT, search criteria are for books not music.
  - DI: Would like to be able to find paper score along with recording in same search.
- I need to find more information
  - Goes to "bad" results page; not clear which results pages are best.
  - Wanted the bio. info. purely for her own knowledge.
  - DI: Include a link to info. about the performer.

Work Redesign

Based on what we had learned about users of Variations, we brainstormed ideas for making improvements that would better support people's work, creating rough vision sketches on flipchart paper. We decided to focus on addressing three recurrent issues: figuring out how to use the system, finding the desired media, and doing detailed listening. We created storyboards showing improved methods for each of these tasks. The storyboards were summarized in a redesign diagram that became the basis for the paper prototypes. Figure 8 shows one part of the redesign sketch, indicating the ability to navigate by measure number.

Live Help: To help users more easily figure out how to use the system, we decided to take advantage of current instant messaging technology to design a means for users to ask for help from a librarian right when the help is needed. This way, instead of having to flounder or ask students working nearby, users could instead get immediate expert advice from reference desk personnel.

Search for Music: A second observed difficulty was searching for a listening piece. The current library catalog system does not make this easy. Students could do keyword searches for the name of the composer or the piece, but then had to sift through many bibliographic records, visually scanning for the name of the piece or composer amid many other fields of data. Our improvement idea here was to allow for more specific searches such as

Figure 8: Part of the Redesign Diagram

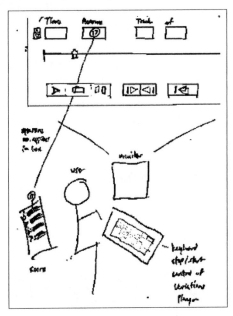

composer, performer, and/or genre, in effect introducing music-specific concepts into the search and retrieval process.

Set Loop/Navigate by Measure: The Variations tool provides a slider control and typical media control buttons (previous/next track, fast forward/rewind, pause, stop, and play). Nevertheless assignments often required students to answer questions about specific segments of a musical work, e.g., "Discuss several ways in which Beethoven creates disruption, or discontinuity, in the music between measures 37-59." To locate the exact measures, students referred to a paper-based score and typically played with the slider trying to find the right location so they could answer the question. Often, students wanted to listen to the same segment repeatedly in order to complete their analysis. Yet the only precise locations in the audio by which students could navigate were the beginnings of each track. So they resorted to using the slider to try to find the right location. In our work redesign, we provided two ideas: allow students to navigate by measure number and to set specific repeat loops.

Given that these redesign ideas emerged from acquaintance with the data in isolation from the development team, it was interesting to note the extent to which our redesign correlated with the Variations2 design work. Of these three redesign ideas, the first one (Live Help) was wholly absent from the Variations2 plans. This is not surprising, because Contextual Design, with its comprehensive look at what people are doing to accomplish their work, often uncovers problems that are systemic and reach beyond the feature set of a particular piece of software. The second redesign idea (Search for Music) is squarely in the center of one of the main emphases of Variations2, so the Contextual Design work merely confirmed the need for cataloging schemes that work well for music. The third redesign idea (Set Loop) had mostly emerged in Variations2, which can provide measure-by-measure navigation and offers a bookmarking mechanism somewhat analogous to the "set loop" functionality. Version 1 of Variations2 provides a way for users to add a bookmark at any point in a recording or score. These bookmarks can then be brought up in a separate window and used for navigation. Our research results yielded a mechanism more tuned to the student tasks we observed — listening repeatedly to a segment with a defined beginning and end.

Paper Prototyping

Paper-based prototypes based on the redesigns created were taken back to the music library, where we put them in front of music students and asked them to attempt to "use" the prototype to do a task they needed to do or had recently done. Figure 9 shows one of the paper prototypes. As can be seen, the

Figure 9: Sketch for a Paper Prototype

prototypes are quick and easy to construct and invite correction or improvement.

In the earlier discussion of paper prototyping, I mentioned that paper prototyping interviews gather data on three levels. Data may address the user interface, the underlying system structure, or our understanding of the user's work practice. The 31 issues we gathered from our paper prototyping interviews were therefore categorized appropriately. Table 4 shows a few examples from each of these three categories.

User interface problems tend to be the easiest to fix. In the Table 4 examples, re-labeling will solve any of these issues. Issues with system structure run a little deeper and have a large impact on design. For example, providing "in-depth information about a musical piece from within Variations" would certainly require additional user interface elements and would likely require significant changes to the underlying implementation in order to provide this additional data within (or from) the listening window. Work practice issues have the potential to transform a design completely. In the Table 4 examples, the first two work practice issues have fairly minor impact, but the last issue rules out the entire mechanism used by the paper prototype to set markers — a separate dialog box with data entry requirements is too disruptive; students need a simple way to set a mark while listening. So the impact of this work practice issue ripples through the system design and the user interface design.

The paper prototypes were rapidly developed and tested, and after only four interviews, we gathered a wealth of user data that validated and invalidated aspects of our user interface design, system structure, or understanding of the work practice.

Table 4: Sample Categorized Feedback from Paper Prototype Interviews

Category	Issue
User Interface	"Ask the Librarian" should include the word "live" or some other note to let users know that the function is live help.
User Interface	Better name for theory listening may be bookmark repeat or loop listening.
User Interface	Likes "Set Loop" and recognizes this terminology to set marks in music; didn't care for the term "bookmark". She suggested "begin loop" and "end loop".
System Structure	Students want the ability to get in-depth information about a musical piece from within Variations.
System Structure	Leave theory listening window open while repeating.
Work Practice	Many students may not know in advance how many times they want a section repeated, so maybe just keep repeating until the user stops.
Work Practice	Grads want to compare recordings often -- this subject would like to see unique information in the title window to distinguish between different recordings.
Work Practice	There is a whole type of listening we missed in the first round of interviews. This is listening for some sort of theme that needs to be supported by a marker that won't stop the piece, but allows the student to go back easily and hear again.

The Ongoing Value of the Data

Although the Contextual Design piece was only a small and somewhat disconnected effort in the scope of the overall Variations2 project, results from the study continue to influence the requirements and design for future versions. For example, in response to the loop concept, we are now planning to include, in version 2, the ability to define an excerpt — a segment with a beginning and end (not just a beginning as with the bookmark concept). In addition, having observed the difficulty students have finding the right listening piece, we have prototyped a visual syllabus that would allow students to go to an online syllabus with a link directly to the pieces or segments for each assignment (Notess & Minibayeva, 2002).

CONTEXTUAL DESIGN AND INSTRUCTIONAL SYSTEMS DESIGN

Having now seen Contextual Design described and having also seen an example of its use, what can we conclude about the relationship between it and

ISD? I offer several thoughts. First, Contextual Design may be both susceptible and resistant to two recent criticisms of ISD. Second, Contextual Design may offer some needed process commonality between the design of instruction and the design of the technology used in instructional delivery. And finally, Contextual Design offers a vision for the future, a future in which Contextual Design enables cross-functional teams to deliver superior learning solutions.

Contextual Design and Criticisms of ISD

Recently, ISD has been the target of significant criticism (Gordon & Zemke, 2000). Among the criticisms are the assertions that ISD:

- is slow and cumbersome, and
- focuses designers on following a process rather than on achieving meaningful results.

I call out these two criticisms because, over the years, I have heard these same criticisms leveled at Contextual Design by casual observers of the process. Seeing the work that goes into Contextual Design and the bewildering (to outsiders) array of flip-chart paper and sticky notes it generates, some people assume that Contextual Design is a long, slow process. In my experience, the slowest part of the process is not the data gathering, analysis, redesign, or prototyping — these can move very quickly. In our case study, the first three phases of Contextual Design — interviewing, interpreting, and consolidating — were all completed within two weeks' time, by people who were working at other jobs and/or enrolled in other classes. The redesign, prototyping, prototype interviews, and the consolidation of the results took even less total time although they were spread over a month of calendar time due to a vacation break and delays in recruiting students for the prototype interviews. It is this latter problem of recruiting interviewees and scheduling the interviews that can stretch out Contextual Design schedules. But that problem becomes manageable as design teams gain more experience with the issues. Any disciplined process takes time to learn and execute. Beyer and Holtzblatt (1990) offer many suggestions on how to make Contextual Design fast and effective for a variety of situations.

The second criticism of ISD mentioned above is that it can focus people on following a process instead of achieving results. Certainly this can happen with Contextual Design too: it is always a risk when there is a detailed process to learn. However, Contextual Design may be less susceptible to this weakness than other processes because of its insistence on putting all members of the design team face-to-face with real users. Most users don't particularly care what process we use, but they do care a great deal about the results we give them. Having the images of those users imprinted on our minds and their work breakdowns called out in red on the work models we've built, we are less likely to disregard users' needs in favor of following a process for its own sake.

In a follow-up article, Zemke and Rossett (2002) summarize some of the responses received to the original Gordon and Zemke article that criticized the ISD process. They divided the responses into two groups. The first group blames ISD itself as a faulty process and the second group blames practitioners of ISD for faulty practice. Zemke and Rossett conclude that, though ISD may be flawed, it is (quoting Marc Rosenberg) "the best thing we have if we use it correctly" (p. 34). In both the original article and the follow-up, there is repeated emphasis on the expertise of the practitioner having a large impact on the quality of the results. Contextual Design, in my experience, has a similar dependency. In all of the Contextual Design projects I've seen that could be termed successful, there was strong leadership from one or more skilled practitioners who had developed those skills under the watchful eye of an expert. Typically, an expert has internalized the principles a process expresses, and can therefore adapt and streamline the process to become effective in a given situation. Contextual Design needs this expertise as much as does ISD.

Technology Design and Instructional Design

In our case study, we see Contextual Design used to guide the design of a software system deployed in an educational context, and indeed it seems as useful here as it is for other systems' design problems. It also seems apparent, even though our case study did not examine this, that Contextual Design might provide a useful approach for integrating technology design and instructional design. The need for this integration is experienced whenever an instructional designer and a software developer try to work together on a project or whenever the instructional designer tries to fill the role of both technology designer and instructional designer. Consider, for example, if our case study had involved not only the development of software for music listening and analysis, but had also included the development of instructional content—a set of lessons to teach music theory, for instance. Table 5 illustrates, by partial example, both the dichotomy and unity of interests between an instructional designer and a software designer during just the analysis and design phases of such a project.

Instructional designers have their own expertise: learning theory, evaluation, message design, etc. Software designers also have their own expertise:

Table 5: Dichotomy and Unity of Interests Between Instructional and Software Design

	Instructional Designer	**Software Designer**
Analysis	What music theory content do the students need to learn? What are the characteristics of the music students? In what contexts will they be learning (classroom, library, dorm room, computer lab)?	What kinds and amounts of data will be needed (audio, image, video, text)? What kinds of user interaction with the data are needed? What technical constraints do we face (network bandwidth, display resolution)?
	Who will be using the system (how many users, how often, etc.)? What tasks does the system need to support? What other people besides students will need to interact with the system (e.g., faculty? librarians? administrative staff? graduate assistants?)	
Design	What are the instructional objectives or outcomes we are trying to achieve? How should the content be sequenced? What instructional strategies best fit the goals and content?	What technologies (e.g., database, user interface, programming languages, software packages, networking, security) should we use? What software architecture best meets the requirements?
	What should the user interface look like? How can we best support collaboration and communication among users?	

programming, software architecture, characteristics of different technologies, etc. But both types of designers have a common interest in understanding the intended users and uses of the system, and both have a large stake in the design of the user interface. Contextual Design might help address the common information and design needs in such a cross-functional team.

A Vision for the Future

Imagine a cross-functional team, including both technologists and instructional designers as well as graphics designers, editors, and other stakeholders. All team members participate in all phases of Contextual Design: observing users/learners, building work models, consolidating the data, redesigning the work, and then designing and prototyping the new solution, refining the design through prototype interviews. The technologists bring their expertise in what can be done with different technologies, and the instructional designers bring their expertise in designing effective learning experiences. Other stakeholders bring their own expertise. Each role has its own responsibilities in delivering the final system, but all are designing based on a shared understanding of the users, and all have learned a common representation for modeling that understanding. All have learned a common process for arriving at and refining that understanding.

For the vision just described to be tenable, we have to continue exploring the usefulness of Contextual Design for instructional designers. The present case study offers an introduction to the approach and, I hope, enough encouragement to continue the exploration (see Appendix A at the end of this chapter for a summary of Contextual Design steps and benefits). One major area of need is to investigate the extent to which Contextual Design is valuable for instructional content design. Contextual inquiry and work modeling look promising for the job/task analysis pieces of instructional needs analysis. An unanswered question is whether subsequent steps of designing content such as sequencing and the selection of instructional strategies are helped, or at least not hindered, by Contextual Design.

Others are recommending or exploring the application of Contextual Design methods to educational problems. Maish Nichani points to Contextual Design as one of several approaches which exemplify what he calls "empathic instructional design" (Nichani, 2002). Allison Druin, in her work with designing technologies for children, has developed a design approach called "Cooperative Inquiry," which leverages in particular the contextual inquiry piece of Contextual Design (Druin, 1999). She has applied this approach in designing a digital library for young children (Druin et al., 2001). If future studies in these areas offer good results, it may well be that Contextual Design or a derivative can provide a process whereby user-centered technology design and learner-centered instructional design work together for the benefit of all.

ACKNOWLEDGMENTS

I would like to thank my students who helped with this research: George Bergstrom, Rovy Branon, Jason Cooper, and Cynthia Spann. I would also like to thank Elizabeth Boling and Karen Holtzblatt for providing expert critique. This material is based upon work supported by the National Science Foundation under Grant No. 9909068. Any opinions, findings, and conclusions or recommendations expressed in this material are those of the author and do not necessarily reflect the views of the National Science Foundation.

ENDNOTES

[1]   The principles of context and partnership are mentioned by Beyer and Holtzblatt as principles of contextual inquiry (1998, pp. 47-56), but these principles are important motivators for Contextual Design as a whole.

REFERENCES

American Society for Training and Development. (1988). Basics of instructional systems development. *Info-Line* (Issue 8803).

Beyer, H. & Holtzblatt, K. (1998). *Contextual Design: Defining Customer-Centered Systems*. San Francisco, CA: Morgan Kaufmann Publishers.

Beyer, H. & Holtzblatt, K. (1999). Contextual design. *Interactions, 4*(1), 32-42.

Curtis, P., Heiserman, T., Jobusch, D., Notess, M., & Webb, J. (1999). Customer-focused design data in a large, multi-site organization. *Proceedings of the CHI 99 Conference on Human Factors in Computing Systems,* 608-615.

Dick, W. & Carey, L. (1996). *The Systematic Design of Instruction (4th ed.)*. New York: Harper Collins.

Druin, A. (1999). Cooperative inquiry: Developing new technologies for children with children. *Proceedings of the CHI 99 Conference on Human Factors in Computing Systems,* 592-599.

Druin, A., Bederson, B., Hourcade, J.P., Sherman, L., Revelle, G., Platner, M., & Weng, S. (2001). Designing a digital library for young children: An intergenerational partnership. *Proceedings of the ACM/IEEEE-CS Joint Conference on Digital Libraries (JCDL '01),* 398-405.

Fardouly, N. (1988). *Instructional Design of Learning Materials*. Retrieved August 3, 2002, from University of New South Wales Faculty of the Built Environment website: http://www.fbe.unsw.edu.au/learning/instructionaldesign/materials.htm.

Gordon, J. & Zemke, R. (2000). The attack on ISD. *Training, 37*(4), 42-53.

Holtzblatt, K. (1994). If we're a team why don't we act like one? *Interactions, 1*(3), 17-20.

Holtzblatt, K. (2001). *Creating New Work Paradigms for the Enterprise Portal*. SAP Design Guild. Retrieved on August 3, 2002, from: http://www.incent.com/pubs/SAPDGPortal.html.

Kemp, J., Morrison, G., & Ross, S. (1998). *Designing Effective Instruction (2nd ed.)*. Upper Saddle River, NJ: Prentice-Hall.

Nichani, M. (2002, February). *Empathic Instructional Design.* Retrieved on August 7, 2002, from: http://www.elearningpost.com/features/archives/001003.asp.

Norman, D. (1988). *The Psychology of Everyday Things.* New York: Basic Books.

Normore, L. (1999, January/February) Reference in context explores the reference process. *OCLC Newsletter,* n. 237. Retrieved on August 3, 2002, from: http://www.oclc.org/oclc/new/n237/research/01research.htm.

Notess, M. (2001, August). Usability, user experience, and learner experience. *eLearn Magazine.* Archived at: http://www.elearnmag.org/subpage/sub_page.cfm?section=4&list_item=2&page=1.

Notess, M. & Minibayeva, N. (2002). Variations2: Toward visual interfaces for digital music libraries. Presented at the *Second International Workshop on Visual Interfaces to Digital Libraries* at the *ACM+IEEE Joint Conference on Digital Libraries,* July 18, Portland, OR, USA. Paper available online at: http://vw.indiana.edu/visual02/Notess.pdf.

Rockwell, C. (1999). Customer connection creates a winning product. *Interactions,* 4(1), 50-57.

Tripp, S.D. & Bichelmeyer, B. (1990). Rapid prototyping: An alternative instructional design strategy. *Educational Technology Research and Development,* 38(1), 31-44.

Variations. Retrieved August 3, 2002, from: http://www.dlib.indiana.edu/variations/.

Variations2: The IU Digital Music Library. Retrieved August 3, 2002, from: http://variations2.indiana.edu.

Zemke, R. & Rossett, A. (2002). A hard look at ISD. *Training,* 39(2), 26-34.

APPENDIX A
OUTLINE OF CONTEXTUAL DESIGN

Step	Activities	Benefits
Contextual Inquiry	Observe people doing their real work in its actual setting. During and/or afterwards, ask questions to determine what was going on and why.	Can be used for instructional system design (study potential users of the system) or content (study people doing the work you want people to learn).
Work Modeling	Build models from observational data: work flow, sequence, cultural, physical, and artifact. Highlight breakdowns in current work process.	Modeling is best done by a cross-functional team. Technologists, instructional designers, subject matter experts, etc., can work from a shared understanding of the data.
Consolidation	Look for the patterns across observation sessions. Identify the patterns in consolidations of the above models without losing the detail.	Model consolidation helps designers see the core work patterns the system needs to support. Consolidation also allows key differences to be identified.
Work Redesign	Create a vision for improved work practice. Develop storyboards to elaborate and illustrate the new design.	Tying the storyboards back to the consolidated models increases the chances of user acceptance and avoids technology-driven design.
User Environment Design	Develop a system "floor plan" showing the needed modules and how they connect.	This phase lets instructional designers participate in the technology design and help ensure it stays grounded in real user work practice.
Paper Prototyping	Create low-fidelity, paper-based prototypes. Interview users with these prototypes to validate (and improve) the design.	Prototype interview feedback addresses multiple levels of the design: the models, the system, and the user interface.

Chapter VII

What You See is All That You Get! A Practical Guide to Incorporating Cognitive Strategies into the Design of Electronic Instruction

Anne-Marie Armstrong
US Government Printing Office, USA

ABSTRACT

Incorporating good instructional strategies based on learning theory is vital for electronic instruction. After all, the instruction must stand on its own without any fallback to a "live" and experienced instructor. What you see is not only what you get, but it is all you get! As with most forms of instruction, planning and preparation are key to instructional delivery and ultimately to stimulating the user's learning processes. An instructor, trainer, or teacher brings many important skills and talents to the learning environment. Many of these skills and talents can be incorporated into the electronic learning environment. This chapter describes how cognitive strategies can be incorporated into each step of the ADDIE process. The chapter also contains many examples of design plans and templates that have worked in the real world of designing instruction for businesses and training organizations.

INTRODUCTION

Electronic instruction, that is, computer and Web-based instruction, differs from other forms of instruction in that it both represents the content to be learned *and* the teacher, trainer, or instructor. What you see is not only what you get, but it is all you get! Therefore incorporating good instructional strategies based on learning theory is vital for electronic instruction. After all, the instruction must stand on its own without any fallback to a "live" and experienced instructor.

As with most forms of instruction, planning and preparation are key to instructional delivery and ultimately to stimulating the user's learning processes. An instructor, trainer, or teacher brings many important skills and talents to the learning environment. Many of these skills and talents can be incorporated into the electronic learning environment. Most expert instructors have a "bag of tricks" which they bring with them. This "bag of tricks" contains their experiences from many years of presenting many different kinds of content to many different kinds of learners. Some of these tricks of the trade are cognitive strategies. Cognitive strategies are an outgrowth of cognitive science that views learning as an internal process of storing and retrieving information. That internal process of storage and retrieval can, in turn, be influenced by external events (West, Farmer, & Wolff, 1991).

There already exists a mechanism which can be used to ensure that cognitive strategies are incorporated into electronic learning, and that mechanism is the instructional design process, commonly known in its simplest form as ADDIE, i.e., analyze, design, develop, implement, and evaluate. This chapter describes how cognitive strategies can be incorporated into each step of that process. The chapter also contains many examples of design plans and templates that have worked in the real world of designing instruction for businesses and training organizations.

ANALYSIS

In this first phase an instructional designer sets forth the types of learners for whom the instruction is being designed, the conditions under which it is presented, and the content and skill levels of the proposed outcomes of the instruction. The course content is broken down into learning types. In my work I use the learning types that conform to the five kinds of learned capabilities (Gagne, Briggs, & Wager, 1992). Those learning types are verbal information, intellectual skills, cognitive strategies, motor skills, and attitude. Up till now, the great majority of electronic learning being produced attempts to teach the verbal information and intellectual skills.

Verbal information consists of labels and facts. It is usually something that the learner can state. Intellectual skills according to Gagne, Briggs, and Wager are what "makes it possible for an individual to respond to his environment through symbols" (Gagne, Briggs, & Wager, 1992, p. 53). Intellectual skills are further delineated according to complexity — from simple discriminations to the higher levels up to and including problem solving.

Cognitive strategies are also intellectual skills, but are distinct in that they are internal processes unique to the individual and based on his or her own successful or unsuccessful experiences. They also differ from metacognitive strategies. Metacognitive strategies are the individual control processes which monitor, evaluate, and ultimately select or reject the use of specific cognitive strategies. Motor skills generally involve the senses and the muscles. And attitude skills consist of the emotions and action.

PERFORMANCE ANALYSIS

Using documentation, job shadowing, and interviews, one goes from the written job description to a listing of the learning objectives. An instructional designer analyzes the performance goals and the learning required to accomplish those goals by listing the specific skills needed and then differentiating them by learning type.

Table 1: Sample Learning Objectives

Apprentices will be able to:
1. Name the various roles and responsibilities of the Agency.
2. Discuss and explain the department's technical processes.
3. Define and use the department's technical terms, e.g., folios, extension, sluglines, etc.
4. Discuss and explain the department's print-based and Web-based processes
5. Define and use common printing terms, e.g., typefaces, measure, type size, etc.
6. List and define common terms and acronyms used within the department.
7. Name, discuss and demonstrate proof and copy markup duties.
8. Name, discuss and demonstrate keyboarding duties.
9. Demonstrate following oral directions.
10. Demonstrate using department procedures for work assignment/reporting and documenting.

Table 2: Learning Analysis Job Aid for Intellectual Skills

Intellectual skill outcome level needed	Suggested objectives would include (measurable actions or verbs)	Possible cognitive strategies employed	Matching testing strategies
Background -- knowledge is for general use, not direct application	Arrange Label List Recall Name	Framing Association Chunking Mapping	State exactly Fill in blanks Order a list Fill in diagram Identify from group
Important -- reasonably high level of knowledge is required	Define Duplicate Match Relate Classify	Listing Applying steps Finding patterns Using rules	State essentials Copy all fundamentals Group with like Place in supra group
Essential -- 100% mastery is required	Order Reproduce Discuss Explain	Simulating Reasoning Inductively Deductively	Arrange accordingly Perform on demand Answer and elaborate State the reasons

Now, it is also common for objectives and enabling objectives to be written for each skill and for a testing or evaluation plan for each skill assessment to be included in the learning analysis report. Table 2 is a job aid that a designer could use to analyze learning outcomes from an intellectual skills level, and to produce a learning analysis and a design plan based on that type of learning, the level of achievement or performance needed, the written objectives, cognitive strategies, and matching testing strategies. The resultant learning report can then recommend a high-level design plan for the design of the electronic learning using the same strategies.

DESIGN PLANS

The next step then is to produce the design plan that can be easily used to produce storyboards, scripts, or the actual prototypes of the electronic instruction. The design plan or blueprint will state enabling objectives as derived from the learning analysis report. Then it will list the instructional events that enable the internal learning process of that objective in the most cognitively effective manner, that is, in a manner that is both meaningful and easily assimilated by the learner. The cognitive strategies can be incorporated at this point so that the objectives and the testing plan both reflect appropriate strategies. As a guide in writing the strategies, I use the nine events of instruction as advocated by Gagne, Briggs, and Wager (1992). Table 3 provides examples of ways that electronic instruction can utilize all nine events of instruction.

The specific instructional events may vary according to the learning type and the objective. The first two instructional events are not always listed in the design plan. The first event for every learning objective is "to gain the learner's

Table 3: Examples of the Events of Instruction

Events of Instruction	Examples, Explanations
1. Get learner attention	Lights, sound, color, pictures, dramatic examples, questioning, etc.
2. State the learning objective	State or list all objectives in Student handbook, on presentation slide, at the top of the web page, at beginning of CBT, video, etc.
3. Relate to previous learning	Give purpose of instruction and relate to job assignment and product being assembled.
4. Present the material	Use appropriate instructional strategy, i.e., lecture, diagram, flow chart, modeled behavior, etc.
5. Provide guidance	Stop and point out important steps, elicit examples, use bulleted statements, show a variety of situations, summarize and repeat.
6. Practice	Simulated activities and demonstrations followed by question on specifics. Provide more than one type of exercise.
7. Provide feedback	Scaffold the performance. Break into small chunks. Give hints and guidance.
8. Assess the performance	Provide scores and meaningful measurement for self-checks.
9. Ensure retention and transfer	Summarize in different presentation. Provide real examples. Suggest real or on-the-job applications. Provide downloadable job aids. Provide frequently asked questions and coaching sections.

attention." The second event is to inform the learner of the objective. Classroom teachers or standup instructors can clap their hands, flip the light switch off and on, or raise their voices to make certain that the learners know that they now must be attentive.

In electronic learning, color, graphics, animation, and sound are used to gain attention and cue the learners. Learning objectives are often listed on the first screen and then repeated in certain screen locales. On Web pages, learning objectives can be placed as banners or as semi-permanent menu items. Frequently electronic instruction lists primary learning objectives as part of a lesson map, as a permanent side menu, in the site map, or in an overview that is accessible by clicking on a button at the bottom of the screen.

Finally, the design will be exemplified and/or described in some way so that the clients, customers, developers, instructors, and other team members can get a quick overall view of the strategy and its presentation. They will then be able to add to it, offer alternatives, or improve upon it. I have included samples of three different design plans that I used with different organizations. In fact, they were customized according to the audiences. The first design plan was used when I knew that I would have to hand over the project to the organization's developers. The design time was very limited. The product would be CBT. The customer wanted something akin to storyboards. They wanted a plan that included flexibility along with guidance. The plan worked.

The developers were able to grasp the plan and the strategies through the use of the listing the instructional events and the provision of many visuals.

Note that the strategies chosen for each enabling objective are appropriate according to the type of learning identified in the learning analysis (see Tables 2 and 3). In other words, match the learning type to one or more specific instructional strategies. For example, a concrete concept could be taught by presenting it graphically and pointing out its identifying characteristics. Then its learning would be evaluated by whether or not the learner could choose it from among similar but not identical objects, whereas an abstract concept would be taught by describing its instances and non-instances, and it would be evaluated

Table 4: Design Plan One

Event 1. Gain attention
Event 2. List learning objective

Enabling Objective	Instructional Events	Strategy Example
2.3 Describe the functions of and support provided by the office manager {Intellectual Skill: Defined Concepts}	3. Relate information to previously learned administrative work 4. Organize information from most important or most common to least 5. List the essential functions and support for each duty or topic 6. Link the functions into a "Story" or generalized example 7. Use metaphor of the manager's desk or office with drawers and files containing essential functions 8. Allow repetition as needed 9. Summarize and then provide multiple choice comprehensive check	
2.4 Apply the steps of the materials management process {Intellectual Skill: Rules and procedures}	3. Organize information into subcategories 4. Use flow charts to represent parts of process 5. Number and present steps consecutively or use arrows and animation 6. Allow learners to simulate process using mouse interaction 7. Allow multiple reviews 8. Learner uses click and drag function to rearrange functions presented out of order 9. Summary and fill-in-the steps exercise	

Table 5: Matching Instructional Events to Cognitive Strategies

Learning Objective	Instructional Event			
	Stimulate Recall	Present Material	Guide Learner	Elicit Performance
Name or lbel	Show association with concrete object	Provide examples	Relate to previous experience or learning	Point and ask for identification
Abstract concept	List relevant features	Describe instances and non-instances	Draw Table of Attributes	Have identify from field of many
Rule use	Review needed concepts and steps	Present instance and non- instances of rule application	Demonstrate rule use and provide any needed memory aid	Request performance using rule
Problem solve	Review all subordinate rules	Present novel task or problem	Model rule usage or problem solving	Request performance in problem solving task

by asking the learner to fill in a table of attributes or by identifying "real" cases (see Table 5 for more examples).

I have used variations on this design plan for organizations that wanted highly technical material presented using the Web and a blended approach. In this case, the developer was the designer and a visual reinforcement of the strategy was not needed.

Another variation of the design plan was used for a governmental agency. The contact was time-limited. The agency was not certain if and when they would implement the plan. They were also not certain if the final instruction would be electronic, classroom, or blended. The same basic elements of learning objective, presentation, strategy, and assessment were used. I simply added another column for the recommended delivery. I was also told that it was possible that the agency's present trainers wanted to use the plan to rewrite their present instructional material. For this reason, the plan was designed so that most of the learning objectives could be implemented individually. This type of design plan, that is, one where it is not even known if the plan will be implemented or not, will be the most detailed. It is possible that it will not be implemented for one year or more.

DEVELOPMENT AND IMPLEMENTATION

Many times instructional designers must move on to other tasks or projects once the design has been laid out. In those cases, they expect that the developers can then implement their design. Using a blueprint-like design plan as shown in the preceding tables can ensure that the developers will have a clear idea of the plan, the learning objectives, and the strategies recommended for presenting material. At the same time, the more general recommendations of the

Table 6: Design Plan for Technical Lesson — Designer is Developer

Enabling Objectives	Instructional/Evaluation Strategies	Examples/Suggestions	Comments/Tag
Module One: Overview of product including database architecture. WBI or Virtual Classroom with pre and posttest. 85% on pre or post = successful completion			
Participants will demonstrate knowledge of capabilities and architecture of BP			
1.1 Identify BP databases and their functions	Describe architecture, use metaphors, list characteristics Relate to db structures and population methods Define configurable and dynamic data and give attributes and examples Present product database population methods using rules and examples and any exceptions Animate relationships Define Core and Shell using examples, rules, exceptions Self-Assess and feedback	Graphical representations of generic database architecture morphing into Architecture, including Catalog, Customer and Admin database Core vs. Shell processes in layers with Bill Format overlapping (animation) Assess with drag and drop exercise with feedback on examples of dynamic and configurable data. Assess with drag and drop exercise with feedback on type, contents and population of product database. Assess with fill in the blanks with feedback and guidance on Core and Shell items	Animation, database architecture, BP architecture, abstract concept Graphic software development exercise database exercise database exercise software development
1.2 Demonstrate knowledge of product's role in billing and customer care	Relate billing to learners' personal experiences Present various information that a bill contains Describe the functions that a bill must perform Describe challenges of a billing system in a dynamic environment Present Life cycle of account using role play or as historical date line. Self-assess and feedback	Present typical scenario in story form. Include account hierarchy, different products, bill cycle, contacts, billing responsibilities, different charges. Introduce product entity icons as parts of story. Use graphic of bill with rollover descriptions Give examples of differences from country to country and product to product. Give examples of future changes and possibilities Simple animation populating a dateline Drag and Drop exercise "What is Billing", page 9 of BP 9.1	Text, narration, billing overview Graphic, product data entity icons Graphic, Telcom Bill Text, product examples Animation, dateline exercise, billing systems
1.3 Identify BP features	Present overview of BP features Self-assess and feedback Emphasize key points, review and summarize Module one	Table of features with descriptions and explanations Fill in the blanks of a table of BP features Chunk information in table form.	Table, BP features Exercise, BP features Table, summary, BP features

design plan allow the developers to be creative and flexible in their choices. Because the strategies are matched to learning types, developers can also keep a file of templates categorized by type for rapid prototyping.

Following is an example of a template that was created to implement the presentation of verbal information. Notice that the information is presented in a pleasant manner that is also familiar to the learner, and it is framed by related chunks of information.

Frequently used screen designs can also be subcategorized by "Standard Video Template," "Flowcharts with Graphics," "Bulleted Text," or "Popup Screens." All such templates can be designed so that they can be used over and

Table 7: Design Plan, May or May Not Implement

Learning Objective	Learning Level	Instructional Events	Testing/Evaluation Strategy	Instructional Strategy and Material Suggestions	Instructional Delivery
1. Name the various AGENCY roles and responsibilities	Knowledge and understanding	3) Relate a brief history of the AGENCY and show a functional chart. 4) Learners to take turns suggesting what the roles and responsibilities of the AGENCY would be today given that history and list their guesses on board or on flip charts. 5) Fill out list with any that were not suggested. 6) Show sample documents and publications. 7) Learners discuss the AGENCY roles and responsibilities as related to one of the samples. 8) Give feedback. 9) Point out where DEPARTMENT is found on the functional chart.	Instructor assesses group knowledge via the participation in the discussion. If self-study, use multiple choice or matching questions with self-scoring.	Informational graphic of AGENCY roles and responsibilities using icons, symbols, arrows and text.	CR, Field Guide, CBT or WBT
2. Discuss and explain the DEPARTMENT technical processes.	Knowledge and understanding	3) Orient DEPARTMENT on the functional chart. 4) Use a walk around to show and explain the technical processes—receiving files, scanning, tagging, database storage, etc. 5) Relate the processes to learners' backgrounds, especially those who have been with the AGENCY. 6) Show samples from each process 7) Probe for understanding 8) Give feedback and correct where needed. 9) Summarize	Instructor assesses group knowledge via the participation in the discussion and answers to probes. If self-study, use multiple choice or matching questions with self-scoring.	Informational graphic of AGENCY roles and responsibilities using icons, symbols, arrows and text. Walking tour of processes	CR, Field Guide, CBT or WBT

Table 7: (continued) Design Plan, May or May Not Implement

3. Define and use DEPARTMENT technical terms	Knowledge, Understanding, Application	3) Recall and repeat the DEPARTMENT technical processes. Ask learners if they heard any new terms while viewing the processes and list on board or on flip charts. 4) Present a glossary of DEPARTMENT terms and have learners take turns reading aloud the term and definition. 5) Explain and show examples where needed. If possible show sample or demonstrate procedure. 6) Use game format to reinforce meanings. 7) Provide correction and feedback 8) Have matching quiz or fill-in the blank 9) Learners correctly use the term(s) in a sentence.	Quiz on terms and definition.	Glossary of terms Examples of extensions, extracts, bar codes, slug lines, yellows, dup list, etc. Jeopardy format would work well. Show definitions and learners give the terms.	
4. Discuss and explain the DEPARTMENT print-based and we-based processes.	Knowledge and Understanding	Combine with Learning Objective 2 above.			
5. Define and use common printing terms.	Knowledge, Understanding, Application	3) Assess learners on previous knowledge of common printer terms. List on board or on flip charts. 4) Present a glossary of common Printer terms and have learners take turns reading aloud the term and definition. 5) Explain and give examples where needed. If possible show sample in document. 6) Use game format to reinforce meanings. 7) Provide correction and feedback 8) Have matching quiz or fill-in the blank 9) Learners correctly locate the use of the term on a printed document.	Quiz on terms and definitions.	Glossary of common printing terms, e.g., EM space, composition, galleys, type face, measure, folio, drop folio, etc. Go from easy to difficult and use Millionaire format.	CR, Field Guide, CBT or WBT

over again by simply changing the text, graphics, and animation as needed. And for quick access, they can be filed and cross-checked by category and subcategory in a database of learning objects.

Some clients prefer to have blueprints and storyboards for documentation. They may plan to outsource the development of the courseware. Here, too,

Figure 1: Template for Presenting Verbal Information, Subcategory "Standard File System"

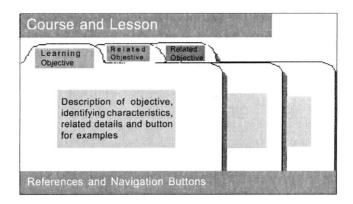

having a design plan based on the events of instruction that also includes strategies for implementation and assessment will facilitate the production of storyboards. Such storyboards need to accurately convey the strategies for each learning object. As insurance, the design plan should accompany the storyboards.

Implementation will also consist of additional reviews and pilots by the target audience, experienced instructors, and other stakeholders. And the original designer can set up a session during which the materials are compared to his or her design plan. Discrepancies and changes can be reconciled and the design plan updated at that time.

STORYBOARDING

Some clients prefer to have blueprints and storyboards for documentation. Frequently they plan to outsource the development of the courseware since they do not want or need to invest in the many resources involved in development. In these cases it is even more important to have a detailed design plan that uses the events of instruction and includes strategies for implementation and assessment. This greatly facilitates the production of storyboards and the hand-off of the production to an outside source.

The following storyboards were developed for another governmental agency. The intention was to outsource the development of the CBT. These storyboards represent one Learning Objective from the design plan.

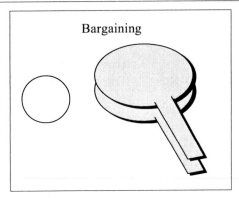

Bargaining

Screen Design: 3-D animation of ping pong game

Voice Over: The bargaining process is a series of steps that operate a lot like a ping pong game. The first thing you are required to do when one of your decisions puts the ball in play is to notify the union of the intended change before you put it into effect. That puts the ball in the union's court.

SME COMMENTS:

FRAME NUMBER: LINK 1:
TOPIC: The Bargaining Process Definitions   LINK 2:
                                                                                          LINK 3:

Collective Bargaining

Mutual obligation of both parties to meet at reasonable times and to consult and bargain in good faith effort to reach agreement concerning conditions of employment.

Screen Design: Standard Definition Screen.

Voice Over: Collective bargaining is defined as the mutual obligation of both parties to meet at reasonable times and to consult and bargain in good faith effort to reach agreement concerning conditions of employment.

SME COMMENTS:

FRAME NUMBER: LINK 1:
TOPIC: The Bargaining Process Definitions   LINK 2:
                                                          LINK 3:
OBJECTIVE: 2.01 Define collective bargaining   LINK 4:

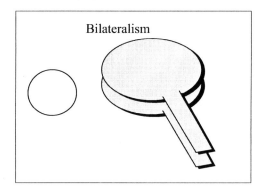

Bilateralism

Screen Design: Repeat animation of ping pong game. Game ends and the two players shake hands.

Voice Over: Collective bargaining agreements are based on bilateralism. This means that both management and union join to determine policies and practices affecting the working conditions of employees.

SME COMMENTS:

FRAME NUMBER: LINK 1:
TOPIC: The Bargaining Process Definitions   LINK 2:
                                                          LINK 3:
OBJECTIVE: 2.01 Define collective bargaining   LINK 4:

EVALUATE

The evaluation phase of the design process is where evaluation strategies that will measure the effect of the particular instructional strategies used are implemented. The design plan has already recommended appropriately typed evaluation strategies for each learning objective. Those evaluation strategies are linked to the ways that most people are able to receive, organize, store, and retrieve information and experiences. In the military they use an expression, "Train the way they fight." Here it is, "Test the same way you taught." Tests and

Table 8: Linking Evaluations to Objectives

Level of Proficiency Required	Beginner	Novice	Expert
Training objective	Arrange Label List Recall Name	Define Duplicate Match Relate Classify	Order Reproduce Discuss Explain Create
Training strategy	Frame info Use association Chunking Mapping	List attributes Know and apply steps Find patterns Use Rules	Use prototype Reason inductively Reason deductively
Training evaluation	Order a list Fill in a diagram Fill in a blank Identity from a group	State essentials Group with like parts Place in supra group Choose from supra group	Arrange accordingly Perform on demand Answer and elaborate

evaluation instruments should be linked to both the instructional objectives and the instructional strategies as is shown in the Table 8.

As with instructional strategies, templates can be used to speed up the development of the screens for the evaluation of the learning. These templates might even be specific to the identified learning type or need.

SUMMARY

Electronic learning necessitates a very special and very exact form of instruction. Since a teacher or trainer is not present with the materials, appropriate cognitive instructional and evaluation strategies must be built into their presentations. The standard instructional design process is the perfect mechanism for incorporating cognitive, instructional, and evaluation strategies

Figure 2: Template for Evaluating Procedures or Rules

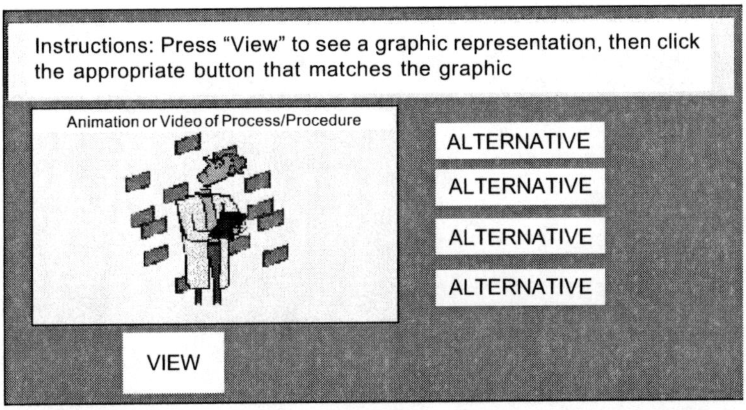

Figure 3: Template for Evaluating More than One Correct Answer (Process, Rules, Problem Solving, Etc.)

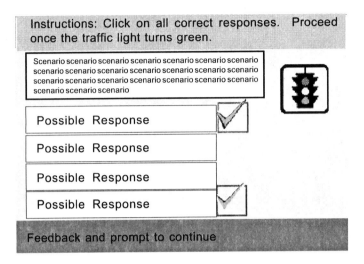

into the design plan, thereby ensuring that the electronic instruction mimics, as much as possible, the instruction of an experienced teacher or trainer.

The designer must keep in mind that electronic instruction not only fulfills the function of content but also the function of teacher or trainer. The design plan can be used to make certain that the teacher's "bag of tricks," intuition, and experiences with a variety of contents and learners are included as much as possible.

REFERENCES

Gagne, R.M., Briggs, L.J., & Wager, W.W. (1992). *Principles of Instructional Design (4th ed.)*. Harcourt, Brace Jovanovich.

West, C.K., Farmer, J.A., & Wolff, P.M. (1991). *Instructional Design, Implications from Cognitive Science*. Allyn & Bacon

Chapter VIII

KABISA:
Evaluation of an Open
Learning Environment

Geraldine Clarebout
University of Leuven, Belgium

Jan Elen
University of Leuven, Belgium

Joost Lowyck
University of Leuven, Belgium

Jef Van den Ende
Institute of Tropical Medicine, Belgium

Erwin Van den Enden
Institute of Tropical Medicine, Belgium

ABSTRACT

This chapter focuses on the last phase of the systematic instructional design approach, ADDIE. This evaluation phase is illustrated through means of a case study, namely the evaluation of a computer-based training program, KABISA. The leading evaluation questions were whether students followed a criterion path and whether students used the embedded help functions. Ninety-seven physicians following post-graduate training in tropical medicine participated in this evaluation. Log files were kept of the students and 21 students participated in thinking-aloud sessions. Results indicate that students do not follow the criterion path and that only poor use is made of help functions. This evaluation study shows that a systematic approach to instructional design remains highly valuable.

INTRODUCTION

Educational goals have generally shifted from knowing everything in a specific domain, to knowing how to deal with complex problems. Reasoning and information processing skills have become more important than the sheer amount of information memorized. In medical education the same evolution occurred. Diagnostic reasoning processes get more strongly emphasized. Whereas previously knowing all symptoms and diseases was stressed, reasoning skills have now become educationally more important. They must enable professionals to distinguish between differential diagnoses and to recognize patterns of illnesses (e.g., Myers & Dorsey, 1994).

Authentic or realistic tasks have been advocated to foster the acquisition of complex problem-solving processes (Jacobson & Spiro, 1995; Jonassen, 1997). In medical education this has led to the use in education of expert systems. Such systems were initially developed to assist practitioners in their practice (e.g., NEOMYCIN in Cormie, 1988; PATHMASTER in Frohlich, Miller, & Morrow, 1990; LIED in Console, Molino, Ripa di Meanan, & Torasso, 1992). These systems simulate a real situation and were expected to provoke or develop students' diagnostic reasoning processes. However, the implementation of such expert systems in regular educational settings has not been successful. Instead of developing reasoning processes, these systems assume them to be available. They focus on quickly getting to a solution rather than on reflecting on possible alternatives. Consequently, it was concluded that students need more guidance in the development of diagnostic reasoning skills (Console et al., 1992; Cromie, 1988; Friedman, France, & Drossman, 1991); instructional support was lacking.

KABISA is one of the programs that was purposely designed to help students in the development of their diagnostic reasoning skills (Van den Ende, Blot, Kesten, Gompel, & Van den Enden, 1997). It is a dedicated computer-based training program for acquiring diagnostic reasoning skills in tropical medicine.

The evaluation of students' performance while using KABISA involved comparing students' paths to a pre-specified 'criterion path' for working with KABISA and analyzing the use of embedded help functions. The evaluation concludes with a discussion of the results, a reflection on the evaluation process itself, and the implications for the evaluation phase within the ADDIE instructional design-model.

DESCRIPTION OF THE KABISA PROGRAM

KABISA confronts the user with cases or 'virtual patients.' The virtual patient is initially presented by three 'arguments'[1] randomly selected by the computer. After the presentation of the patient (three arguments), students can ask additional arguments gathered through anamnesis, physical examination, laboratory, and imaging (see Figure 1). If students click on a particular argument, such as physical examination or test, they receive feedback. Students are informed about the presence of a certain disease characteristic, or whether a test is positive or negative. If students ask a 'non-considered' argument, i.e., an argument that is not relevant or useful in relation to the virtual patient, they are informed about this and asked whether they want to reveal the diagnosis they were thinking about. After selecting a diagnosis, students receive an overview of the arguments that are explained by their selection and which

Figure 1: User Interface of KABISA

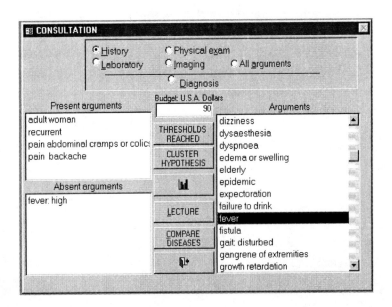

ones are not, as well as the place of the selected diagnosis on a list that ranks diagnoses according to their probability given the arguments at hand. If students do not want to show the diagnosis they were thinking about, they can just continue asking additional arguments. A session is ended with students giving a final diagnosis. KABISA informs them about its correctness. If their diagnosis is correct, students are congratulated.

If the diagnosis is not correct, students may be either informed that it is a very plausible diagnosis but that the threshold is not yet reached, or they may get a ranking of the diagnosis and an overview of the disease characteristics that can and cannot be explained by their answer (this feedback is similar to the one students receive when they show the diagnosis they were thinking about after asking a non-considered argument).

In addition to the information on non-considered arguments, students may use other support systems available in KABISA. KABISA offers the following support systems:

1. *Threshold reached:* this tool gives a ranking of the possible diseases at that moment and provides information on whether a threshold is reached. Reaching a threshold means that, given the disease characteristics present and absent at a certain moment, a diagnosis can be given, although one is not absolutely certain, but sufficiently certain to start a treatment.

2. *Cluster hypothesis:* presents an overview of all possible diagnoses, given the disease characteristics known at a certain moment.

3. *Graphic:* presents the different diagnoses with the disease characteristics known by the student. The graphic indicates the contribution for each disease characteristic and how it contributes to thresholds for different possible diseases.

4. *Lecture:* in this section, students can ask for information about a certain disease. They get all disease characteristics that occur if a patient has a particular disease, or by clicking on the characteristics they get information on their diagnostic power.

5. *Compare diseases:* gives the opportunity to compare disease characteristics of two diagnoses. The comparison reveals the unique and shared characteristics of the alternatives considered.

There are two different versions of KABISA, a junior and senior version. These versions do not differ in structure or content, but with respect to difficulty level. In the junior version virtual patients always have all the typical arguments for a disease. If a student asks an argument that should be present given a 'textbook' description of the diagnosis, the program will confirm its presence. In the senior consultation, some of the arguments that should typically be present for a specific diagnosis might be missing.

Parallel to these two versions, there are also exam-versions of KABISA. These versions are similar to the junior and senior version. However, students can no longer use the support systems.

EVALUATION METHODOLOGY

In order to gain insight in how students use KABISA, an evaluation was performed. To do this, first a criterion path was drawn that represents the 'ideal' way of working with KABISA. This criterion path served as the benchmark for the evaluation. This criterion path was elaborated in close collaboration between the evaluators and the domain experts.

Evaluation Questions

Two evaluation questions were focused upon, namely:
1.   Do students follow the criterion path when working on KABISA? And if not, how many, and how serious do students deviate from this path?
2.   Do students use the different embedded help functions?

To answer these questions, relationships between program and student characteristics were explored.

Participants

The students involved in this evaluation are general physicians following a post-graduate training in tropical medicine at the Institute of Tropical Medicine in Antwerp. Thirty-seven Dutch-speaking students and 60 French-speaking students participated. For the complete group log files were kept, and 21 volunteers (10 from the Dutch-speaking group and 11 from the French-speaking group) participated in think-aloud sessions.

Evaluation Instruments

For the first question, two evaluation approaches were used: the analysis of think-aloud protocols and the analysis of log files. For the second question, only log files were analyzed. The think-aloud procedure involved students performing two consultations on KABISA (one with the junior version and one with the senior version), while externalizing their reasoning processes. Students were instructed to think aloud and work with KABISA the way they would normally do, i.e., without an evaluator sitting next to them. It was explicitly mentioned that they could use all functionalities of the program. If students did not say anything while working on KABISA, they were prompted by the evaluator to think aloud with a question like: "What are you thinking of?" Everything students said was audiotaped. Notes were taken of the different steps students took. The think-aloud method allows detailed insight in the reasoning process of students, and the path they follow during a session (Karat, 1997; Ericsson & Simon, 1993).[2]

Audiotapes and notes were transcribed and used for protocol analysis.

For analyzing the log files, a dedicated program was developed. The program registered different actions of students while working on KABISA. For data gathering through log files, students were asked to do three junior and three senior consultations, and three exams (junior version) on KABISA. The advantage of log files is their unobtrusive character. The registration of students' actions has no effect on the behavior of students (Jackson, 1990).

Procedure

Question 1: Do students follow the criterion path? And if not, how many, and how serious deviations do students make?

As previously mentioned, a criterion path was constructed. This path was compared to students' paths when working with KABISA. Actual paths followed by the students were reconstructed based on the think-aloud protocols.

For the second part of this evaluation question, all possible deviations from the criterion path were identified and scored on their 'seriousness' by two experts of the Tropical Institute. Both experts gave a score for the possible errors on a six-point scale (from 0, not serious, to 5, very serious mistake). The sum of these scores was used in further analyses.

This approach corresponds to what Elstein and Rabinowitz (1993) call a 'normative approach.' Uncertainties and risks involved in a clinical situation are translated in probabilities that allow the construction of an ideal model.

A comparison was made between sessions with the senior and the junior version as well as between consultations by the French-speaking and the Dutch-speaking groups.

Using the think-aloud protocols, students' deviations from the optimal path were identified, summed, and given a score. An average number of deviations and an average score for the seriousness of the deviations were calculated for every student think-aloud. Different groups and different versions were compared.

Question 2: Do students use the embedded help functions?

For this question, the frequency students' use of help function was analyzed. A mean was calculated per help function for each session. These means were used as dependent variables. Three-way ANOVAs or MANOVAs were performed (depending on the correlation between the different help functions) with 'group,' 'version,' and 'finding the correct diagnosis' as independent variables.

RESULTS

Question 1a: Following the Optimal Path

Of 21 students participating in the think-aloud procedure, only one French student followed the criterion path during a session with the senior version. All other students did not follow the criterion path. Log file analysis reveals only eight consultations in which the criterion path was followed. Five out of 44 students followed this path (see Table 1).

Question 1b: Number of Deviations

For the number of mistakes, the analysis of the think-aloud protocols reveals that with the junior version, on average four mistakes are made per session. Almost five mistakes per senior version are made. The French group makes fewer deviations from the criterion path than the Dutch group. Concerning the seriousness of the mistakes, it seems that the Dutch group makes more serious deviations than the French group, both for sessions with the junior and the senior versions (see Table 2). It should be noted, however, that the data presented here relate only to a limited number of students (N = 21) and

Table 1: Number of Students Following the Optimal Path

Group (max. N sessions)	Version	N students	N sessions
French (n = 218)	Junior	1	2
	Senior	1	1
Dutch (n = 142)	Junior	2	4
	Senior	1	1

Table 2: Means for the Number of Mistakes and Seriousness of Deviations

		Number of deviations ($\overline{x}$)		Seriousness of deviations ($\overline{x}$)	
Junior	Dutch	4.70 (SD = 3.16)	3.95 (SD = 2.57)	14.40 (SD = 10.37)	11.38 (SD = 8.77)
	French	3.20 (SD = 1.93)		8.64 (SD = 6.30)	
Senior	Dutch	7.00 (SD = 5.70)	4.90 (SD = 4.72)	20.00 (SD = 17.40)	13.43 (SD = 14.09)
	French	3.10 (SD = 2.69)		7.45 (SD = 6.50)	
Total		4.40 (SD = 3.65)		12.41 (SD = 11.40)	

consultations (N = 42). Hence, no statistics were performed to test the significance of the observed differences.

However, the log file analysis reveals that even if students deviate from the criterion path, the correct diagnosis is found in more than half of the sessions (Table 3). This result will be discussed later as an implication for other evaluation studies.

Question 2: Use of Help Functions

For this question a difference is made between the response to discuss a non-considered argument and the remaining help functions. For most help functions students themselves have to take the initiative to use it. In case of a non-considered argument, however, KABISA explicitly invites students to provide a response.

Non-Considered Arguments

To gain insight in the way students deal with non-considered, or irrelevant arguments, the average number of considered and non-considered arguments was calculated. Within the last group, the average of non-considered discussed arguments was calculated as well. From Table 4, it can be seen that students ask more for considered arguments than for non-considered ones. On average, three non-considered arguments are asked for almost 13 considered ones.

Table 3: Cross Table for Finding the Diagnosis

		Version		
		Junior	Senior	Total
Diagnosis found	No	23	47	70
	Yes	155	134	289
Total		178	181	359

Table 4: Number of Considered, Non-Considered, and Discussed Non-Considered Arguments

	Version	N sessions	x̄	SD
Number of considered arguments	Junior	178	13.11	68.32
	Senior	181	12.10	48.32
Number of non-considered arguments	Junior	178	3.28	17.32
	Senior	181	2.59	12.34
Number of discussed non-considered arguments	Junior	178	.90	6.06
	Senior	181	.85	4.47
Total amount of arguments	*Junior*	*178*	*16.39*	*85.45*
	Senior	*181*	*14.69*	*60.41*

However, less than one out of three non-considered arguments are discussed. In other words, students who ask a non-considered argument ignore the opportunity to discuss the diagnosis they were thinking about.

The large standard deviation (SD) reveals large differences between the sessions with respect to the number of arguments asked.

To study the influence of group, version, and finding the diagnosis, proportions were calculated for the number of considered and non-considered arguments, by taking the sum of the considered and non-considered arguments as 100%. For the number of discussed non-considered arguments, the proportion was calculated by taking the number of non-considered arguments as 100%.

To decide whether a MANOVA or ANOVA should be done, a correlation (Pearson) was calculated between the proportion of considered arguments and the proportion of non-considered discussed arguments. This resulted in a low but significant positive correlation ($r = .16$, $p = .02$). The larger the

Figure 2: Main Effect of Version on the Proportion of Considered, Non-Considered, and Discussed Arguments

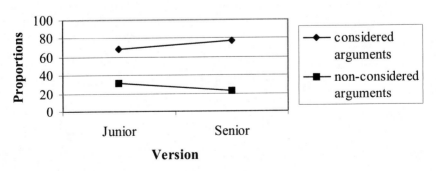

Figure 3: Proportion of Non-Considered Discussed Arguments

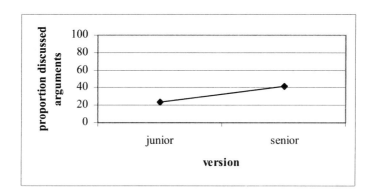

proportion of considered arguments asked during a session, the greater the probability that students will discuss non-considered arguments.

Given this correlation a multivariate three-way analysis of variance (MANOVA) was performed with group, version, and finding the diagnosis as independent variables and the proportion of considered and non-considered discussed arguments as dependent variables. A significant main effect of version was found (λ = .95, F(2,221) = 5.43, p = .01) (see Figure 2[3]). In the senior version the proportion of considered arguments is significant higher than in the junior version.

Looking only at non-considered arguments, results also show that significantly more non-considered arguments are discussed when working with the senior version than with the junior version (Figure 3). The more difficult the consultations are, the higher the proportion of considered arguments (Figure 2) and the more students discuss non-considered arguments (Figure 3). No significant effects were found for group and finding the diagnosis.

Other Help Functions

In Table 5, an overview is presented of the frequency of consulting a particular help function; the number of sessions, and the number of sessions in which a help function was consulted; and a correct diagnosis was found. From this table it can be derived that 'clusters' and 'thresholds' are consulted most frequently. Results also indicate that these help functions are consulted repeatedly in a session. The number of consulting thresholds is almost twice the number of sessions.

Table 5: Consultation of the Different Help Functions (HFs)

Help function	N consulted	N sessions in which a HF was consulted/ total N sessions	N correct diagnoses/ N sessions in which a HF was consulted	N students consulting a HF
Clusters	150	108/350 (= 30.86%)	80/108 (= 74.07%)	34/51 (= 66.67%)
Thresholds	297	174/350 (= 49.71%)	137/174 (= 78.44%)	40/51 (= 78.43%)
Graphic	45	33/350 (= 9.43%)	24/33 (= 72.73%)	18/51 (= 35.29%)
Lecture	69	47/350 (= 13.43%)	32/47 (= 68.09%)	17/51 (= 33.33%)
Compare diseases	29	25/350 (= 7.14%)	12/25 (= 48%)	25/51 (= 49.02%)

In order to detect the influence of group and version on the consultation of these help functions, first correlations (Pearson) were calculated for consulting the help functions (Table 6). A positive correlation indicates a tendency to use several help functions during one session.

Table 6: Correlation Between the Use of the Different Help Functions

	Thresholds	Graphic	Lecture	Compare diseases
Clusters	.35**	.22**	.31**	.35**
Thresholds		.18**	.38**	.26**
Graphic			.28**	.35**
Lecture				.26**

A MANOVA with group and version as independent variables and consultation of help functions as dependent variables resulted in two main effects, one for group ($1 = .91$, $F(5,350) = 6.81$, $p = .01$) and one for version ($1 = .96$, $F(5,350) = 3.20$, $p = .01$). For all help functions, (except for clusters where there was no significant difference between the versions), students more frequently consult the help functions in the senior consultation than in the junior version. With respect to differences between the two groups, the French-speaking group more frequently consults the help functions than the Dutch-speaking group does. Graphic is an exception; the Dutch group (see Table 7 for an overview) more frequently consults it.

Table 7: Two Main Effects for Group and Version on the Use of the Different Help Functions

	Version			
Help function	x̄ junior (SD)	x̄ senior (SD)	(F1,357)	p
Clusters	.32 (.61)	.52 (.82)	.96	.33
Thresholds	.63 (.87)	1.02 (1.68)	13.26	.00
Graphic	.01 (.26)	.19 (.64)	4.04	.05
Compare diseases	.00 (.15)	.14 (.41)	4.26	.04
Lecture	.01 (.35)	.29 (.77)	11.46	.00
	Group			
Help function	x̄ Dutch (SD)	x̄ French (SD)	F(1,357)	p
Clusters	.37 (.71)	.45 (.85)	4.08	.04
Thresholds	.51 (.82)	1.04 (1.57)	3.92	.05
Graphic	.18 (.67)	.01 (.33)	7.60	.01
Compare diseases	.00 (.22)	.17 (.35)	10.20	.00
Lecture	.01 (.26)	.28 (.73)	6.25	.01

CONCLUSION AND SUGGESTIONS FOR OPTIMIZATION

The evaluation of KABISA reveals that students do not follow a criterion path when working with KABISA. As evidenced by log file analysis, a criterion path was followed only in eight sessions. The think-aloud procedure reveals only one such session. These findings might be explained by the perception of students of consulting help functions. In the think-aloud protocol analysis, indications were found that students conceive consulting a help function as cheating or as failing:

"I'm going to cheat now and have a look at the thresholds."
"I really don't know what it is (...) I'm going to look at the thresholds."
"I give up, can I look at the thresholds?"

The students anticipate the feedback provided by KABISA when a non-considered argument is asked for. They rephrase it to 'stupid argument':

"If I would now ask fever, he will tell me that this is a stupid question."
"Stool, but he will say that it is a stupid question."
"I will ask something but the computer will probably not find it very interesting."

Log file analyses reveal also that students seldom consult help functions. Given the limited use of help functions, their impact on the learning process cannot be but limited.

Concerning version and group, differential effects were found for the use of the help functions. The Dutch-speaking group less frequently discusses non-considered arguments. In general, students in the French group more frequently consult help functions. For version, the proportion of considered arguments is larger in the senior version than in the junior version. Similarly, non-considered arguments are more often discussed in the senior version than in the junior version. Help functions are more consulted in a senior consultation than in a junior consultation.

However, in spite of the limited use of the help functions and in spite of the observation that in only a small number of consultations the optimal path was followed, students do find the diagnosis in 80% of the consultations (Table 3).

It might be concluded that KABISA provides easy tasks for students. Or, the program may allow too easily for guessing and may not sufficiently link the criterion path to finding the correct diagnosis. Students can easily follow another path and still make the correct diagnosis. Overall, students approach the program as being product directed rather than learning directed. Finding the correct diagnosis seems to be more important than the reasoning process to arrive at a diagnosis. Differences between the French-speaking and the Dutch-speaking group further suggest that the way in which KABISA is introduced to the students influences their use of KABISA.

The results of this evaluation suggest that KABISA is currently not used by students to foster their diagnostic reasoning skills. Rather, it enables them to train readily available skills.

IMPLICATIONS

Looking at the ADDIE-model, it can be said that the evaluation phase remains important. Through the use of evaluation methods, feedback is given with respect to other phases of the design process. In the case of KABISA for example, the evaluation gave some indications that more attention should have been given to the analysis phase. A more thorough analysis of student characteristics could have provided a means to adapt the difficulty level to the level of the students or to identify what guidance students actually need. Apparently, the feedback given to students does not encourage them to adapt their problem-solving process. Being product rather than process oriented, feedback may not be adapted to students' actual needs. Or, students' perception of the program (a game versus an educational application) may influence the use of the program. These perceptions should be taken into account throughout the design process of the program.

The difference between the French-speaking group and the Dutch-speaking group indicates a need for a different type of introduction for the program. In the introduction, the aims of the program, the different functionalities and the relationship with the different courses are clearly defined (see Kennedy, Petrovi, & Keppell, 1998 for the importance of introductory lessons). This relates to the implementation phase.

In order to perform a thorough evaluation, the use of different evaluation instruments provides more information than using only one instrument. With respect to the evaluation of KABISA, the think-aloud method resulted in both quantitative and qualitative results and, hence, a more detailed insight in the reasoning process of student. This think-aloud method allowed, for example, to find out why students make only limited use of these help functions. However, given the time investment that is needed for collecting the information and analyzing the protocols, the method may not always be applicable. Log files on the other hand are automatically generated and allow one to easily gather data from a large group. However, they do not provide insight in the reasoning processes of students (Drury, 1990; Kirwan & Ainsworth, 1992). This underscores the need for multiple evaluation tools and methods to obtain optimum results.

Open and realistic learning environments make it difficult to anticipate and to take into account during the design phase potential problems or difficulties students might encounter. A recommendation in this respect would be to break the linearity of the ADDIE-model and to introduce a formative evaluation after each phase. This would enable the redirection of the program while developing it, rather than after the implementation of the program. Rather than only evaluating a final product, the development process should be taken into consideration as well. Rapid prototyping for testing the program at different phases of the development might be indicated.

The presented case study of KABISA illustrates the importance of the evaluation in the ADDIE process. It revealed students to be able to state a correct diagnosis without using the diagnostic skills the program purports to be training.

For various reasons (limited time, limited budget, etc.), this phase often receives limited attention or is quickly dealt with through a questionnaire measuring students' attitudes towards the program. Restricted evaluations on the other hand may be both cheap and non-productive. Kirkpatrick (1994) has already revealed that such restricted evaluations have only limited value. However, a more thorough evaluation can point out weaknesses and flows otherwise remaining undiscovered, thus making an investment in evaluation (formative and summative) worthwhile.

ENDNOTES

[1]   The term 'argument' refers to either a symptom or disease characteristic, as well as a request for results of a physical examination, laboratory test, or imaging.

[2]   There is an ongoing discussion whether thinking aloud interferes in the reasoning process of students and whether the results are reliable. Criticisms have been made and have been rejected (e.g., Karat, 1997; Veenman, Elshout, & Groen, 1993). But given the structured environment of KABISA, it is assumed that thinking aloud does not interfere to the extent that students change their behavior.

[3]   In Figure 2, the proportion of non-considered arguments is also presented, although this was not entered as a variable in the analysis since it is the inversed proportion of the considered arguments.

REFERENCES

Console, L., Molino, G., Ripa di Meana, V., & Torasso, P. (1992). LIED-liver: Information, education and diagnosis. *Methods of Information in Medicine, 31*, 284-297.

Cromie, W.J. (1988). Expert systems and medical education. *Educational Researcher, 17*(3), 10-12.

Drury, C.G. (1990). Computerized data collection in ergonomics. In Wilson, J.R. & Carlett, N.I. (Eds.), *Evaluation of Human Work* (pp. 229-243). London: Taylor and Francis.

Elstein, A.S. & Rabinowitz, M. (1993). Medical cognition: Research and evaluation. In Rabinowitz, M. (Ed.), *Cognitive Science Foundation of Instruction* (pp. 189-201). Hillsdale, NJ: Lawrence Erlbaum Associates.

Ericsson, K.A. & Simon, H.A. (1993). *Protocol Analysis: Verbal Reports as Data* (revised ed.). Cambridge, MA: MIT Press.

Friedman, C.P., France, C.L., & Drossman, D.D. (1991). A randomized comparison of alternative formats for clinical simulations. *Medical Decision Making,* 11(4), 265-271.

Frohlich, M.W., Miller, P.L., & Morrow, J.S. (1990). PATHMASTER: Modeling differential diagnosis as "Dynamic Competition" between systematic analysis and disease-directed deduction. *Computers and Biomedical Research,* 23, 499-513.

Hannafin, M.J., Hall, C., Land, S., & Hill, J. (1994). Learning in open-ended learning environments: Assumptions, methods, and implications. *Educational Technology,* 34(10), 48-55.

Jackson, G.A. (1990). Evaluating learning technology. *Journal of Higher Education,* 61(3), 294-311.

Jacobson, M.J. & Spiro, R.J. (1995). Hypertext learning environments, cognitive flexibility and the transfer of complex knowledge. *Journal of Educational Computing Research,* 12(4), 301-333.

Jonassen, D.H. (1997). Instructional design models for well-structured and ill-structured problem-solving learning outcomes. *Educational Technology Research and Development,* 45(1), 65-91.

Karat, J. (1997). User-centered software evaluation methodologies. In Helander, M., Landauer, T.K., & Brabhu, P. (Eds.), *Handbook of Human-Computer Interaction (2nd ed.)* (pp. 689-704). Amsterdam: Elsevier Science.

Kennedy, G., Petrovic, T., & Keppell, M. (1998). The development of multimedia evaluation criteria and a program of evaluation for computer aided learning. In Corderoy, R.M. (Ed.), *Proceedings of the Fifteenth Annual Conference of the Australian Society for Computers in Tertiary Education (ASCILITE)* (pp. 407-415). Wollongong, Australia: University of Wollongong.

Kirkpatrick, D.L. (1994). *Evaluating Training Programs. The Four Levels.* San Francisco, CA: Berrett-Koehler Publishers.

Kirwan, B. & Ainsworth, L.K. (1992). Observational techniques. In Kirwan, B. & Ainsworth, L.K. (Eds.), *A Guide to Task Analysis* (pp. 53-58). London: Taylor & Francis.

Myers, J.H. & Dorsey, J.K. (1994). Using diagnostic reasoning (DxR) to teach and evaluate clinical reasoning skills. *Academic Medicine,* 69, 429.

Shaw, E., Johnson, W.L., & Ganeshan, R. (1999). *Pedagogical Agents on the Web.* Available online at: http://www.isi.edu/isd/ADE/papers/agents99/agents99.htm.

Van den Ende, J., Blot, K., Kestens, L., Van Gompel, A., & Van den Ende, E. (1997). KABISA: An interactive computer-assisted training program for tropical diseases. *Medical Education, 31*, 202-209.

Veenman, M.V., Elshout, J.J., & Groen, M.G. (1993). Thinking aloud: Does it affect regulatory processes in learning? *Tijdschrift voor Onderwijsresearch, 18*(6), 322-330.

Chapter IX

Guerilla Evaluation: Adapting to the Terrain and Situation

Tad Waddington
Accenture, USA

Bruce Aaron
Accenture, USA

Rachael Sheldrick
Accenture, USA

ABSTRACT

This chapter provides proven strategy and tactics for the corporate evaluator. Topics include: adopting a performance-based operating model (the V-model) to shift focus from training for activity to training for results; using the V-model to plan and structure communication; leveraging modern measurement and statistics to save time and money (e.g., Item Response Theory, sampling procedures, regression); leveraging available data to calculate training ROI (return on investment); determining when to hire or contract skills and knowledge; using technology to save time and money; and making the most of your available applications.

INTRODUCTION

Most corporate evaluators confront an assortment of decisions and trade-offs between the prescribed models of their discipline and the demands of the current business and technological situation. These exigencies demand flexibility in measurement and evaluation approaches. Adapting successfully to the situation and the reality of the corporate terrain often requires creative or "guerilla" tactics. In this chapter we share some of the tactics that have served us well in our endeavors to conduct effective evaluation in the larger corporate system within which we operate. For us, guerilla evaluation means adapting to two primary domains or constraints:

1. *Terrain*—the unique demands of the modern corporate training environment. Successfully navigating the corporate terrain requires tactical planning and communication, and a good map. Our map is a systems development model adopted from our corporate methodology and repurposed for evaluation and performance improvement work. This model guides our work as well as our communication plans. It helps us identify the unique characteristics and requirements of each stakeholder group, and deliver the information that each group needs in a timely manner.

2. *Situation*—constraints on resources of time, money, people, skills, and technology. We respond to these situational constraints with a second set of guerilla tactics based on lessons learned: leveraging data and statistical skills, using contractors and consultants, and maximizing our use of available technology.

It is important to note that what we describe in this chapter is based on our experiences as a small team with a large agenda. Our group of four is the evaluation team for the central learning organization of Accenture, a leading global management consulting and technology services organization, with more than 75,000 people in 47 countries. Our team's defined mission probably reflects that of other corporate evaluation teams:

To be an integral partner within our organization and provide valued information that enables us to improve the products and programs necessary to build capabilities within our company.

In essence, our mission is to use evaluation to create and drive value.

Our collective background includes graduate training in evaluation, statistics, and measurement, as well as applied measurement and evaluation in the public and private sectors. In recent years our business context has become more challenging (but more interesting) and our strategies have evolved in response. This chapter will describe and illustrate a few of the important challenges confronting today's corporate evaluator, and what can be done to meet these challenges with resourcefulness, flexibility, and creativity.

NAVIGATING THE TERRAIN

Evaluation within a business context and the discipline of measurement as practiced and taught within academic settings are different enterprises and require different approaches. In our experience, successful corporate evaluators place themselves "in the trenches" and frame their work in the business context, rather than attempt to organize their efforts around lofty theory. As we'll describe later, academic training and acumen in statistics and measurement are critical levers for adding value, but in the corporate arena, the alignment of evaluation strategies with the business needs of the organization is of primary importance. Two strategies we have employed for the purpose of adapting to the business terrain are:
1. Adopting a performance-based operating model
2. Planning and structuring communication effectively in a business context

As is usually the case in adapting to any terrain, it helps to have a map. Ours is a model that guides our evaluation work and relates our work to the goals that the organization values. It is also vital for organizing our communication with stakeholders about our processes and results.

Creating a Map of the Terrain

It is widely purported that the Human Resource Development (HRD) field is evolving of necessity from its traditional training paradigm to a performance-based approach. In this approach, the objective of the training function is no longer the activity of training but the production of performance and business results (Stolovich & Keeps, 1999; Fuller & Farrington, 1999). Naturally, a shift in the training enterprise requires a shift in the evaluation of that enterprise. Phillips (1997) describes the characteristics of this shift, as shown in Table 1.

If an organization has not emphasized this shift, the evaluator has a unique opportunity to help clients and colleagues make the transition to performance-based solutions by leveraging the evaluation function in pursuit of ROI (return on investment) data. Because the bottom-line results of ROI analyses are attractive to today's clients, requests for ROI results are common. In address-

Table 1: Paradigm Shift in Training Evaluation

Training for Activity	Training for Results
No business need for the program	Program linked to specific business needs
No assessment of performance issues	Assessment of performance effectiveness
No specific measurable objectives for behavior and business impact	Specific objectives for behavior and business impact
No effort to prepare the work environment to support transfer	Environment prepared to support transfer
No efforts to build partnerships with key managers	Partnerships established with key managers and clients
No measurement of results or cost benefit analysis	Measurement of results and cost benefit analysis
Planning and reporting on training is input focused	Planning and reporting on training is output focused

ing these requests, an evaluator can demonstrate that ROI is integral to a larger performance-based framework that involves needs analysis and identification of the relevant business issues and results. In effect, the evaluator can use ROI to sell a performance-based approach.

Consider, for example, a typical request for the ROI of a course or program. Such requests are not usually based on deep experience in HRD ROI methodology, but rather on the client's desire to know what bottom-line return will be achieved on the investment made in a learning solution. An evaluator engaging this client can demonstrate the need and value of a performance-based approach by illustrating how determination of ROI for the learning solution must be based on the measurable business results that are at the core of the client's need and central to the client's request for a solution. By structuring this conversation clearly, the evaluator can test the links between the learning or performance solution that's on the table, and the ROI and business results that should be realized. Often, these links have not been clearly defined, which puts the client's return at risk. A clear performance model will help structure these conversations with clients. By guiding the client through this process of mutual discovery, the evaluator enters the realm of performance-based HRD through ROI. In fact, doing this extends the evaluator's role to that of performance consultant, and small efforts such as these can help an organization transition from a training mode to a performance mindset.

As HRD organizations journey from an activity-based training culture to a performance-based and results-based approach, the evaluation model should likewise shift to a performance-based framework. The evaluation model should address each of the following fundamental objectives:

1. Measure the extent to which training meets the business goals and needs of the organization.
2. Link HRD intervention efforts to measurable results and estimation of return on investment (ROI) of training dollars.
3. Provide valuable information about training to the key decision makers for the purpose of continuous improvement.

In our effort to meet these requirements, we adapted a model from Accenture's core business methodology to map out the process for evaluating learning assets. Referred to as the V-model, it bridges our local business context, best practices in evaluation, and the shift in emphasis from traditional training activity to performance improvement approaches. The original V-model is an industry best practice for quality control in the development of applications, providing a structured development framework comprising verification, validation, and testing processes. The HRD adaptation of the model is shown at a basic level of detail in Figure 1.

Figure 1: V-Model

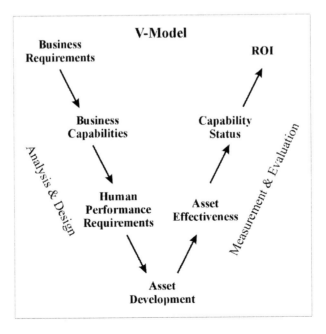

The model proceeds down the left side of the V, moving from broad analysis activities (starting with the business need and definition of business requirements) through finer detail specification and specific design decisions. This essentially is a process of analysis and decomposition of broader objectives into more granular requirements, with verification at each step to validate links to the preceding set of requirements. During this analysis phase, the business need is translated into human performance requirements and solution designs. Development of the intervention occurs in the middle of the process, at the bottom of the V. Then, proceeding up the right side, each step signifies a specific set of measurements or products for its left-side counterpart. The process unfolds upward, finally resulting in Level 4 evaluation metrics (Kirkpatrick, 1994) and their monetary transformation into ROI estimates. In this reflective fashion, business results and ROI are measured in a manner that matches the business needs that were the original drivers of the problem or opportunity.

The key to the V-model is its symmetry. During the analysis and design stages (left side of the V), the model requires simultaneous development of metrics that reflect and link plan with result, gap with measurement, and ultimately, investment with return on investment. This 'testing' process, as well as the validation and verification processes inherent in the V-model, ensure the integrity of the system and provide tight linkages between the analysis-design phase and the measurement phase. When implemented properly, this results in performance solutions that are tied to the business needs that defined the original problem or opportunity, and metrics that are tied to performance objectives. Because it is adopted from our internal business culture, the V-model has been effective both for organizing our work and communicating our processes and results to stakeholders. It orients our clients in evaluating learning and performance interventions, guiding us from point A to point B.

Using the Map as a Guide to Communication

The V-model not only maps the terrain and guides evaluation work, it also helps in planning communication. The importance of communication in corporate evaluation seems underrated. The corporate evaluator must realize that in a real-world business context, the value of the evaluation effort is transaction-based and depends on the communication and reception of information. The evaluator's work is complete only upon an effective information transaction, with results delivered in a language that the audience understands and at a time that is useful for decision making. Communication and dissemination of evaluation results therefore require as much attention as any other aspect of the evaluation effort and should be planned, designed, delivered, and managed.

In order to be deliberate and effective, communication planning should be mapped to the overall evaluation model. The V-model is useful for identifying the level and characteristics of target audiences for evaluation results. These audiences are identified for each set of evaluation results on the right side of the V-model (e.g., effectiveness of a course or program, its impact on business capabilities in the field, and return on investment). When mapped to the corresponding front-end processes of the performance model (the left side of the V), the identified target groups represent those whose needs, assumptions, and expectations have been clarified and incorporated into evaluation planning. These front-end requirements provide the basis for reporting results. Figure 2 displays the types of audiences within our organization that correspond to each of the levels of the V-model.

In addition to focusing results and reporting, identifying these groups allows us to consider their unique characteristics and needs. For example, at the bottom of the V, where courses are developed, instructional designers and project teams need rich, detailed information at the level of individual learning objectives as they pilot and revise a course. It is important for evaluators working with these project teams to report and interpret patterns, and to

Figure 2: V-Model Communication Map

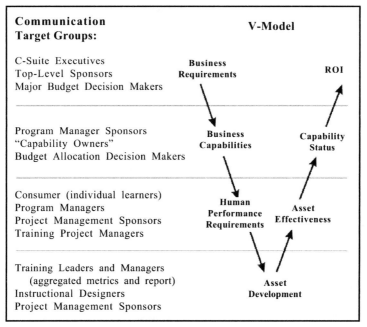

integrate qualitative and quantitative data to provide solid formative information for continuous improvement. At the other extreme, near the top of the model, executives typically need a much bigger picture of how the course or program is delivering results. If the project has been selected for ROI evaluation, they will want monetary estimates, and evaluators should be prepared to provide details on the method used and the basis of the results. But, these stakeholders will typically need a more comprehensive and global summary of the course or program effectiveness across levels. Simple indices or scorecard presentations will summarize the big picture.

Similarly, mapping the communication plan onto the larger model allows evaluators to anticipate the flow of evaluation information between target audiences, and effectively plan the structure and timing of dissemination. This involves evaluating the consistency of messages released to each level of the target audience, and considering how each audience might use the information in reporting to others.

Piloting the Communication

An evaluator should feel confident that the information planned for delivery exactly answers the questions posed at each level of the model and for each stakeholder group. If necessary, the communication can be piloted before releasing results. Ideally, this should be done on the front end of the process while working with stakeholders to define needs and requirements. An easy way to do this is by producing mock reports with simulated data. This helps ensure that the right kind of information is being given in the right way. It can also save time on the back end of the project, because the simulated data can simply be replaced with actual data, and the tables and graphs refreshed. Because stakeholders use evaluation information to make decisions, piloting the communication will help clarify that the right questions are being addressed in order to make those decisions, that the right data will be collected, and that the best analysis method will be applied to the data.

Timing the Communication

When communicating evaluation results in today's business environment, timing is nearly everything. When developing the communication plan and working with stakeholders, it is important to assess their context to determine exactly when they will need the information. Of course, their answer is often "yesterday," but the reality is that various pressures drive stakeholder needs, and a pretty-good evaluation today may be worth much more than a perfect one tomorrow. The stakeholders' external pressures should be identified in order to determine the most appropriate time to disseminate information. Well-crafted evaluation, delivered at the right time to the right decision makers, is the fundamental achievement of the corporate evaluator's work. Conversely, it is very frustrating to deliver results of a well-crafted and labor-intensive evaluation effort to stakeholders who have already made their decisions. They will respond to their pressures, make a decision for better or worse, and proceed to other pressing issues. If the decisions aren't optimal because they didn't have good data, everyone loses.

To Give is to Receive

Since knowledge is said to be power, one might be tempted to hoard it. We have found, however, that the opposite is true — the value of our work increases with the size of our audience. We choose to publish evaluation reports to an internal intranet site with open employee access. Organization productivity is dependent on collaborative efforts among strategic partners and allies throughout the organization, and these partners depend on information. Making information easily available serves to decrease transaction costs for program improvements within the organization and increase the entrepreneurial efforts of a wider audience to add value.

Users are not likely to misuse or inappropriately slant evaluation output if we succeed in delivering a cohesive and meaningful presentation of results and follow the communication plan. We have also found it helpful to identify early on those who used and found value in the reports in order to share their positive experiences with colleagues.

ADJUSTING TO
SITUATIONAL CONSTRAINTS

Another major challenge for corporate evaluators is doing more with less and making the most of available resources. By effectively leveraging available resources, the evaluation effort can succeed in its goal to demonstrate the relationship between performance improvement interventions and bottom-line impact. This, in turn, will help improve the quality of solutions and ensure that training and performance improvement expenditures are seen as investments, not merely costs. Demonstrating the value of performance improvement interventions helps protect budgets for important training and evaluation projects during challenging periods in the economic cycle and ultimately ensures the health of the human resource system in the organization. We have developed four strategies for coping with the frequent lack of resources encountered during evaluation efforts in a business context:

1. Leveraging statistics to save time and money
2. Leveraging available data to deliver value
3. Hiring or contracting needed skills
4. Using technology to save time and money

Leveraging Statistics to Save Time and Money

With skills in statistics and measurement, an evaluator has a wider range of tools for doing good work. Following are four examples from our experience.

Case 1: The Fickle Flexibility of Raw Score Ratings

We were asked to evaluate an ongoing and extremely expensive annual event for our company's leadership. Three years of data showed a statistically significant *decline* in ratings of the event, but qualitative comments suggested that people thought the event was getting better each year. In resolving this conflicting information, we applied IRT (Item Response Theory) analysis techniques, which allow raters and rated items to be separately and objectively measured on a common scale, independent of any particular sample of respondents. Because unique identifying information had been collected along with the ratings, we knew how each person had rated the event and could take into account individual differences in how the event was rated (e.g., some people are easier "graders" and tend to give higher ratings). With these biases factored out, we found that the event was actually receiving significantly higher ratings each year. Investigating further, we discovered that each year the event planners had been inviting fewer managers (who tend to be more positive in their ratings) relative to higher-level executives (who are more severe raters). By systematically eliminating the easy "graders," they had accidentally biased the data against themselves. Resolving this conflict of information (decreasing ratings but positive comments) gave the managing partner for the event better information with which to make decisions. The importance of having reliable and valid information was made clear when she told us, "You've just earned your pay for the year."

Case 2: Using Sampling to Save Thousands of Dollars

Another tactic we used in the analysis for this annual event was to sample wisely. The event was attended by several thousand people whose hourly bill

rate was extraordinarily high. Previous evaluators had surveyed every participant with a lengthy survey. If each survey took 10 minutes to complete and
3,000 people completed them, the cost to the company was $250,000 — a
very expensive way to gather information. We needed information on the
quality of the event, but we did not need to know what every participant thought
of every aspect of the event. The large size of the event allowed us to gather
information on different parts of the event from different participants and still
have a reliable measure of the event's quality. In other words, we sampled both
people and items. A few items remained common to the four different surveys
sent to participants so that all of the items could be calibrated with IRT
techniques, ensuring psychometrically valid measures, independent of the
sample used to collect the data. By sampling both items and people, the length
of each survey was cut to two minutes and the number of people completing the
survey to 1,000. The total estimated opportunity cost thus dropped to
$17,000, saving the company $233,000 while still delivering valid results.

*Case 3: Providing Valid and Reliable Measures — Even When You
Can't Choose the Items*

We also used Item Response Theory both to develop valid measures of
our company's e-learning products and to avoid a series of political battles.
Our e-learning group had developed millions of dollars worth of training
products, but no evaluation data had been collected. When the organization's
leadership required that comprehensive evaluation be put in place, the product
managers took different approaches and selected different items to collect
evaluation data. While all of these items consisted of general evaluative
statements reflecting perceived value of instruction, the selection criteria in
many cases appeared to be the manager's perception that the item would
produce high ratings (since subtle manipulations of item wording and rating
scales can influence the raw score ratings). When our team was asked to
provide a comprehensive evaluation of these products, some resistance was
evident within the development group (as is often the case when evaluation is
perceived as externally mandated). In working through the political issues and
compromises, each development manager was still allowed different selections
of items for their products' evaluation surveys, rather than being constrained to
a common set of identical items. We created an item bank that consisted of
general evaluative statements reflecting perceived value of instruction. These
items were calibrated using IRT techniques since a data matrix could be built
in which some people rated multiple products and some products were rated
by the same items. A common measure was derived across all products that

was both valid and reliable, and allowed legitimate comparisons between courses. Because the items were psychometrically calibrated, it did not matter which specific items appeared on any product evaluation. For any combination of items, we could calculate an overall measure of value that allowed us to directly compare the e-learning products. Even though we lost the battle (managers controlled which items appeared on the surveys), we were able to win the evaluation war (regardless of the items chosen, we were able to provide valid and reliable measures).

Case 4: Using Data to Drive Course Design

One current project also leverages IRT. To date we have data from more than 75,000 evaluations of roughly 3,000 courses. Each course is coded on variables such as course length, format (e.g., classroom or e-learning), learning objective level (e.g., skill building or knowledge dissemination), and course-design variables (e.g., goal-based scenario). We will be able to develop an objective calibrated measure of instructional value as the dependent variable and use multiple regression to identify those aspects of course design (described above) that predict the perceived value of courses. This information should be useful to course developers and will further enable "data-driven design." This should help answer the question, "For this audience and with these constraints, how should we build this course?"

Leveraging Available Data

Depending on their skill sets and experience with data analysis, corporate evaluators might be asked to perform various analyses and answer questions beyond the scope of the planned evaluation of specific courses. Tackling these broader research questions usually involves working with extant data, and these data from various sources can often be used creatively to deliver exciting results. Three examples from our experiences demonstrate this theme.

Case 1: A Unique Way of Calculating Training ROI

Most people think about the value of training in terms of how a specific course gives a specific person a specific skill that allows that person to accomplish a specific task. While this is not inaccurate, our work on training ROI revealed larger effects of training—effects in recruiting, chargeability, bill rates, and retention. Ignoring these effects risks underestimating the broader value of the training program. The benefits gained from taking a single course may be fleeting, but the benefits gained from taking many courses can be pervasive. We chose, therefore, to look at how training histories (rather than individual courses) affect broad business concerns — how to attract and keep good people and make them more productive during their tenure. Our work on training ROI has been recognized for its innovation; in June 2002 we won the Corporate University Xchange Excellence Award in the category of Measurement.

To calculate the ROI of training, we analyzed over a quarter-of-a-million human resource records on all employees who have been with the company. We began by calculating net per-person Contribution [(Chargeable hours * Bill rate) – (Cost rate * total hours)], the individual's margin over his or her career with the company. We used regression to determine how training histories (e.g., hours spent in training) affected Contribution, making sure to remove the effect of potential biases in the data such as career level, work experience, inflation, and business cycles. The results of the analysis showed that people who take the most training (those in the top 50th percentile) were both more billable and charged higher bill rates than those who had taken less training. These employees were also more likely to stay with the company longer. We based our analysis on actual data collected within the company and were able to document a 353% ROI for training expenditures.

Case 2: If You Scratch My Back, I'll Scratch Yours

A common constraint in corporate evaluation is the availability and quality of data. Evaluators are the quintessential knowledge workers, often required to generate meta-knowledge (i.e., measuring what the organization knows). Evaluation involves creating knowledge from information and intelligence from data. In addition to the data generated through course evaluations and knowledge/skill assessments, other existing sources of data generated or collected by internal organizations that might be of use to the training organization include employee or customer satisfaction data, and marketing or market research data. Often the data needed to answer the business question being asked are not accessible. Helping the owners of the data realize value by providing evaluation expertise and methodology is a valuable tactic in gaining access to these additional sources of data. For example, gaining access to human resources records was essential for our ROI analysis. By assisting HR in an analysis of personnel performance ratings and the promotion process, we not only added more value to our organization, but were able to gain access to the data we needed for our own analyses.

Case 3: Know the Nature of the Task

Ideally, evaluators are asked to evaluate a project by providing objective summative or formative feedback. It is not uncommon, however, to find that what is actually expected is a kind of positive, quantified advertisement. Stakeholders might be influenced by the "drive for 5s" approach to evaluation, where the primary object of conducting evaluation is to achieve a maximum "grade" on a five-point rating scale. Such motivations are understandable, and typically are not informed by a sense of the importance of constructing items that produce variance and balancing item difficulty (i.e., the ease with which an item can be rated highly). In general, data will be more accurate and informative when there is increased variance in responses, which cannot occur if everybody gives a rating of a 5. To balance the need for good measurement with good advertising, evaluators can include both types of items — tougher questions that provide good measurement information and easier items that provide good press. Both types of items can be used ethically, if you are mindful that consequential validity — the degree to which the intended actions and inferences based on the data are supported by the data — is maintained. A course that gets a lower percentage of 5s on a difficult item may be an outstanding course, but a statistically naive stakeholder might not take into account the difficulty of the item and decide to cut funding for the course because of its "low" score. Paradoxically, the "advertising" items (a lot of 5s), though statistically spurious, might allow for the right decision to be made (e.g., this course had a lot of 5s so I'll continue to fund it). The paradox is that sometimes you can only get the right decision by providing bad data, a truly guerilla tactic.

We have been successful in persuading people to use items with greater item difficulty by convincing them that it is in their long-term interest to have these tougher items. Suppose 95% of participants rate a program as some form of "Excellent." The sponsors of the program may increase the funding for the program for the next year and expect higher results for the increased investment. Because the ratings are already near the upper limit (100%), they cannot get much higher, and future results may be misinterpreted as a lack of progress. While course sponsors might prefer "feel-good" items for advertising purposes, this must be balanced with the high-quality measurement provided by tougher, more valid questions.

Hiring or Contracting Skills and Knowledge

Even under the best of circumstances, an evaluator at times might not have the time or level of skill necessary to complete a project. Multiple projects may be imposing serious time demands, or there may be an opportunity to deliver value that requires familiarity with new techniques or processes. When such demands or requirements are too great, assistance can be sought in external sources, such as university students or consultants. Both sources can provide the skills needed (and provide the opportunity to develop those skills within the evaluation team) and free up time for the evaluators to complete more pressing or valuable projects.

It is useful to maintain contacts with local universities, as students can be an excellent resource; they are also generally more cost effective than external consultants. In addition, if you have positions opening, the experience can be a useful trial period for the organization and the student to assess the fit. We have had great success using graduate students from a nearby Ivy League school. These contractors are paid more than they could make on campus and less than the typical cost for employees (a tactic that keeps both our company and the students happy), and we strictly follow the law for employing temporary contract workers. These contractors can be invaluable in consolidating research relevant to current projects, providing statistical assistance, and handling time-consuming tasks.

The internal staff should define the target problems and break them down into manageable steps. The contractors then can work on the tasks and develop potential solutions. With this assistance, the evaluation staff can work on more projects and deliver valuable results more quickly than would be possible otherwise. The internal staff might also proactively identify areas that would be of interest to the organization and create reports based on the work of the contractors. For instance, one of our contractors read and performed content analysis on over two million words of qualitative comments from various surveys that we have in place and provided a well-synthesized qualitative summary that was quite useful and well received by many stakeholders.

Another type of external consultant that can be leveraged is a highly specialized expert with recognition in the field. These consultants are hired because of their specialized evaluation expertise and the unique value they can deliver to an evaluation project. For example, an external expert with deep expertise and experience in calculating the ROI of human performance interventions can be contracted for assistance with such analyses. Unlike lower cost contractors that require some level of supervision, these higher-level consultants work more like partners, and different strategies are needed to manage and leverage these relationships.

In any contracting relationship, make the scope of the project clear. Define the expectations for work, roles, and responsibilities. In setting the parameters of the relationship, a long-term view should be maintained in order to take full advantage of the partnership. To the extent possible, opportunities and expectations for knowledge transfer should be built in, so that at the end of the project, the evaluation team has gained new competencies in the expert's domain. The scope of this knowledge transfer will vary according to that domain and the project circumstances, but such experiences are among the best professional development opportunities around, and they should be capitalized on. The ultimate goal should be the ability to tackle the same type of project independently as a result of the experience.

A number of tactics can be used to reach this goal. An evaluation consultant's typical service might include tasks that an evaluator or evaluation team can assume (e.g., production of survey instruments, data collection, or internal communication with project stakeholders). Relieving the external consultant of these tasks can free up time and an expectation can be set for collaboration on evaluation design or for more frequent meetings to discuss problems and options.

It also helps to do some research on the area of expertise prior to engaging the consultant. Initially, an evaluator should have enough background to know that the consultant's particular expertise is a good match for the organization's performance issue, and that this expertise or resource is not available internally. Investing time up front, and demonstrating some knowledge and expertise while setting expectations with the consultant, will earn their confidence and assist in the development of a close working relationship that will result in deeper learning.

A final report or document should be developed that has sufficient depth and documentation to provide guidance for conducting similar projects in the future. This should include whatever elements are deemed helpful for reproducing the processes. Such elements might include sufficient background on the theoretical bases of the approach, description of the processes involved, detailed evaluation design or planning documents, and copies of instruments used. As an expert in the field, the consultant should have no trouble generating this sort of document. It can probably be synthesized easily from the body of her work, which could include books and professional papers. Also, given the consultant's direct engagement in the evaluation project and organization, she is ideally suited to tailor this body of work to an evaluator's particular context.

Using Technology to Save Time and Money

Evaluating courses can be a time-consuming task, particularly when the evaluations are developed and distributed manually. Because of the time involved in designing, developing, distributing, and analyzing the results of a course evaluation, it may not be possible to evaluate every course that a company offers its employees. By leveraging technology, however, the task of evaluation cannot only become more manageable, but time and resources may also be freed up to allow more intensive and valuable data analyses that further benefit the company. The following examples illustrate this use of technology.

The Leap from 200 Customized Surveys to 3,000 Standardized Surveys

Before June 2001, course evaluations at Accenture were done on a case-by-case basis, and evaluations were developed specifically for individual courses. The responsibility of deciding whether a course should be evaluated usually fell to the course sponsor. If the decision was not made early enough in the course development process, the course was not evaluated until well after it was released, or it was simply not evaluated at all. When these post-course surveys were created, the design process often included considerable iterative input from the course sponsor and others in an effort to provide quality client service. However, the expectations of the sponsors had to be balanced with survey design standards (i.e., questions and rating scales that provided reliable and valid metrics), and many hours were often spent in discussions over the wording of particular items or a number of questions. These individual course surveys were distributed on an ad hoc basis via e-mail, and the reports that presented the survey results were created and updated manually.

While customized surveys provided value, the process behind such evaluations (from survey design to distribution to reporting) was hardly efficient. The time needed to support course evaluations left little room for reflection on evaluation processes, and no time to work on more interesting and business-relevant projects, such as training ROI. By leveraging technology, however, the course evaluation process was greatly streamlined. A system was created that not only provided evaluation services for *all* of the learning assets provided by Accenture, but also allowed us the chance to provide more valuable evaluation services to the company at large, rather than limiting it only to individual course owners.

In June 2001, Accenture rolled out myLearning, a personalized, Web-based portal that gave its employees immediate access to all information related to company-sponsored learning assets. The myLearning portal includes:

- A Course Catalog and Learning Management System (LMS), which provide a list of required and recommended courses based on an employee's role within the company and gives employees the ability to register for courses online.

- A Decision Support Center, which provides a comprehensive and immediate snapshot of learning metrics, including expenditures per area and course evaluation ratings.
- A Course Evaluation System, which provides "5-star" ratings and detailed course reviews for every course to guide employees in their learning decisions.

The 5-star ratings and course reviews provided by the Evaluation System are based on participant responses to end-of-course surveys. These surveys are automatically distributed by the LMS upon course completion; data are stored in a SQL server, which warehouses data, feeds 5-star ratings and course reviews back into the LMS for publication to end users, and transfers learning metrics data to the Decision Support Center (DSC) reports.

Rather than creating individualized surveys for every course, which would be time consuming to create and of limited utility due to lack of standardization, we created four distinct surveys based on the following types of assets:

- Instructor-Led Training (e.g., classroom training)
- Virtual Training (e.g., Web-based seminars)
- Online Course (e.g., CBT)
- Books/Publications

We selected survey questions based on the results of an Item Response Theory analysis of over 10 million data points culled from six years of in-depth classroom evaluations (our earlier custom evaluations), test scores, follow-up surveys, faculty ratings of student learning, and supervisor ratings. Though brief, the 5-star rating system is a psychometrically reliable and valid proxy for the previously completed in-depth course evaluations. As might well be expected, a few clients were not pleased with the systemic changes to evaluation processes. Sponsorship and support from key leaders was essential in articulating the new value that was to be realized from adopting the widespread changes.

Not only are surveys distributed automatically, but reporting is also provided automatically, via myLearning's Decision Support Center (DSC). The DSC integrates information from a variety of sources — including course evaluations, accounting, and global personnel tracking (all of these data have been stored on an SQL server to facilitate integration) — to make immediately available the information that learning stakeholders need to make better education investment decisions. The reports are pre-formatted as Excel pivot tables that can be customized by user groups so that they may examine their learning programs from a variety of perspectives and make appropriate modifications.

Because the reports are linked to the SQL server that houses evaluation data, the results of those evaluations become immediately available when surveys are returned. And, because the reports are also linked to usage and financial information, the reports become more valuable to multiple groups. Accenture executives can quickly create reports that provide an organizational summary of educational spending and effectiveness, learning sponsors can easily manage the day-to-day learning activities of their employees, and course owners can determine which courses provide the greatest benefit, based on course selections, evaluations, and expenditures.

This universal and automatic evaluation system has several advantages that drive continuous improvement:

- Surveys are distributed automatically, rather than manually.
- All learning assets are now evaluated, rather than just a handful of courses. In its first year, the 5-star rating system collected over 75,000 evaluations on more than 3,000 courses. This much data allows for the data-driven course design mentioned above.
- To help Accenture employees make better and more informed learning asset selections, the 5-star rating and participant comments associated with the course are posted in the course catalog.
- The 5-star rating system allows Accenture to use statistical process control methods on all of its courses in order to weed out those that aren't performing up to standard.
- With myLearning Decision Support, Accenture learning stakeholders have on-demand access to all measurement data, course usage information, and financials.

Online Surveys

The myLearning LMS delivers surveys through the Internet; participants are either sent a link to the survey in an e-mail message or click a button in their transcript to open the survey in a new browser window. There are many benefits to creating online surveys, most notably their ease of use. Because online surveys are accessible via the Internet, they can be completed at any time and from nearly any computer. Rather than distributing the surveys manually, participants can be given a link to the survey. A link to the survey can also be added to the website for a specific course or organization, making it easy to find and complete.

Although Accenture uses an LMS to distribute its online surveys, an LMS is not necessary to develop online surveys. All that is needed is web space that can be accessed by everyone who should complete the survey, a person who can develop an HTML form (i.e., the actual survey), a repository to collect the data (e.g., a database or XML file), and a spreadsheet or other analysis package to analyze the data. Even if these things are not available, it is still possible to create and distribute online surveys. Many companies provide services for the creation and storage of an online survey (search online for "online survey solutions" or "create online survey"), as well as basic analysis and reporting services as the data are collected.

"High-Tech" Paper Surveys

Developing a learning management system that incorporates evaluation and reporting is just one way to make the most out of technology. While an LMS can incorporate a highly efficient evaluation system, it requires a large investment of time and resources to develop. There are many other ways to make evaluations more efficient and valuable without requiring such an investment. Even paper surveys and processing can leverage technology well. At times, paper surveys are the best alternative for survey administration — for instance, when those taking the surveys do not have access to the Internet or a computer, or clients insist on immediate and tangible administration of the questionnaire. But hand-entering data from paper surveys can be an onerous and error-prone task, that ties up valuable resource hours.

Nonetheless, if the paper survey relies on a selected-response item format, it can use "bubble" responses (e.g., fill-in-the-bubble formats found on standardized tests), and can be scanned into a computer and processed using software that can read optical marks. Such software does not require "bubble sheets" (e.g., standardized testing forms) in order to process the surveys; even surveys created in Microsoft Word can be scanned and processed. This software automatically codes and enters the data into a spreadsheet, which can then be saved into many other common database formats, such as Microsoft Excel or Access. With a scanner and scanning software, even paper surveys can be a high-tech and efficient way to provide evaluation services.

Another alternative for paper survey data processing is professional data entry. Data entry companies are fairly common and provide a cheap and flexible (i.e., variable-cost as opposed to fixed-cost) way to handle data entry. Usually if you ship them the data overnight, they can e-mail you hand-entered results within a day or two for a reasonable price. Because they are experts, the error rates are much lower than having an in-house non-expert enter data.

Making the Most of Applications

One of the best ways to make the most of technology is simply to make the most out of your applications. One of the most widely used applications, Microsoft Excel, is also one of the most under-used, in terms of the flexibility and power it offers. Three of the most powerful features this program has to offer are formulas, pivot tables, and macros. (Visual Basic for Applications is also a powerful tool, and is available beginning with Excel 2000, but can be more difficult to learn. VBA gives users a way to add highly interactive and dynamic features to their reports. Many books, as well as the Excel help menu, are available to help users who are interested in VBA for Excel.) With these tools, you can create appealing and informative reports quickly and easily. You can also create surveys that look and act much like HTML surveys do, with features such as drop-down menus, checkboxes, and option buttons.

Excel's features make it a reasonable option for automating reports. If the data can be stored in an Excel worksheet (not to exceed 65,536 rows or 256 columns), a blank report template can be created with all of the formulas, charts, and tables already entered and formatted. A blank worksheet can be reserved to hold the data, and the formulas, table cells, and chart sources can be entered such that they reference the appropriate cells on the data sheet. Of course, this means that some thought will have to go into how the data sheet will look (both when the data are compiled and in the report template), and how the tables and/or charts should look. Once the template is set up, however, a few macros can be recorded to automatically update the report with the click of a button once the data are copied into the reserved data worksheet.

If your evaluations produce too much data to be stored on an Excel worksheet, Excel can still be used to generate customizable reports to meet the needs of your clients. Pivot tables and charts can be created that draw upon data stored in an external database, such as Microsoft Access or SQL server, by using ODBC connections (they can also use data stored in an Excel worksheet). Pivot tables are an excellent way to create interactive, modifiable tables that can be easily refreshed and updated as new data come into your database. They offer a variety of summary functions to present your data — including means, standard deviations, counts, and percentages — and also give you the flexibility to create your own summary functions; for instance, a formula can be created that divides one variable in your dataset by another (e.g., course price by number of training hours), without having to add the formula to your original data. Filters allow you to display different summaries of the data by limiting the report to only those categories you are interested in. A report on course evaluations can include filters based on student demographics so that results from a particular geographic location or office can be quickly accessed. With a few clicks of the mouse, the report can drill down to increasing levels of detail (e.g., from broad industry category, to a specific industry within the category, to an office location). Pivot charts can similarly present an interactive and modifiable report in chart format.

Excel can be used not only for reporting, but also to create the actual surveys used in course evaluation. Forms can be created that have a look and functionality quite similar to HTML surveys, are easy to create, and can be distributed and collected via e-mail. The Control Toolbox and Forms toolbars provide multiple options to create dynamic survey questions. Drop-down menus, checkboxes, text boxes, and lists are just a few of the choices available. Multi-page surveys can easily be created with macros programmed to direct the user from worksheet to worksheet. A "thank-you" page (or other announcement) can appear at the end of the survey to thank users for their participation. Best of all, the data do not have to be hand-entered in a spreadsheet when the surveys are returned. The survey questions can be linked to a data sheet hidden behind the survey such that the data are automatically collected in a spreadsheet as a user completes the survey.

Excel is described here only to provide a few examples of how a commonly used application can make course evaluation easier. This is certainly not to suggest that Excel is the only application that can or should be used. Many applications have a great deal of flexibility and power that can be used for data collection and reporting, but often this power is unrecognized or underutilized. While it might take some time, it is important to become familiar with all of the features available in the applications you use. You may be surprised how much time-consuming work is minimized by simply making the most of your everyday applications.

CONCLUSION

Every evaluation team should exist to add value to their organization. But, as Peter Drucker (2001) says, quality isn't what you put into your work; quality is what others get out of your work. Therefore, in order to deliver quality, the corporate evaluator must creatively navigate the business terrain. Adopting an appropriate performance model is key to such navigation. We use the V-model to link training to business goals, link intervention efforts to measurable results and ROI, and support continuous performance improvement. The V-model also helps plan effective communication by identifying which decision-makers should receive what type of evaluation results and when. It makes our work more valuable, because our work is tied directly to business goals and it makes our communications more effective, because they are targeted to the appropriate audiences and timed to be valuable in aiding decisions. This is important, because evaluation work that is not understood by the organization or that is not delivered when it is needed for decision-making will not be valuable in business no matter how valid and reliable the results.

An evaluator not only needs to be aware of and adaptive to the terrain, or business context, but must also have the strategies and flexibility necessary to adapt to situational constraints. Evaluators are often faced with constraints on the money available for evaluation work, the data available for analysis, and the time or skills available to complete projects. Statistical and technological tools can give an evaluator the ability to provide quality work more efficiently (e.g., using sampling to send out fewer and shorter surveys, creating automated processes). If data exist that would improve the quality of evaluation work, but access to the data is limited or denied, using evaluation or statistical skills to help another group achieve quality results can add value to the organization and provide access to the needed data. When time or skills are at a premium, hiring contractors or external consultants can free up time to tackle larger projects and create an opportunity for skill development within the evaluation team.

In summary, guerilla evaluation tactics allow you to adapt to rugged terrain and to changing situations, thereby creating and driving value in your organization. As such, guerilla evaluation requires deliberate innovation, and deliberate innovation is the first step toward innovation delivered.

REFERENCES

Drucker, P.F. (2001). *The Essential Drucker.* New York: HarperCollins Publishers.

Fuller, J. & Farrington, J. (1999). *From Training to Performance Improvement: Navigating the Transition.* San Francisco, CA: Jossey-Bass Pfeiffer.

Kirkpatrick, D.L. (1994). *Evaluating Training Programs*. San Francisco, CA: Berrett-Koehler Publishers.

Phillips, J.J. (1997). *Return on Investment in Training and Performance Improvement Programs*. Houston, TX: Gulf Publishing.

Stolovich, H.D. & Keeps, E.J. (1999). *Handbook of Human Performance Technology: Improving Individual and Organizational Performance Worldwide (2nd ed.)*. San Francisco, CA: Jossey-Bass Pfeiffer.

Chapter X

Standards for Online Courses: Can We Do It? Yes We Can!

Noel Estabrook
Michigan Virtual University, USA

Peter Arashiro
Michigan Virtual University, USA

ABSTRACT

This chapter provides a real-world example of how instructional design theory can be used in academe, industry, and business to aid in the design and evaluation of online courses. It also describes how theoretical, philosophical and pragmatic aspects of instructional design were combined to develop standards and a model for an online instructional design system. We begin by establishing a need for standards in the field, followed by an outline and description of our standards. The chapter then describes how we used these standards to build an actual course. Examples are also provided of how the standards can be used to effectively evaluate online courses.

A NEW BEGINNING —
IT'S ALL ABOUT LEARNING RIGHT?
Instructional Design vis á vis Rubber Tree Plants

For the past several years, my colleague and I have worked at the Michigan Virtual University, a very unique organization that deals with a variety of different organizations, from K-12 to higher education; from manufacturing to government. In addition to serving different populations, we also fulfill various roles for those institutions. We build learning centers, design custom courses and curriculum, and help make decisions in buying off-the-shelf learning, as well as provide a host of consulting services. This experience has given us a very broad and, we think, distinctive view of the e-learning world.

Since we aren't just a single company cranking out courses and modules "our way," we are able to see how different entities are thinking about and producing e-learning materials. Sometimes, the results are quite impressive; more often, they are not. So, we set about doing our utmost to try to get the best courses into the hands of our constituent learners.

But then a funny thing happened at the office one day. There we were, minding our own business, doing our own thing, when we started hearing the same question over and over again — how do we *know* that the courses we're building, buying and recommending are any good? After the requisite initial blank stare, we started to think, "Yeah, how *do* we know?"

As instructional designers, we like to think that we know what good instruction looks like. But how could we communicate that knowledge to internal and external clients who don't possess this expertise? Furthermore, how could we talk about the quality of online instruction with various groups, with any kind of consistency, when everybody has their own ideas about quality? And what an online course should look and be like? There are educators who use pedagogical strategies of instruction. Then there are those in the corporate world who are more interested in "training" than "education" who have been conducting standup training for years. Then there are those in the LCMS and Web development fields who have their own ideas about what's important in an online course with all of their talk about user interfaces and learning objects.

What's an instructional designer to do? What should be like music to our ears, with all voices coming together to create beautiful instruction, in reality is more like the noise on the floor of the New York Stock Exchange, with everyone shouting to be heard. And it's not that these voices aren't important

— they are. However, it is again important to remember our prime directive when developing online courseware: to enable students to learn.

Should we maintain our comfortable townhouse in Babel and be content? Or, should we make an attempt to get everybody speaking the same language? Should we be satisfied with a cacophony of voices, or do we want to hear beautiful music? We at MVU have chosen the latter route, and it's all about learning, and it's all about standards. Only by unifying the voices from these different sectors into a set of principles and standards that lead to effective instruction can we really begin to design and evaluate good instruction.

You Are Not Alone

Somewhere along the line, it seems that perhaps a major focus of online instruction has been lost. It's very simple, really; when all is said and done, has anyone actually *learned* anything from our instruction? Is there really any more important measure of course quality than that? With all of the talk about interactivity, motivation, collaboration, and many other (good) things, we think it's time to "go back to the beginning" and start examining these elements in light of whether or not they are instructionally effective.

At MVU anyway, that is where we decided to start. We examined the work of Merrill (Merrill, Drake, Lacy, & Pratt, 1996, 1997, 1999), Yelon (1996; Yelon & Berge, 1988), Reigeluth (Reigeluth & Moore, 1999), Gagné (1988), van Merriënboer (1997), as well as others and detected a common thread — one which is concerned with the effectiveness and the efficiency of instruction. But when we looked at what were considered to be standards in the field of e-learning, such as AICC (2001) and SCORM™ (Advanced Distributed Learning Initiative, 2001), we were surprised to find that none of them addressed standards as it relates to meeting instructional objectives.

At first, it seemed that we were all alone. Try as we might, we saw very little in the field that talked about establishing standards for the effectiveness and efficiency of online instruction. Then, slowly, we began to see awakenings: a monograph by the Pew Technology and Learning Program (Twigg, 2001) here, some work by ASTD (2001) there. We knew we were on to something. We began to really believe that the e-learning community could truly benefit from an attempt to establish standards for online instruction.

If All Your Friends Jumped Off of a Cliff…

Just because it appears that people are starting to jump on the standards bandwagon doesn't mean that it's something we should be doing. We still need to know *why* we should develop them and *how* they could be used.

Since we're writing this chapter, we obviously believe that the *why* and *how* can be sufficiently answered. Since we want to deal with many of the practical applications of standards, we will provide the executive version of the answers here:

Why should we have standards and how should we use them?

- Standards allow people to make apples-to-apples comparison of courses. This is extremely important for those who are considering the purchase of course libraries or custom builds from different vendors.
- For course design, it lays out an instructional blueprint that has a high probability of success.
- By using standards, all parties involved in producing courses can be "on the same page" and can know exactly what is to be expected going into a project.
- If used correctly, standards can represent a common starting point from which to improve and change the quality and nature of online instruction.

TOO MANY COOKS — FINDING THE RIGHT INSTRUCTIONAL RECIPE

Course Development by Committee

In the real world, it is very rare for one person to sit down and build a course alone from start to finish. Far more likely is the scenario where a number of key players have a hand in designing and developing online instruction. Such development teams can typically include subject matter experts (SMEs), instructional designers, website developers, programmers, and more.

This scenario is further complicated by the fact that, quite often, these people may not just be in different departments, but in different companies, states, or even countries! We have developed courses where the manufacturing SME resided in Ohio, the instructional designers were in Michigan and California, and the lead programming team was in India. Without some very tight development *and* content quality constraints in place, such a project would have little chance of success.

In practical terms, then, we have had to pay attention to two primary factors when dealing with such a large number of contributors and stakeholders to ensure quality: process and materials. The first, process, is actually quite straightforward. Whether it be ADDIE, a variation thereof, or some other accepted process, the key is simply in making sure all of the developmental bases get covered — there must be analysis, design, development, implementation, and evaluation — and this will be talked about in more detail later in the chapter.

The second item, materials, is the one that we will focus on most closely in this chapter. We are using the word "materials" here in the broadest possible terms to represent the actual "stuff" of a course — user interface, navigation, content, etc. We have found that, in many cases, attention to process has become so narrowed and focused that issues of course quality are often ignored. This is generally due to the assumption by many that a quality process will ensure a quality product. However, we firmly believe that it takes both a quality process and quality material to generate a quality product. Whereas we can apply models such as ADDIE to ensure a quality process, we believe that we can use standards to ensure quality materials.

Alas, Poor Addie, I Knew Her Well

Assume you are a car manufacturer. You have a process for building your cars and getting them into the hands of consumers. However, you find that your cars are in need of repair at an alarmingly high rate. At first, you have a hard time understanding this, since you use basically the same process to build your cars as do other manufacturers. But, upon looking at your entire production cycle, you realize that you don't have any standards to make sure you are receiving quality components and materials. As a result, your cars are less reliable.

Because of this, you decide to create standards for the quality of the materials you receive from your suppliers and, as you find higher quality supplies, you find that the reliability of your cars improve. In addition, you probably find that you can change some of your manufacturing processes to be more efficient — with better cars being the result.

Apply this analogy to courseware development. Using the ADDIE model is to simply apply a *systematic* process. This process, if applied using faulty or inappropriate material, will produce courses of mixed effectiveness. However, if we can apply principles of effective instruction, which consider the *systemic* nature and effects of instruction, to help identify, develop, and apply sound and appropriate instructional design standards, then we can begin to produce better courses. In addition, we may find that the application of such principles may allow us to modify our process in ways that improve instruction even more. This basic tenet provides the foundation for the rest of this chapter.

So, should online course standards spell the end of the ADDIE model? Yes and no. ADDIE will continue to help designers and development teams guide the development process, but we need to constantly remind ourselves that a development process is only as good as the materials it uses.

United We Stand

There are a number of experts in the field, such as Merrill et al. (1996) and Clark (2002) who treat instructional design as a science. Clark posits that design sciences share certain characteristics. Among these, they have in common:

- Systematic process that involves stages of planning, development, and testing
- Scientific and technical principles in the design of products
- Products designed to be functional and appealing to users (Clark, 2002)

It is the second and third points that create the impetus behind using standards for the development and evaluation of online learning. The first is covered by ADDIE and other development processes. Still, we have yet to really get a handle on the last two points, and that's where principle-based standards come into the picture.

And this is what we, at the Michigan Virtual University, have been working on for over two years. The result of that work is a set of over 100 e-learning standards in the areas of Technology, Usability, Accessibility, and Instructional Design. While not dictating style, strategies, or personal taste, they do define the elements that are needed for "effective, efficient, and appealing" (Reigeluth, 1983) instruction to occur.

Further, we have released our standards in the open source tradition of Linux (a computer operating system that has benefited from hundreds of fixes and enhancements provided by the field). By simply going to our standards website at http://standards.mivu.org, one can view our standards, a companion course evaluation tool, and most importantly, provide feedback and ideas that can expand and enhance the standards for the field at large.

TEACH ME TO FISH — PRINCIPLES VS. STRATEGIES

Adding an 'O' to Instructional Design

At MVU, we refer to online instructional design (OID) instead of instructional design quite often. Why? Because we feel that there are a couple of fundamental challenges that exist in online instruction that aren't present in face-to-face instruction. In addition to sound instructional design theory to guide our standards, we feel that any principles that can be derived from these theories must take these challenges into account in order to be effective.

Online instruction must control, reduce, or eliminate the variability of the uncontrolled and interactive e-learning environment

In a face-to-face course, most elements of instruction are fairly well controlled. Everyone reads the same textbook, listens to the same lecture, takes the same tests at the same times, etc. However, in an online course, all of this can go out the window. For instance, what one student sees while viewing a 14" monitor displaying at 640 X 480 over a modem connection using Netscape 4.7 may be radically different than what another student sees while viewing a 17" monitor displaying at 1024 X 768 over a cable-modem connection using Internet Explorer 5.5. Because of this, OID must come up with a way of setting standards to account for this variability.

Online instruction systems must provide reasonably complete, accessible, and timely feedback and support mechanisms for the learner

Trainers and educators agree — feedback is crucial to learning and performance. In a face-to-face setting, feedback is almost built in — a teacher can see the quizzical look on the face of a student who doesn't understand or can jump in and help correct a crucial mistake before it's too late. Online, however, an instructor (if there even is one) may be removed from the situation by hours or even days. Because of this, online courses must be designed so that the system and/or instructors can provide adequate guidance and feedback for the learner.

Laying the Foundation

So, what can we say about instructional design, OID, and how principle-based standards can be applied to online learning? Our main foundational principles are as follows:

1. Instruction is as much science as it is art. As such, rigor can be applied to the ID process to produce consistently effective materials (Merrill et al., 1996).
2. The application of ID, referred to as instructional technology, is rigorous and takes time to complete. This requires more planning, preparation, and effort for designers. However, when applied, this process produces more efficient, effective, and appealing instruction for the learner.

3. All of our standards are based on ID principles and not specific practices. Principles such as active engagement of the learner, appropriate practice and feedback, evaluation, establishment of goals and objectives, and mapping to real-world performance are all vital to our process (Yelon, 1996; Yelon & Berge, 1988).

4. We also believe that the technological learning environment should be as "transparent" as possible. In other words, navigation, layout, access, and speed should be designed in such a way that the learner can concentrate on the material instead of worrying about the delivery vehicle, thus reducing anxiety and increasing learning.

5. Real learning is measurable and must be measured. All online instruction activities should be tested to find out if they are effective. Though helpful, we believe that evaluations should go beyond "Did you like the course?" to "What did you score on the evaluation that determines whether you learned something?"

Based on this foundation, we established our Technology, Usability, Accessibility, and Instructional Design standards that are outlined in the next section. Each category is broken down into standards and sub-standards, which have a variety of attributes that are intended to help in both the design and evaluation of online courses. The components of each standard are:

- **Standards and Sub-Standards:** Each one of our standards is carefully broken down into its smallest component parts. For example, the **Technology** category has three main standards, one of them being **Identification of Technology Requirements**. This standard is then broken into 11 distinct sub-standards — for instance, **Identification of Audio Capabilities**.

- **Measurement Criteria:** Each standard has a Measurement Criteria that gives a description of how that standard should be met.

- **Benchmarks:** Each standard's measurement criteria will include Benchmarks that will give the evaluator or designer general criteria and key things to look for in evaluating or using the standard.

- **Weight:** Each standard is also given a weight. This is basically a determination of how vital a standard is to the functioning of a course.

- **Prescriptions:** Each standard also contains a Prescription. A Prescription can be used to help improve a course if a standard is not met. Quite often, a Prescription will restate or further clarify the information provided in the Measurement Criteria.

Technology — The First Frontier

Before anything else can occur, an online learning system must *work*. This category is primarily involved with the functionality and appropriateness of the technology. The Technology category does not encompass such things as navigation, but rather issues of whether or not the technology works, if it's appropriate for the audience, etc.

There are three main standards in the Technology category — ***Identification of Technology Requirements***, ***Identification of Audience Capability***, and ***Technical Functionality***. The purpose of this chapter is not to go into extensive detail regarding the standards themselves; anyone may visit the standards website for that. However, this category is primarily concerned with:

- Identifying for the user exactly what they'll need before starting the class (minimum browser, connection speed, audio, video, plug-ins, etc.)
- Identifying for the user exactly what Internet skills a course requires (basic Web browsing and e-mail, of standards, advanced skills such as downloading, and any special software skills needed). This can help the learner determine if a course is right for them **before** they spend money and time on it.
- Assuring that all technical aspects of a course (hyperlinks, programming, images, and multimedia) are fully functional to reduce frustration for the user.

Usability — Can I Use It?

All of the technology can work, but if the learner can't use the technology, it doesn't matter. This category also deals with technology, but goes beyond mere "does it work" issues and deals primarily with function as it pertains to promoting an optimal learning environment.

There are five standards in our Usability category — ***Interface Consistency***, ***Learner Support***, ***Navigational Effectiveness and Efficiency***, ***Functionality of Graphics and Multimedia***, and ***Integration of Communications***. This category is primarily concerned with:

- Ensuring the consistency of the course or system's learner interface to reduce distraction or confusion.
- Ensuring the presence and quality of learner support so that help can be provided when needed during a course.
- Providing for consistency in the course or system's user interface and navigation so the learner can progress through the course quickly and easily.

- Ensuring that graphics and multimedia all function in a usable way. For instance, multimedia must do more than just work; it must load quickly enough and be large enough to actually be usable.
- For instructor-led courses, an assurance that communication channels such as bulletin boards, chats, and e-mail are integrated into the course in a usable manner.

Accessibility — Can Everyone Use It?

Many course providers require that persons with disabilities have equal access to learning. We have established standards based on WAI's Priority 1 guidelines (W3C, 1999) for *Basic Content*, *Tables and Frames*, and *Media*. This category of standards ensures that all content provides accessible equivalencies for people with disabilities.

Instructional Design — Getting to the Heart of the Matter

This category represents what is most often missed in online instruction. That is, is the material itself instructionally sound? Our standards ensure that all

Table 1: PK Pairs

Type of Instruction by Performance				
Discrete Skills and Knowledge			Complex Skills and Knowledge	
Remember	Identify	Apply	Derive Method	Derive Solution or Answer
Recall or Identify Facts (F)			Students are presented with a unique scenario or situation in which they must decide how to reach a stated objective (M)	Students hypothesize, infer or draw a conclusion about a unique scenario or situation (S)
Describe or Identify the Location of Elements in a Whole (E)				
Recall or State a Concept (C1)	Recognize or Identify Instances of a Concept (C2)	Use a Concept (C3)		
Recall or State the Steps of a Task (T1)	Recognize or Identify the Steps of a Task (T2)	Perform a Task (T3)		
Recall or State a Principle (P1)	Recognize or Identify a Principle at Work (P2)	Apply a Principle (P3)		

necessary components of successful instruction are present: Explanation, Demonstration, Practice, Feedback, and Assessment. Further, they ensure that content, practice, and assessment are consistent with the type of skills and knowledge being taught, consistent with the stated or implied objectives of the instruction, as well as being consistent with each other.

We have developed a set of ID standards that allow all instruction to be mapped to a particular Performance/Knowledge type (what we refer to as PK Pairs). Depending upon the type of knowledge and performance that is required of the instruction, our standards define a unique set of standards for that content. This allows for a totally customized design or evaluation of the Instructional Design of an online course.

Table 1, on the previous page, represents the PK Pairs our standards have identified.

Our standards for Discrete Skills and Knowledge come primarily from Merrill's (1983) Component Display Theory, and those for Complex Cognitive Skills are derived largely from the work of van Merriënboer (1997).

COURSE DESIGN CASE STUDY — ONLINE LEARNER'S ORIENTATION TOOL

Singing from the Same Book

How do you get SMEs, vendors, and your clients to buy in to standards? As far as we're concerned, it's all about conditions (or circumstances) and communication. Our case study for this chapter revolves around a course we built called the Online Learner's Orientation Tool (OLOT). OLOT is a short course intended to prepare students for the world of online learning.

Prior to the design and development of OLOT, MVU had developed and released a similar course called the Distance Learner's Orientation Tool (DLOT). External resources were hired to make all of the instructional design and development decisions for this initial product. Unfortunately, DLOT turned out to be less than stellar for a number of different reasons. Chief among these was a development process absent of standards and a lack of sound instructional design to guide the project. So, management set out to try again.

Ironically, it was while DLOT was being developed that we had already completed a number of drafts of the OID standards and were actively promoting and seeking feedback throughout the organization about how best we could use the standards as part of doing business. While we were certain of the value of standards, we knew they couldn't exist in a vacuum. If the standards were ever going to become operational, explaining them to others and gaining company-wide acceptance was going to be crucial. And, as it turned out, our strategy worked: there's now an expectation that any design or evaluation project that comes across our desks will have the OID standards applied to them to determine quality.

But even though we now had company-wide acceptance of our standards, we still hadn't proved that they could work in the real world. So, we were asked to "put our money where our mouth was" and given the task of developing the new OLOT. Presenting our plan to use the OID standards to our production vendor was probably the easiest part of the coordination activity, as they appreciated working with a client that could provide them with consistent and well-designed content and ideas to work with.

Analysis First

The analysis phase was fairly straightforward and involved two major activities to determine the needs and current conditions for the course. The first analysis activity was actually conducted prior to the start of this project, and it involved using the OID standards to evaluate the quality of the original DLOT course. This allowed us to use the standards to generate some consistent and categorized data about the quality of the course, which would eventually be used to help design and develop an improved course: OLOT. We also took this opportunity to see what would happen if a non-instructional designer used the standards to evaluate DLOT. Though not as succinct as our evaluations, we were pleased to find this person not only could apply the standards, but that the results were consistent with ours.

For the second activity, we hired a firm to conduct a focus group study to identify the skills, knowledge, and attitudes that target audiences were going need in order to be successful online learners. Of course, the goal was to determine if there was indeed a need for a course such as this and, if there was, what such a course would need to include. Even at this early stage in the process, we were already able to envision what some of the instructional activities would be like, based on the standards. For example, any content having to do with an identifying concept would have to involve providing examples, non-examples, instruction that explained and highlighted the discriminating characteristics of the concept, and an opportunity for the learner to identify instances of the concept being taught.

Instructional Design — Developing the Content

Merrill (1997) is often quoted as saying "information is not instruction." This simple and profound statement seems to make a whole lot of sense; there's a lot more to teaching than just telling students about something and then expecting knowledge and skills to magically appear. Yet what we find in a majority of textbooks, lecture halls, and online courses is a whole lot of telling and not much instruction. We certainly didn't want our course to be categorized as just another "electronic page-turner."

As we mentioned earlier, Performance-Knowledge (PK) Pairs are the foundation of our Instructional Design. The acknowledgment of different types of performance and knowledge, combined with Gagne's (1988) assumption that different types of instructional outcomes require instruction that is appropriate for and consistent with that outcome, allowed us to quickly get a sense of what learners would need from this course if intentional learning was to happen.

Rather than trying to contrive different kinds of interactions and activities for learners for the sake of "motivating," "engaging," or "creating an active learning environment" for them, we simply identified a PK Pair for each piece of content and the principle-based standards for each PK Pair to determine the nature of the instruction. The following is an example of how we applied the standards to design our instruction.

In one of the lessons, we wanted to teach Web browser basics. From a PK standpoint, the kind of Knowledge we were designing for was a combination of Concepts (e.g., what a hyperlink is and the different kinds of hyperlinks) and Principles (e.g., what happens when you click on a hyperlink, or what you should do if a page fails to load properly). In terms of Performance, we wanted learners to Apply (e.g., be able to recognize instances of hyperlinks within the context of a Web page and be able to troubleshoot when a problem occurs with the Web browser). In other words, this particular unit would have Apply-Concept and Apply-Principle PK Pairs.

Based on the standards, the instruction for Apply-Concept includes the following:

- An Explanation of the situation or context where the concept can be found or used, and what one should do when it is recognized.
- A Demonstration or illustrations of the concept as it would appear or be applied within a situation or particular context.
- An opportunity to Practice recognizing and acting upon (applying) the concept.
- Feedback to inform the learner on their performance.
- An Assessment that is similar in nature to the Practice.

How this translated into actual instruction that taught learners about "hyperlinks" was a combination of text to explain what hyperlinks were and graphic examples of different kinds of hyperlinks that are commonly used on Web pages. To allow learners to practice applying this concept, a Macromedia Shockwave interaction was developed to guide learners through a Web page and browser simulation that asked them to click on certain hyperlinks. When they performed correctly, the simulation continued. If they didn't perform correctly after three attempts, they were given guidance. For the assessment, a question that required the learner to know the concept "hyperlink" was used to determine whether they were able to apply the concept of "hyperlink" in order to answer the question.

Technology and Usability — Making Sure It Works

Our Technology standards require informing the learner what technology is required to take a course, as well as providing them with enough skill-appropriate directions and instructions to successfully use the course. Informing learners about the required technologies was simply a matter of making a list available to them before they signed up for the course. We listed them in the online course catalog as follows:

- PC with a 200 Megahertz Pentium processor (Macintosh version NOT available at this time)
- Windows 95
- 64 Megabytes of memory (RAM)
- Monitor capable of displaying 800x600 screen resolution
- 28.8 Kbps Modem (connection speed is determined by your computer's physical location, the speed of your modem, your phone lines, and the plan you purchase from your Internet service provider [ISP])
- Internet Explorer 4.xx - 5.xx or Netscape Navigator 4.xx (AOL browsers and 6.0 versions of Internet Explorer and Netscape Navigator are NOT supported)
- Macromedia Shockwave Player (available from http://www.macromedia.com/shockwave/download)

Of all the technical requirements, the one that we were particularly concerned with was the Shockwave Player plug-in, as this requires a user to download and install software from a website. Our standards suggest that when a novice user is expected to perform a relatively technical procedure, such as downloading a plug-in, they are given very specific directions on how to perform the task. Conveniently enough, detailed instructions for downloading and installing the Shockwave Player are provided on the download site, so we didn't have to re-invent the wheel.

The more obvious standards for Technology deal with whether the course is free from technical errors, such as broken hyperlinks, broken images on pages, multimedia not playing, and server errors. Though it's very easy to tell when things aren't working on a page, the process of finding these errors throughout a course is really the key to successfully meeting this standard. Our developers gave us many opportunities to preview the course content before it was integrated into the learning management system (LMS) that we were using to launch the course. They basically provided a Web-based index from which we could go through and view each of the content pages and review roughly 90 percent of the technology-related items. The only things we couldn't check at this time were the course navigation, tracking, and reporting features, as they could only be reviewed after the content was integrated into the LMS.

Just as instructional design standards allowed us to quickly determine what the instruction was going to look like and how it would function, the Usability standards made it easy for our developers to create interface, navigation, and support features that would allow the student to focus more of their energies on the lessons and less time figuring out how to make the course "work." Of the five sub-standards that had to be incorporated into the course, the one that would have the most impact on usability was the Navigational Effectiveness and Efficiency sub-standard. Therefore, much time was spent on designing a solution that met these sub-standards.

The first Navigation sub-standard states that the course "must provide a 'home base' where the learner can always return to and access whenever needed. In addition, a link to the Home or Course Map must be available at all times and clearly visible to the learner." To meet this sub-standard, the interface shown in Figure 1 was created.

This global toolbar, which includes a link to the homepage, is available at the top of every content page throughout the course.

The second Navigation sub-standard states, "Ideally, learners should be able to quickly and freely get to anywhere within the course very quickly (three clicks or less is ideal)." This includes allowing the learner to move forward or

Figure 1: Global Toolbar

Figure 2: Section-Unit Navigation

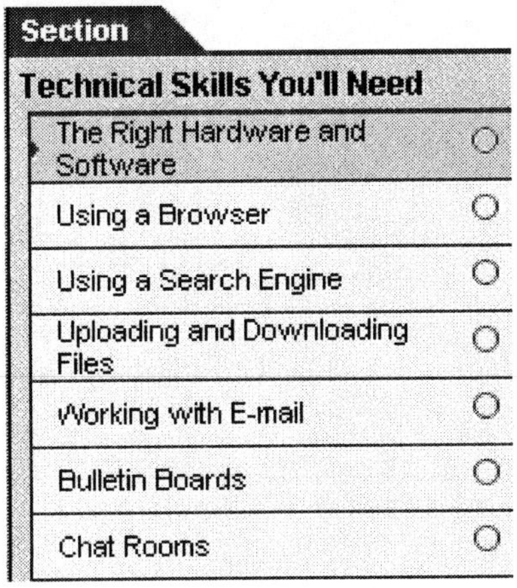

backwards through pages, move forward or backwards to units or sub-units in the course, and that courses that contain multiple-page units should allow the learner to jump directly to specific pages in a non-linear manner. Since our course had this complex structure, it was important that we come up with a navigation solution that met the standards but wasn't too overwhelming for the learner.

The global toolbar (Figure 1) also allows learners to navigate between the four different sections of the course. As you can see from the global toolbar graphic, this learner has navigated to the section on "Technical Skills You'll Need."

Each section of the course is broken down into a number of units, which are listed in a menu bar located on the left-hand side of every page (Figure 2). As the learner moves between different sections, the units change. Also, the lessons that make up each unit are listed directly below each unit and dynamically change relative to the section and unit the learner is currently going through.

To provide page-to-page navigation, buttons that represent the pages in the unit are included on every screen. This allows the learner to go through the lesson or unit in either a linear or non-linear fashion, as Figure 3 indicates.

Figure 3: Page Navigation

Figure 4: Course Map

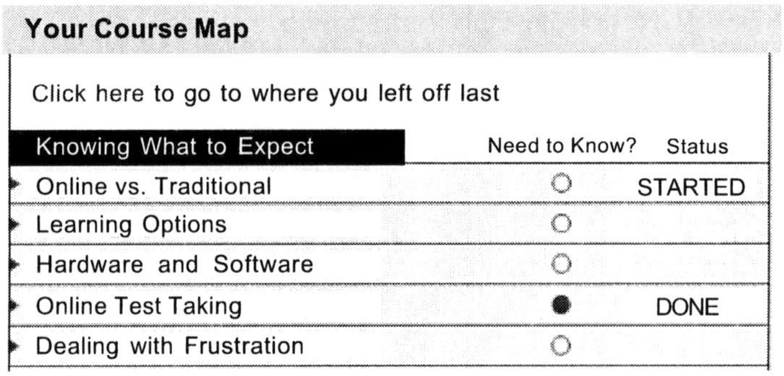

Your Course Map

Click here to go to where you left off last

Knowing What to Expect	Need to Know?	Status
► Online vs. Traditional	○	STARTED
► Learning Options	○	
► Hardware and Software	○	
► Online Test Taking	●	DONE
► Dealing with Frustration	○	

The third Navigation sub-standard states, "It is vital that learners know what materials they have accessed, completed, and still need to complete every time they access the course." To meet this standard, we designed a course map that allows learners to access the different units in the course and provides completion status for the units they are required to go through (which are determined by a pre-assessment). There is also a "bookmark" feature included that allows the learner to return directly to the page they last visited (Figure 4).

The final Navigation sub-standard deals with the issue of "giving the learner cues as to where they are in the context of the course at all times." Providing a sense of orientation and location reference at a micro-level within the course helps the learner know where they are and how much they have left to go.

In this example, the page indicator is highlighted to show what page the learner is currently reading and also shows how many more pages are left in this unit (Figure 5).

The Iterations and Variations

As suggested in the descriptions of our design and development process, in some sense our process did go through the ADDIE steps, though it's clear that we also utilized the strengths of the standards to determine the kinds of

Figure 5: Page Indicator

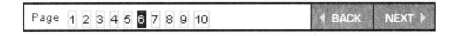

Page 1 2 3 4 5 6 7 8 9 10   ◄ BACK   NEXT ►

activities that were going to take place within each of these steps. We feel that there's some advantage to using the standards to guide the design and development of instruction. Throughout the entire process, we are reviewing and refining the course, making the necessary and goal-specific adjustments needed to create a quality course.

This is in contrast to models, such as Dick and Carey's (1999), that suggest reviews and revisions be made after some or all of the course is launched. While this kind of review and revision procedure is also important right before and/or soon after the course is actually launched, it would seem to make sense to get things working closely to some standard first and then have learners try the course out. So, even though we followed the ADDIE model, in reality, it proved to be a "mini-ADDIE" in which shorter versions of each step were performed multiple times throughout the course development and deployment.

APPLYING OID TO COURSE EVALUATION
Passing the Test

Because both MVU, and our clients, build and buy online courses, the results of an evaluation can aid greatly in making any one of three decisions:
1. For builds, fix it if the quality is low, continue using as is, or stop using it.
2. For buys, decide to keep it or stop using it.
3. Decide to make a purchase or not.

Thus, in order for our evaluations to be of any value, the results would have to provide information that would allow clients to make decisions and take appropriate action based on their situation. Figure 6 is an actual evaluation shows the basic reporting features that we've determined are valuable across all situations.

This Usability evaluation of the Navigational Effectiveness and Efficiency standard starts out by describing the sub-standard in general so the client understands what is being evaluated. The next set of information displays the scores from the evaluation. This table shows how the course scored on each of the sub-sections, a total standard score, and an associated descriptive rating (in this case "Poor"). Below the figure is a narrative of the data, followed by prescriptive suggestions on how this part of the course could be improved to achieve a rating of "Excellent." We see these prescriptive suggestions as being of most value to those who have the ability to change or request changes to the course.

Figure 6: Sample Usability Evaluation

U3 – Navigational Effectiveness and Efficiency

This category looks at how well a course or system's navigational elements allow the learner to get around in the online course environment. In other words, this standard determines whether or not there are any navigational elements that will prevent the learner from finding all necessary learning elements quickly and easily. For a course to be effective, there must be a number of navigational supports present to support the learner as he/she progresses through a course.

U3 Standards	Rating	Weight	Score	U3 Score
U3.1	5	SERIOUS	5.0	2.8
U3.2	2	SERIOUS	2.0	Poor
U3.3	1	SERIOUS	1.0	
U3.4	3	SERIOUS	3.0	

The overall rating for U3 was "Poor" with a score of 2.8. The ratings ranged from 1 to 5, with 1 sub-standard rating a 5, 1 sub-standard rating a 3 (Presence of Course Orientation), 1 sub-standard rating a 2 (Intracourse Navigability) and 1 sub-standard rating 1 (Presence of Course Progress Indicators).

In order for this course to achieve an overall rating of "Excellent" for this standard, the following needs to be done:

- Include a means to indicate to students where they last left off in the course.
- Include page-to-page navigation that allows students to go from different pages within modules, rather than allowing for forward-only, page-by-page navigation.
- Improve upon Course Orientation to include specific instructions on how to use navigational buttons.

While the same basic information is reported for the Instructional Design section of the evaluation (i.e., description of the standard, scores, ratings, and prescriptive suggestions for improvement), the only significant difference is the data reported in the table (as shown in Figure 7).

The figure is broken down by Performance Objective (PO) for a particular Module or Unit, and then shows how each of the instructional components for the Performance-Knowledge (PK) Pair for that PO is rated and scored. In this example, there are three POs for this Module, and each of the POs is identified as a PK type of Recall-Fact. According to the standards, instruction for Recall-Fact should include Explanation (F.1), Practice (F.2), Feedback (F.3), and Assessment (F.4). Each component is rated and scored, then a total ID score and rating for that PO is provided. Finally, a cumulative score and rating for the entire Module is provided.

The results of this evaluation show that the first two modules of this course had a few Usability and many Instructional Design issues that needed to be

Figure 7: Sample ID Evaluation

PO 2.1	F.1	F.2	F.3	F.4		Total	
Rating	5	2	5	3		3.8	
Score	Excellent	Poor	Excellent	Average		Average	
PO 2.2	P1.1	P1.2	P1.3	P1.4		Total	
Rating	5	2	5	2		3.5	
Score	Excellent	Poor	Excellent	Poor		Average	
PO 2.3	P3.1	P3.2	P3.3	P3.4	P3.5	Total	Unit 2.0 Total
Rating	1	1	1	1	1	1.0	2.8
Score	Inferior	Inferior	Inferior	Inferior	Inferior	Inferior	Poor

addressed in order to reach at least an average score. Whether or not any action will be taken is now up to the client, but they at least know where the strengths and weaknesses of the course are and how to go about fixing the areas that need improvement.

Comparing Apples to Apples

We have shown you how our standards are used in the real world. The primary power behind any set of standards is in their ability to produce repeatability. In other words, if they're really going to work, they should either allow us a basis upon which to do things faster or do them better. We believe our standards do both.

In our example from the previous section, a standardized report on a course was produced for a client. If the client had given us a second similar course to evaluate for them in order to assist them in making a decision as to which one to buy, we could have produced an identical report on the second course, allowing the client to look at both courses in the same way and make an informed decision. This process would result in a higher quality product for the client. Presently, such decisions are made based on a vendor's sales pitch or color brochure or some other highly subjective criteria.

In the production of courseware, using standards can help ensure that the course is built right the first time, saving both time and money in terms of user frustration, lack of course acceptance, ineffective training, and extensive course revisions. The carpenter's credo is "measure twice, cut once." When it comes to building courses, we could say, "design and evaluate using standards, build or buy once."

GOING TO THE FRONT LINES — WHAT'S NEXT?

Who Do You Think You Are?

So, who is MVU really, and why should anyone pay attention to our standards? That's a good question, and certainly one that we, as instructional designers, are accustomed to hearing. As mentioned earlier in the chapter, one of our initial challenges regarding the standards was their acceptance within our organization; we needed to go through a process to validate them. By openly sharing the standards with our colleagues and continually seeking commentary and feedback, we were able to, over time, establish them company-wide. Gaining acceptance and validation from the field, however, is another matter.

Our approach towards field validation and acceptance was to first compare our work against what had already been developed and utilized in the field. The only published standards that we could locate at the time, that were similar in nature to the MVU OID standards, were those created by ASTD (2001) for their E-Learning Courseware Certification (ECC) program. In fact, we were quite surprised to find how our early work closely resembled ASTD's initial standards, even though our development work had been completely independent. While we were pleased to see some indication of comparative validity based on the work of a reputable organization such as ASTD, we were very concerned that some might feel we had "lifted" our standards from ASTD, potentially affecting the acceptance of our standards in the field

We had the good fortune to share our standards with Dr. Merrill before and after our discovery, and asked for his thoughts. His response? "I think that it shows that when trained people take a look at what constitutes effective courseware that they are bound to come up with very similar standards" (personal communication, June 5, 2001). While we are still unsure of the level of acceptance the ASTD standards have gained in the field, their presence and work allowed us to move to the next phase of validation and acceptance testing — releasing our standards to the public.

As mentioned earlier in the chapter, we released the standards on the Web as open source, making them publicly available for review, critique, application, and revision. It was our intention to gather as much solicited and unsolicited commentary from the field as we could in order to determine their value to practitioners.

Since bringing up our standards website, we have received over 500,000 hits from over 40 countries in just six months. We have received dozens upon dozens of personal comments from government, industry, education, and the non-profit sector, almost all of which have been overwhelmingly positive. We hope that continued feedback on how to improve the standards, as well as how people and organizations have used them, will help us determine whether the field has validated and accepted these standards. Only time will tell.

Using Occam's Razor

We have been able to develop and deploy standards for the purpose of guiding the design of online learning, as well as aiding in its evaluation. We have received positive feedback from the field and know that applying such standards ensures higher quality instruction. So where do we go from here?

The answer is clear. We must come up with a way to simplify our tool set. Our standards and evaluation tool were designed by, and for, experts. However, the fact is, there is a *lot* of online learning out there being created and implemented without any instructional design expertise at all. If we expect front-line practitioners to adopt our standards and tools, we must make the standards easier and quicker to use. We must, in essence, produce a "lite" version.

Another aspect of simplification is streamlining. We need, and desire, to create an evaluation tool that is quick, reasonably accurate, and easy to use. We feel that this can only be accomplished by creating an evaluation tool that is Web-based. Our current Excel-based evaluation tool is somewhat clunky to use and can take time to get used to. However, a Web-based tool could be much more intuitive, interactive, and could provide other features, such as instructor and student course feedback based on the standards to give even more complete evaluations.

The Final Word

We are actively pursing the direction outlined in the previous section at this very moment, but such endeavors require funding and partnerships. It is our hope that others will recognize, as we have, the importance of standards and the impact that they can have on the quality of the online learning that is getting to the marketplace. It is our belief that, based on our experience and feedback, the field is ready for this next step — we just have to be willing to take it.

REFERENCES

Advanced Distributed Learning Initiative. (2001, October 1). *The SCORM Overview*. Retrieved July 1, 2002, from: http://www.adlnet.org/ADLDOCS/Documents/ SCORM_1.2_Overview.pdf.

AICC. (2001, April 2). *CMI Guidelines for Interoperability*. Retrieved July 1, 2002, from: http://www.aicc.org/docs/tech/cmi001v3-5.pdf.

ASTD. (2001). *The ASTD Institute E-learning Courseware Certification (ECC) Standards*. Retrieved June 1, 2001, from: http://www.astd.org/ecertification/.

Clark, R.C. (2002). Applying cognitive strategies to instructional design [electronic version]. *Performance Improvement*, 41(7), 8-14.

Dick, W. & Carey, L. (1990). *The Systematic Design of Instruction (3rd ed.)*. Glenview, IL: HarperCollins Publishers.

Gagné, R.M. & Driscoll, M.P. (1988). *Essentials of Learning for Instruction (2nd ed.)*. Englewood Cliffs, NJ: Prentice-Hall.

Merrill, M.D. (1983). Component display theory. In Reigeluth, C.M. (Ed.), *Instructional-Design Theories and Models: An Overview of their Current Status* (pp. 279-333). Hillsdale, NJ: Lawrence Erlbaum Associates.

Merrill, M.D. (1997). Instructional strategies that teach. *CBT Solutions*, (November/December), 1-11.

Merrill, M.D. (1999). Instructional Transaction Theory (ITT): Instructional design based on knowledge objects. In Reigeluth, C.M. (Ed.), *Instructional-Design Theories and Models: A New Paradigm of Instructional Theory* (Vol. II) (pp. 401 - 424). Mahwah, NJ: Lawrence Erlbaum Associates.

Merrill, M.D., Drake, L., Lacy, M.J., & Pratt, J. (1996). Reclaiming instructional design. *Educational Technology*, 36(5), 5-7.

Reigeluth, C.M. (1983). Instructional Design: What is it and Why is it? In Reigeluth, C.M. (Ed.), *Instructional-Design Theories and Models: An Overview of their Current Status* (pp. 3-36). Hillsdale, NJ: Lawrence Erlbaum Associates.

Reigeluth, C.M. & Moore, J. (1999). Cognitive education and the cognitive domain. In Reigeluth, C.M. (Ed.), *Instructional-Design Theories and Models: A New Paradigm of Instructional Theory* (Vol. II) (pp. 51-68). Mahwah, NJ: Lawrence Erlbaum Associates.

Twigg, C.A. (2001). *Quality Assurance for Whom? Providers and Consumers in Today's Distributed Learning Environment*. Retrieved

March 1, 2001, from: http:// www.center.rpi.edu/PewSym/Mono3.pdf.

van Merriënboer, J.J.G. (1997). *Training Complex Cognitive Skills*. Englewood Cliffs, NJ: Educational Technology Publications.

W3C. (1999). *Web Content Accessibility Guidelines 1.0*. Retrieved May 6, 2002, from: http://www.w3.org/TR/WAI-WEBCONTENT/#Guidelines.

Yelon, S.L. (1996). *Powerful Principles of Instruction*. White Plains, NY: Longman.

Yelon, S.L., & Berge, Z. (1988). The secret of instructional design. *Performance & Instruction*, 27(1), 11-13.

Chapter XI

Designing and Reusing Learning Objects to Streamline WBI Development

Pam T. Northrup
University of West Florida, USA

Karen L. Rasmussen
University of West Florida, USA

David B. Dawson
University of West Florida, USA

ABSTRACT

Reusable Learning Objects (RLOs) and reusable information objects (RIOs) are tools that facilitate quick, systematic, and effective design and development of Web-based instruction. Learning objects form the basis of an online professional development program targeted toward teachers who must learn and implement new strategies and approaches for teaching in a convenient and flexible environment. Using learning objects, following the Cisco model, to develop instructional components for repurposing provides designers with the flexibility to meet different goals and instructional needs of a variety of education and training settings.

INTRODUCTION

In the past few years, the World Wide Web has emerged as a primary technology-based delivery environment affecting the way people communicate and do business; it is poised to create a paradigm shift in the way people learn (Wiley, 2001). With this trend, there are new technical and instructional demands being placed on instructional designers to get materials to the Web quickly, provide just-in-time instruction, and make modifications to instructional materials on the fly. These demands have forced instructional designers to re-examine the work processes of designing and developing high-quality instructional materials.

Current instructional design models have been touted as 'slow and clumsy' resulting in instruction that takes too long to get to market (Gordon & Zemke, 2001). Thirty years of evidence supports a systems approach that produces solid instructional products and, in fact, the proposition that students do learn as a result of the instruction. Although the intent of design models is to serve as a heuristic for targeting specific instructional goals to solve organizational performance problems, many designers following the ISD process re-invent the wheel every time new instruction is developed. In one branch of the military, an analysis of courses revealed that there were over 150 courses on 'pumps' and new ones were continuing to be developed. In many organizations, this re-design and re-development continues to occur. (Imagine how many courses on customer service exist!) Rather than re-developing the same course over and over again, it is time to flatten the knowledge silos, see what else is out there, and parcel out components of various types of instruction that can be re-purposed for differing goals and instructional needs. In the 21st century, with the rapid advances in information exchange and mass data storage, these knowledge silos no longer have to exist.

In the past five years, several technological developments have emerged that assist designers in getting content out to end users as quickly as possible. Tools such as learning management systems, content management systems, and task management systems now exist. These systems provide templates that sit on top of high-end databases enabling designers and non-designers to enter content into databases that can then be filtered back into their instructional lessons. The value of directly inputting content into databases lies in the designers' flexibility to locate specific resources to use and re-use for multiple purposes. The problem is that unless data input follows a common standard, it may not be able to be re-purposed and shared with others.

In the late 1990s, the Advanced Distributed Learning movement began as an approach to allow the armed services to create and share their instructional resources rather than to replicate content on similar topics across and even within the branches of the military. This movement has resulted in the development of learning object systems that, to date, have focused on technological attributes, metadata standards, and system specifications that define levels of granularity and interoperability (Singh, 2000). Out of this work, SCORM-compliant standards were developed and are evident in many software applications on the market today.

With research that provides system specifications and standards, it is now time to consider the implications for instructional designers who will be designing and re-using learning objects.

This chapter will provide a foundation for the design of Reusable Learning Objects through discussion of a project to design reusable online professional development in a partnership between the University of West Florida (UWF) and Santa Rosa County School District. Teachers across the State of Florida are being held accountable for student progress at unprecedented levels through a student assessment called the Florida Comprehensive Assessment Test (FCAT). Teachers are being required to learn new strategies and approaches for teaching and learning in Reading, Math, and Science without being provided time outside of the classroom during the school day for professional development. In addition, teachers are at various levels of need and desire for professional development opportunities. The school district is seeking ways to provide professional development to teachers that is convenient and flexible for their busy schedules. In partnership with researchers from UWF, a series of Online Professional Development (OPD) courses were developed as learning objects that could be used and reused, based on the professional development needs of the teacher.

WHAT ARE LEARNING OBJECTS?

The Learning Objects Standards Committee has formulated a definition of learning objects that is quite broad, enabling organizations to classify digital and non-digital sources as learning objects. The definition is as follows:

A learning object is any entity, digital or non-digital, which can be used, re-used, or referenced during technology-supported learning. Examples of technology-supported learning include computer-based training systems, interactive learning environments, intelligent computer-aided instructional systems, distance learning systems, and collaborative learning environments. Examples of learning objects include multimedia content, instructional content, learning objectives, instructional software and software tools, and persons, organizations, or events referenced during technology supported learning. (LOM, 2000, as cited in Wiley, 2001)

Wiley (2001, p. 7) argues that only digital objects supporting learning should be classified as a learning object and defines learning objects as *"any digital resource that can be reused to support learning."* This definition describes reusable digital resources while rejecting non-digital, non-reusable objects. The definition also focuses on the purposeful, supportive role the object plays in learning, not simply its usability in learning activity.

Researchers at UWF define learning objects as a digital resource that is flexible enough to be reused in multiple locations. Going a step further, it is suggested that designers should have the flexibility to reduce the size of a learning object to its most granular form or choose to select the object in its entirety.

INSTRUCTIONAL DESIGN AND LEARNING OBJECTS

Instructional designers typically wrestle with how to generate instructional content, practice, and assessment that is motivating and creative, yet meets the needs of the learners. Designers also struggle with the classification of individual content into larger chunks, which may be considered as lessons, chapters, units, modules, or courses. Designing instruction for print-based materials, Web-based instruction, or designing for reusablility, designers are always questioning, *"Will this solve the performance problem?"* or *"Will learners be motivated to continue in this instruction?"* and a host of other typical concerns. When designing for reusability, the best example is Cisco's model for Reusable Learning Objects (RLOs) and Reusable Information Objects (RIOs). Barritt and Lewis (2001) present a comprehensive model that classifies instructional objects into RLOs and RIOs. The Cisco model frames the processes of how to develop learning objects and provides a clear approach for dealing with the classification of content into domains and how to represent it in structured databases.

The Cisco Model

Demands placed on modern training organizations require a move away from the development of static, custom-designed, single-purpose courses to

"...reusable, granular objects that can be written independently of a delivery medium and accessed dynamically through a database" (Barritt & Lewis, 2001, p. 4). The Internet Learning Solutions Group at Cisco Systems identifies the system as the Reusable Learning Object strategy. The RLO can be classified as an entire course, a module of instruction, or unit of instruction. Based on the RLO classification, the Reusable Information Object is focused on a single objective and is composed of content, practice, and assessment. Using the classification of learning objects proposed by Cisco provides a direction for designers to write new training in smaller chunks that are specifically aligned to job tasks. This process also opens the possibility of learners customizing their own knowledge paths by selecting RIOs and RLOs that most closely align to their immediate instructional needs.

The Components of an RIO

The Reusable Information Object contains content, practice, and assessment that are all tied to a single instructional objective. Designers can create RIOs based on single concepts of instruction. Designers should classify the RIO 'type' as concept, fact, procedure, principle, or process. The key to designing an RIO is to make it 'intact' so that it can be re-used in multiple ways in the future.

Content. Each RIO should include introductions, examples, and instructor notes. Based on the classification of the RIO as a concept, fact, procedure, principle, or process, designers should determine how to best represent the concept through tables, lists, demonstrations, charts, guidelines, analogies, etc.

Practice. Practice items are reinforcement activities that apply the RIO's content. They do not usually contribute to the overall assessment of the learner's mastery of the concept, but usually include feedback mechanisms to reinforce the important elements of the content in response to the learner's performance. Practice items may include matching, multiple choice, true/false test items, text entry, simulations, case studies, and hands-on labs.

Assessment. Assessment items measure the learner's mastery of the RIO's learning objective. They may take the form of questions or any measurable activity, but they must both match the learning objective of the RIO and measure the appropriate cognitive level designated for the RIO.

Determining the RIO Type

Each RIO must be assigned a cognitive level value in the object's metadata that identifies how learners will remember or use the information contained in the RIO. The cognitive level scale is a hybrid of Bloom and Krathwohl's (1994) taxonomy and Merrill's (1983) component display theory (Clark, 1989). Where Merrill (1983) divides cognitive level into two parts, that which must be remembered or that which must be used, Bloom (1994) divides it into six levels: knowledge, comprehension, application, analysis, synthesis, and evaluation. Combining these classifications, all RIOs should be tagged either *remember* or *use*. Assigning the *remember* tag for cognitive level automatically means that it corresponds to Bloom's knowledge level, but if the *use* tag is assigned, a sub-level designation from one of the top five levels from Bloom is required. This tag would be comprehension, application, analysis, synthesis, or evaluation (Barritt & Lewis, 2001). This designation of cognitive level assists the designer in selecting the appropriate instructional strategies to select for writing content, practice, and assessment items.

The Reusable Learning Object (RLO)

The larger instructional unit composed of RIOs, the RLO, is based on *"...a single learning objective derived from a specific job task"* (Barritt & Lewis, 2001, p. 7). The RLO is composed of an overview, between five and nine RIOs, and a summary.

Overview. The overview provides the learner an advance organizer that includes an introduction, an explanation of the importance of the information contained in the RLO, the objectives of the RLO, a list of any prerequisites that may be required before using the RLO, and an outline of the RLO. It may also include a job-based scenario as a model for how the information in the RLO may be applied.

Summary. The RLO summary brings the RLO to a close, provides a review of the material covered in the RIOs, and serves as a transition between the RIOs and the assessment section. Assessment items from each RIO are included in the RLO. The summary may also provide information about the next steps the learner must follow, and point to additional resources the learner might explore.

Comparison to Traditional Design Models

Instructional designers tasked with designing in a learning objects paradigm will be able to see parallels between the Cisco model for generating and reusing instructional content and more traditional instructional systems design models. Designers familiar with learning outcomes, objectives, content, practice, and assessment will likely be comfortable designing learning objects. Designers should also find comfort in searching repositories of content, practice, and assessment by specific instructional objectives when tasked with selecting and reusing learning objects. Using the Cisco model enables designers to still be creative with design, by incorporating motivational elements, "war stories," unique activities, and more, while keeping the goals of instruction in the forefront of the design process.

THE NEED FOR STREAMLINING PROFESSIONAL DEVELOPMENT FOR TEACHERS

During the past decade, many states across the country have engaged in rigorous school reform and accountability efforts, most in direct response to the national Goals 2000 initiative. In some states, high-stakes testing accompany rigorous standards, all with the hope of transforming education and improving student performance. Ultimately, the improvement of performance comes down to how well teachers understand the reform efforts, the standards, and the content for which they are being held accountable (Sparks & Hirsch, 1997). Teachers must have the tools, support, and training to radically change teaching and to infuse change at the school level (Darling-Hammond & McLaughlin, 1995; Sparks & Hirsch, 2000). Schools trying to improve must consider professional development as a cornerstone to success (Fullan, 1999) with strong linkages between professional development and the reform agenda (Darling-Hammond & McLaughlin, 1995).

In Florida, a school improvement and accountability initiative to reform state public schools was implemented in 1996. The major goal is to raise student achievement to "world class" levels. To assist in achieving this goal, standards called the *Sunshine State Standards* have been developed to delineate expected achievement outcomes for all students in seven subject areas: mathematics, language arts, science, social studies, foreign languages, fine arts, and health/physical education.

The *Sunshine State Standards* evolved from previously state initiated Goals 2000 achievement standards that are legislatively mandated in all of Florida's public schools. These standards were the state's method of replying to the national school accountability initiatives and the Secretary's Commission on Achieving Necessary Skills (SCANS) competencies. Therefore, the accountability efforts of the state promote that teachers integrate real-world problems and situations into their teaching practices.

Combined with the need for professional development is the fact that teachers are unable to attend professional development during the school day.

For these reasons, a Web-based model was proposed to meet the challenges of a large-scale professional development initiative. The project team determined that designing the program using the learning objects paradigm allowed maximum customization for schools and districts.

DESIGNING THE ONLINE PROFESSIONAL DEVELOPMENT (OPD) REPOSITORY

In planning for, designing, and field-testing this approach to OPD, there were several decisions that had to be made during the design and development process. In this section, issues surrounding planning for learning object design — including granularity, how to structure and use templates, and how to set up a learning objects manager — will be discussed. The issues related to designing RLOs and RIOs also will be addressed; the section will end by exploring the issues of tracking and managing individual RLOs and RIOs. As part of these discussions, potential solutions and responses are presented.

Planning for Learning Objects Design

The issue of granularity is still being discussed. At this juncture, South and Monson (2001) suggest that a course, lesson, or module can be a learning object. Others suggest that a granule may be a small electronic learning object (ELO) that includes a small piece of text, graphic, audio, video, or other interactive component which is tagged and stored in a database (Muzio, Heins, & Mundell, 2001). With the Cisco model, granularity may be reduced to the RIO level (a cluster of content, practice, and assessment). Although the topic of granularity will continue to be discussed, it provides the opportunity for content to be modularized in a way that is most meaningful to the instruction itself, putting the decision into the hands of the instructional designer. Merrill (2000) contends that the instructional designer's primary role is to determine how granular the knowledge components should be as well as determine their instructional sequence.

Researchers at CEDAR have represented ELOs in small chunks that allow them to be easily used or reused with minimal or no change (Muzio, Heins, & Mundell, 2001). Making the chunks small increases flexibility for designers, as well as providing a repository of reusable objects that are readily available.

Researchers at UWF have represented learning objects based on the Cisco model of RIOs and RLOs. We have chosen to make the RIOs as small as possible, including complete 'chunks' of content, practice, and assessment.

To deal with the issue of making it 'small' for potential reuse and combination with other RIOs, UWF researchers have granularized the RIO into areas of content, practice, and assessment, providing the designer the flexibility of selecting just content, just practice, or just assessment — or any combination of the three levels within the RIO (Northrup & Rasmussen, 2002). This design permits customization of many different situations. In some cases, educators just need access to the content. In other cases, when educators are provided with content through other means, they just require the practice. In other words, this additional flexibility allows the individual learning object to be reassembled in many ways to support individual instructional goals.

Using Templates

For the Online Professional Development Repository, templates were considered essential for the input of content into the database as well as a selection option for the output of the content onto a website for end-users (Northrup & Rasmussen, 2002). The options of output depends on the dynamically created templates, which "pull" the contents of the database.

Input into Database. A Web interface was designed that facilitated entering the content into the database. The Web interface comprises a series of forms that can be used as a guide for instructional input (see Figure 1).

The Web interface sits on top of an Access Database, allowing content developed to be parceled into the correct fields within the database. Designers follow the Web interface to create concept-by-concept, including the instructional elements of content, practice, and assessment in each of the RIOs.

Figure 1: Input Wizard

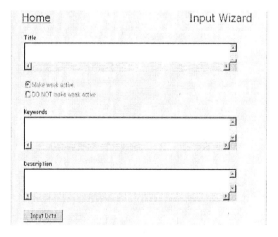

The other major component of the Input Tool was to encourage designers to tag each instructional object using the Cisco framework. Tagging includes:

- title objective and type;
- job function and job task;
- author name and owner name; and
- creation date, publish date, and expiration date.

Table 1 lists the elements or fields items that can be entered into the database. Not all fields are required by the system for the output, providing the designer with a large degree of flexibility in determining the elements actually required to meet the objectives. Blank fields are automatically suppressed when the output Web pages are generated.

Three issues emerged. First, thinking in isolation of the "big picture" is very difficult for some designers. Second, developing isolated chunks of content into a Web-interface form rather than being able to see the final view of the instruction presents problems for the visual, creative designer. And finally, it was noted that Subject Matter Experts (SMEs) inputting data needed a "hold" on their content until it can be reviewed and modified by an instructional designer.

Table 1: Input Wizard Elements

```
Title
Keywords
Description
Introduction
Introduction Threaded Discussion URL
Introduction Graphic
        Show Graphic
        Hide Graphic
        Place Graphic on left
        Place Graphic on right
Concept 1 Opening
Concept 1 Threaded Discussion URL
Concept 1 Examples
Concept 1 Video 1
Concept 1 Video 2
Concept 1 Video 3
Concept 1 Director Movie
Concept 1 Flash
Concept 1 Graphic 1
Concept 1 Graphic 2
Concept 1 Graphic 3
Concept 1 Activities
Concept 1 Assessment
<Repeat for Concept 2>
<Repeat for Concept 3>
Summary
Summary Threaded Discussion URL
Summary Graphic
```

Resolving the Issues

As a result of the identified issues, a series of solutions were generated. The need to explore the "big picture" with a development team was suggested. A "preview" window was created to enable designers to see what the final view would look like in the output template. A status checkbox was also created that made everything draft until it was reviewed by a designer. Only when the designer finalizes individual RIOs and RLOs can they be activated for use and reuse. The following section explores the specific processes that were undertaken to resolve the issues.

Development Team. The establishment of a development team facilitated the design and development of the content and allowed the product to progress from a common framework. The team is typically made up of experts in OPD, instructional design, technology, and content. For this *teacher OPD*, expert teachers were also recruited. The development team framed the OPD; this determination of the framework began with a series of questions (see Table 2). To ensure that all of the team members are "on the same page," extensive discussion and consensus building as to the OPD's elements was undertaken. The questions cover a variety of topics, ranging from the OPD content to how to use the database input wizard

The process began with a series of organizational meetings to formulate the content, objectives, and length of the OPD. Using the questions outlined in Table 2 as a basis for discussion, each member of the team participates in the process to generate the same picture of the process. Through this planning process, a common vision of the product is developed. The final task of the

Table 2: Questions Framing OPD

- What is the context of the OPD?
- What is the content of the OPD?
- What standards (national, state) are to be met by the OPD?
- What are the OPD objectives?
- What is the philosophy of the OPD?
- What is the length of the OPD?
- What writing style/tone should be used?
- What kinds of activities are important in the OPD?
- What kinds of instructional strategies are appropriate?
- How will success be measured? Or, what should the final project or assessment include?
- What kinds of interaction between facilitator and student will be needed?
- What kinds of interaction between and among students will be needed?
- What should be the time commitment for participants?
- How is the database used as a tool for input?
- How will the instruction be tagged for the RLO/RIO?

development team involves organizing and sequencing the instructional content. Content SMEs lead this analysis and the development assignments are made, based on the results.

With the framework established, the developers/writers of the instruction create the instructional content, following the model of the input wizard (see Figure 2) and the instructional content outlines developed in the team meetings. They tag the content appropriately for the RLO/RIO. In the case of the OPD created at UWF, subject matter experts served as the instructional developers. Working with technology experts, the SMEs requested appropriate graphics, videos, and Flash files that support their instruction. Again, only appropriate multimedia were integrated into the product. The database accommodates blank fields, providing the maximum amount of flexibility in the elements that are included. The database also recognizes HTML coding, so technology-savvy designers or technology experts can return to the database and incorporate relevant HTML tags that will be acted upon by browsers when the website is generated.

Preview. One of the identified issues is related to the need to preview the draft instructional product. This preview permits the developer to see the flow of the instruction so that modifications can be entered as necessary. The developer can see the "real-time" impact of combining text and media elements in the template.

In the dynamic Web generation process, the contents of the Access database are "called" by an HTML-coded template using Cold Fusion (or

Figure 2: Input Wizard Completed

similar middleware), developed by the team technology experts. The contents of the database populate the HTML template and appear to the user as an integrated page in the resulting site.

Designer Review. As SMEs completed their content construction, an instructional designer reviews and edits the material. The SME and ID work together using the same database so revisions are immediately viewed in the real-time preview of the output site. Questions of meaning and structure can be addressed via an electronic discussion process. When the SME and ID complete their revisions, the database element is put into final form and available to be part of the field test. This field test requires that the database dynamically generate a website.

Output to End-Users. When following the Cisco RLO/RIO model of designing instruction, designers also have to determine which concepts collectively form an RLO. Having a library of templates from which to choose frees the designer from making screen design decisions and provides time to select or develop high-quality instructional materials. Templates can extend from those that simply designate text left/graphic right to providing a framework for problem-based learning, instructional interaction and collaboration with other learners, and visually rich and stimulating instructional environments. Templates also present a consistent interface that will facilitate predictable tool performance across units as well as throughout an entire system (Barritt & Lewis, 2001). The template used in UWF's OPD is displayed in Figure 3.

Figure 3: Output Template for OPD

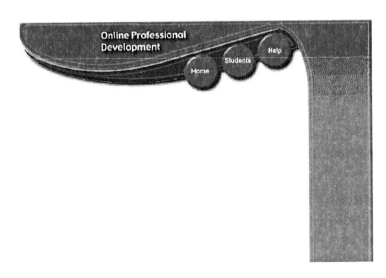

Figure 4: Dynamically Generated Production Website

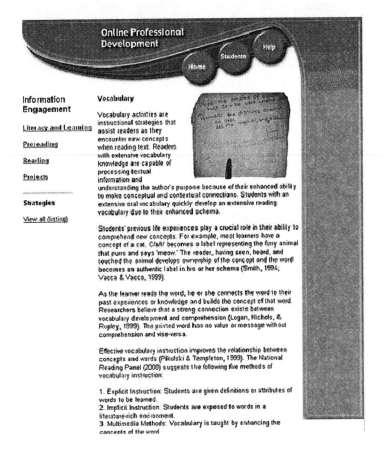

Field Test

The dynamically generated website is used in the field test (see Figures 4 and 5). For the teacher OPDs, the field test was conducted with a small group of teachers who had a variety of technical skills. The evaluator and facilitator held initial and ending focus groups with the field test participants. Teachers kept an evaluation log that identified problems they experienced. Teachers were encouraged to share their thoughts and views of the instructional product with the facilitator and evaluator. Based on comments and suggestions from the participants, the database was modified.

Figure 5

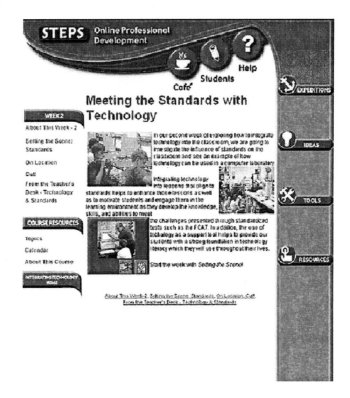

The Learning Objects Manager

In contemplating how to provide ready access to district-level staff development administrators, it was determined that a Web interface should exist that allows "administrators" to create unique professional development opportunities for their staff. The Learning Objects Manager provides a comprehensive list of all items that exist as RLOs and RIOs, provides access to go in and edit as needed, and gives the administrator the flexibility to pick and choose among the RIOs/RLOs to create unique professional development. The district-level administrators, then, have control over the professional development opportunities that they offer to their teaching staff.

CONCLUSION

The notions of RLO/RIO and database repositories offer instructional designers a flexibility not even imagined a few short years ago. As instructional designers investigate how to incorporate these processes and tools into their work processes, the potential for efficiency in use and reuse exponentially expands. Revisiting the "way we've always done things" provides an avenue for streamlining Web-based instructional development.

REFERENCES

Barritt, C. & Lewis, D. (2001). *Reusable Learning Object Strategy: Designing Information and Learning Objects Through Concept, Fact, Procedure, Process and Principle Templates.* Version 4.0, November 2001, Cisco Systems, Inc. Retrieved May 5, 2002, from: http://www.cisco.com/warp/public/10/.

Bloom, B. & Krathwohl, D. (1994). *Taxonomy of Educational Objectives, Handbook 1: Cognitive Domain.* Boston, MA: Addison-Wesley.

Clark, R. (1989). *Developing Technical Training: A Structured Approach for the Development of Classroom and Computer-Based Instructional Materials.* New York: Performance Technology Press.

Darling-Hammond, L. & McLaughlin, M. (1995). Policies that support professional development in an era of reform. *Phi Delta Kappan, 76*(8), 597-604.

Fullan, M. (1999). *Change Forces: The Sequel.* Bristol, PA: Falmer Press.

Gordon, J. & Zemke, R. (2000). The attack on ISD. *Training Magazine, 37*(4), 42-53.

Merrill, D. (1983). Component display theory. In Reigeluth, C. (Ed.), *Instructional Design Theories and Models.* Hillsdale, NJ: Lawrence Earlbaum Associates.

Merrill, D. (2000). *Components of Instruction: Toward a Theoretical Tool for Instructional Design.* Retrieved May 2000 from: http://www.id2.usu.edu/Papers/Components.PDF.

Muzio, J., Heins, T., & Mundell, R. (2001). *Experiences with Reusable e-Learning Objects: From Theory to Practice.* Available online at: http://www.cedarlearning.com/CL/elo/eLearningObjects_sml.pdf.

Northrup, P.T. & Rasmussen, K.L. (2002). A framework for online professional development. *Presentation at the International Conference Ed-Media*, Denver, CO, USA.

Singh, H. (2000). *Achieving Interoperability in e-Learning.* Retrieved March 2000 from: http://www.learningcircuits.org/mar2000/singh.html.

South, J.B. & Monson, D.W. (2001). A university-wide system for creating, capturing, and delivering learning objects. In Wiley, D.A. (Ed.), *The Instructional Use of Learning Objects*. Available online at: http://reusability.org/read/chapters/south.doc.

Sparks, D. & Hirsh, S. (1997). *A New Vision for Staff Development*. Alexandria, VA: Association for Supervision and Curriculum Development.

Wiley, D.A. (2001). Connecting learning objects to instructional design theory: A definition, metaphor, and a taxonomy. In Wiley, D.A. (Ed.), *The Instructional Use of Learning Objects*. Available online at: http://reusability.org/read/chapters/wiley.doc.

Chapter XII

Integrating ICT in Universities: Some Actual Problems and Solutions

Vassilios Dagdilelis
University of Macedonia in Thessaloniki, Greece

ABSTRACT

Universities adopt the most progressive, technologically speaking, methods of research and education. Nevertheless, the adoption of ICTs (Information and Communication Technologies) appears to be necessarily accompanied by a deep shift in the organization of work, and this adoption must to be included in a wider teaching and learning strategy. We present some of the problems arising when ICT systems are integrated in universities and some suggestions to deal with these problems.

INTRODUCTION

Computers and more generally speaking, ICTs (Information and Communication Technologies), have penetrated substantially into every area of human activity: from research to entertainment and from medicine to business management, ICTs have revolutionized the methods used by humans up to now. The field of education is no exception where ICTs have had a strong impact, perhaps the greatest since the invention of printing. Thus, ICTs seem to be advancing at great speed, and generally are being accepted and adopted by educational institutions, especially universities.

Universities and other similar organizations of higher education constitute socially recognized institutions assigned mainly to research, education, and services. By their very own nature, universities adopt the most progressive, technologically speaking, methods of research and education. Under these conditions, it is expected that they will thus adopt the most contemporary instructional technologies, especially ICTs. In addition, universities are obliged to adopt ICTs, not only because of their nature, but also due to the strong economic, political, and social pressures from external sources—and in actual fact, pressures which often appear for the first time. ICTs offer the possibility of expanding the student body, making available a more flexible schedule, as well as the improvement of teaching methods through the creation of teaching environments with multiple possibilities. Nevertheless, the adoption of ICTs appears to be necessarily accompanied by a deep shift in the organization of work, and this adoption must to be included in a wider teaching and learning strategy (Bates, 2000). Further, ICTs are also the means through which institutions of higher education will be able to respond to the new economic and social demands.

Instructional Systems Design methodologies, such as ADDIE, constitute a generally accepted tool for the design of instructional applications. It has been applied successfully in many cases in the design and the development of modern educational applications. Unfortunately, however, ADDIE cannot be applied to the university instructional systems without some additional work and consideration. Furthermore, it must be added that the design of a new instructional system for the university must take into account the fact that the designed system will function within a larger system, the university itself.

Universities have their own structure and by consequence, new systems like an instructional system destined to function within them must be integrated. Moreover, universities and other similar institutions are also part of a system of larger institutions, with society itself as the largest one. Each one of these institutions, as a kind of homocentric cycle, includes the institutions of the "lower" level and is included in the "higher" one. Universities, for example, are part of institutions of higher education, which is part of the educational system and so on. An analogy is that of live organisms living in a specific environment. Their environment (e.g., a lake) is a part of the regional environment, which is part of a larger ecosystem. Thus, in order to study the function of one organism, we must take into consideration its own internal structure, its parts and their interrelatedness, and also the ecological conditions that govern its interaction with the environment.

Returning to the issue of universities, it is argued that the understanding of their function must be based on the study of their internal structure and of their "ecology," i.e., their interaction with the other institutions. Institutions of higher education are influenced both by local as well as general trends which prevail in the economic, political, and social fields. However, it must be kept in mind that the institutions, in turn, also influence these trends (Marginson & Rhoades, 2002).

All the factors, which are included in this interaction, have not been adequately analyzed nor validated — even though many attempts have been made at an international level to create a theoretical framework that would allow for their analysis (Marginson & Rhoades, 2002).

The strong interaction between institutions and the integration of universities into larger institutions creates some complex problems not easily dealt with when tools like ADDIE are used. Traditional ADDIE methodologies are meaningful when applied to a stable environment with known variables. New technologies, besides introducing novel ideas, also change the environment. For this reason, ADDIE does not seem to be a sufficient tool, able to integrate these elements in the construction of a new educational system. In some way, using ADDIE leads to a paradox, because the more a tool like ADDIE is needed, the more insufficient it becomes, as it cannot take into account the consequences of a radical change.

Below, are some of the problems arising and some of the affecting conditions when ICT systems are integrated in universities, and some suggestions to deal with these problems.

SOME IMPLICATIONS FOR ICT IN UNIVERSITIES

As already referred to in the introduction, it is the actual nature of universities that leads them to adopt the most advanced technological systems. However, in the case of ICTs, external factors are applying pressure to the universities more than at any other period in time. Universities are knowledge-driven organizations and thus it is only to be expected that they will be influenced by progress in ICTs, especially since universities themselves were one of the pioneers in this progress.

First of all, ICTs have had an influence on a fundamental activity carried out by universities, namely that of research (Duderstadt, 1998). The influence has been so deep that nowadays it is absolutely inconceivable to conduct research without the use of ICT: from the actual research procedure which may be based on simulations or huge calculations to the communication among the researchers, all stages of the research appear to need ICTs.

Apart from research, ICTs are used to a large extent by university administration and recently they are also being used in teaching. A basic benefit of ICTs in teaching is their ability to create rich learning environments, which at least theoretically, contribute to the development of more successful teaching methods. In other words, their basic benefit, that which most affects the running of teaching institutions, is that they offer new ways of communication. The new technological possibilities that — thanks to ICT — have been opened up today, allow educational services to be delivered to anyone at any place and at any time, without the limitations of space and/or time (Bates, 2000; Duderstadt, 1998; Langlois, 1997). It is estimated that the effect of ICTs will become even greater — given that no other technological invention in the past, neither the radio nor television, influenced educational institutions so intensely and in such a short period of time (Bates, 2000; Duderstadt, 1998; Langlois, 1997).

The network of relationships in institutions of higher education with the other social institutions, of course, includes the interaction of the institutions among themselves. The institutions are not only interacting when they belong to the same administrative area — State or Nation — but also when they are in the same categories: for example the institutions involved with molecular biology obviously are in constant contact with each other and influence one another. This interaction, as a rule, has a number of general characteristics: institutions all over the world, more and more, look alike. Institutions of higher education, for instance, tend to be almost homogeneous. Although this procedure is rather complex, it can be explained, due to two types of mechanisms.

The first type is classical: the same reasons cause analogous results, thus, while globalization tends to equate the economic and cultural environments in which universities function, it also causes similar reactions on their part. The second type of mechanism, connected to the first, is that which can be described as the "snakelike procession of academic drift" (Morphew, 2000). This is the idea that as the snake's tail "follows" the same route as the head, in the same way the least successful academic institutions will follow the most prestigious ones. However, the image of the "snakelike procession" is not fully accurate because the less well-known institutions do not actually follow the same route as the successful ones but just *mimic* them. For example, if a prestigious university adopts a successful strategy after a trial period, then the other institutions will also adopt this same strategy, but without necessarily passing through all the intermediary trial stages. For this reason the process of homogeneity develops faster. If this hypothesis of homogeneity is correct, then strategies adopted by one category of institutions, in this example the most technologically advanced, will in the long run also be adopted by the other institutions all over the world.

An obvious example is the Greek Open University (www.eap.gr), which was established in 1993 and which adopted the successful strategies of other Open Universities around the world. This tendency to be homogeneous comprises a powerful factor that influences the formation of modern universities. Thus, when the large and prestigious universities adopt ICTs, this becomes an indirect factor for the small universities to also adopt them.

SOCIAL AND ECONOMIC FACTORS

However, the most important factors affecting the integration of ICTs in universities are those of an economic and social nature. There is a series of interacting factors which more than anything else not only define the strategy of universities toward ICTs but also, more generally, determine indirectly many of the changes universities make. The study of such complex factors is based on a series of ascertainments or developments. The first development is that the number of students has been increasing much faster over the last 30 years. This increase includes not only the number of "typical" students, i.e., those who go to institutions of higher education straight out of secondary education (18- to 20-year-old high school graduates), but also the number of the mature-aged students who come from a variety of socioeconomic backgrounds. The latter have particular characteristics: they are, as a rule, already employed and have specific training needs that are required in order for them to remain competitive in the employment market. Therefore, neither the regular university schedule nor their presence on campus, nor the typical curriculum of institutions of higher education, meets the needs of these mature students. Their social importance, nevertheless, as well as their economic power makes them as important or even more so than the typical students. Universities are thus called on to readjust in order to cope with the new demands. Mature-aged students have very specific needs, which are directly linked to their type of work. For example, nowadays, production requires the use of a workforce that is computer literate and prepared to undergo independent lifelong learning. Universities are to a degree obligated to readjust under these social pressures.

As is natural, the increased demand for education creates a similar increase in the running costs of universities. The university expenses, however, for research, education, and the rendering of services, have increased at even greater speed: universities function because of the highly trained staff and the facilities and special equipment, which are all very expensive. Universities are driven by an ever-expanding knowledge base; access and exploitation of this knowledge, likewise, have a very high cost.

At the same time as the cost of the running of universities is constantly increasing, government and other funding sources are drastically being reduced (Katz & Associates, 1999; Bates, 2000; Duderstadt, 1998; Langlois, 1997): "Not only in the USA and in the EU, but internationally has public support for higher education flattened and then declined over the past two decades." In the USA, this downward trend is obvious at all levels — for example, the aid toward students in the form of grants has been replaced with help in the form of loans. This reaction, on the part of universities, is analogous to the local conditions.

In the USA, there appears to have been an increase in tuition fees that is much higher than the Consumer Price Index. This fact has provoked public interest as to the profitability of investment (public and private), which is made in institutions of higher education. In the EU, the programs are geared all the more toward the direct needs of the economy. Therefore, universities are obliged to readjust to the new social and economic situation.

INFORMATION AS A COMMODITY AND A BUSINESS

Additionally, the great demand in teaching services has an indirect result: information and knowledge, more than at any other time, have become an economic good — and their use appears to be regulated more by the market forces and less by the current governing policy. This means that universities now face external competition. It appears that they are losing, to an extent, their formerly exclusive production of new knowledge, and the power and authority to educate and certify knowledge and skills. Today, large organizations and businesses are establishing their own educational departments, which offer "just-in-time" and "just-in-case" extra training to their employees. Also, new businesses are appearing, whose only activity is to offer educational and training services. Virtual Universities and "learning-ware" providers are entering the marketplace to compete with traditional institutions (Duderstadt, 1998). It is thus clear that the universities are experiencing multiple external pressures and need to readjust. Clearly, this readjustment is directly connected to ICTs.

The use of ICTs in no way decreases the overall functioning costs of a university since its costs are initially high and the equipment used is very quickly outdated. Nevertheless, under the right circumstances, ICTs can lead to improved cost-effectiveness by enabling new target groups to be reached and new, higher quality learning outcomes to be gained at a lower marginal cost per student than through conventional classroom methods (Bates, 2000).

Universities are also undergoing internal pressure, from their own nature and function. The necessity of adopting new technologies because universities have as a basic aim the adoption of modern methods has already been mentioned. To this must be added the fact that university students, who are not simply computer literate, but are actually the so-called "Plug'n'Play generation," expect the institutions at which they are studying to make extensive use of ICTs — and especially now, since ICTs have been integrated into all levels of human activity such as work and entertainment. Very often, universities are in a position of competition among themselves and their technological infrastructure is an important factor in attracting more and better students.

Finally, the actual members of the academic community who are involved with ICTs also apply a type of pressure either toward the direction of the market for new equipment or toward the direction of employing even more staff for research and teaching that will use ICTs for the institution.

THE UNIVERSITY ECOSYSTEM TODAY

Studying institutions of post-secondary education, within the nexus of their relationships with other institutions, allows for a more complete understanding and interpretation of the problems which arise. In fact, we support the position that the internal and external pressures force universities and in general all higher educational institutions to adopt ICTs and at the same time to alter their own status. This change is so deep-rooted that many believe that universities and institutions of higher education generally will cease to exist in the way that they have been known until now. There are two very important changes: (1) changes in the economic funding of these institutions, especially of universities; and (2) changes in the actual functioning, not only at an internal level of organization, but also the types of services they will provide.

Diversity is a good example. In many countries, diversity has become an important issue in higher education policies. Diversity can be seen as an answer to the continual expansion of universities. It is comparable to the differentiation of studies and services offered by the academic institutions (form, duration, direction) but also in the differentiation between the actual institutions themselves (size, location, type of institution). However, even though diversity has as a general aim the satisfaction of social needs, a number of researchers observe that diversity can and should be analyzed within the framework of a purely economic analysis (Dill & Teixeira, 2000), and believe that diversity and the related concept of innovation are economic concepts and as such they should be analyzed. Considering these concepts from an economic point of view raises a specific *problématique*: "From this point of view, an academic innovation would be considered as a way to better satisfy universities' customers or to create a clear benefit for the innovating Higher Education institution" (Dill & Teixeira, 2000).

Apart from diversity, a second example is the economies of scope, i.e., the fact that complementary products, which are available simultaneously, function successfully. Thus, some researchers include both doctoral and contract research in this category of complementary products (Dill & Teixeira, 2000).

THE UNIVERSITY AS A BUSINESS

The overall activities, therefore, of a higher educational institution can be put to an economic analysis. Universities and other institutions of higher education in general seem to be progressively losing their academic character-istics and acquiring those of a *business*. For many economic researchers, the only plausible response to the pressures that universities are under is based on a conceptual change: universities, from non-profit organizations functioning on the basis of government subsidies, will be considered as "for-profit firms" (Jongbloed, 2002). In this situation, the influence of the general environment on the functioning of universities will be even stronger, since, for example, the most significant factor for the adoption of innovations will be the wider structure of the market (Dill & Teixeira, 2000). These phenomena, i.e., the obligatory restructuring of universities, can be explained by the fact that the economy itself is being transformed in its entirety from a manufacturing economy into a network economy (Jongbloed, 2002).

It is common to refer to the principal aims of the university in terms of teaching, research, and service. But these roles can be regarded as simply the 20th century manifestations of the more fundamental roles of creating, preserv-ing, integrating, transmitting, and applying knowledge (Jongbloed, 2002). Universities perform a basic function in "creating, preserving, integrating, transmitting, and applying knowledge" (Duderstadt, 1998). In the 20th century, this function was realized in a particular way and thus, universities organized themselves accordingly so as to produce new knowledge, to transmit this knowledge, and to offer services in accordance with social, as well as other needs of the century. In the 21st century, universities will therefore function more as a type of knowledge server rather than in the way they are operating today. If the more contemporary language of computer networks were to be used, the university might be regarded as a "knowledge server," providing knowledge services (i.e., creating, preserving, transmitting, and applying knowledge) in whatever form needed by contemporary society.

From this more abstract viewpoint, it is clear that while these fundamental roles of the university do not change over time, the particular realization of these roles *does* change — and in fact, quite fast.

PROBLEMS IN ADOPTING ICTS AT UNIVERSITIES

This whole trend of adopting ICTs and the gradual restructuring of the universities is not without obstacles nor is it unconditional. The main obstacle in the adoption of ICTs comes from the actual nature of the universities, which is basically conservative. For certain academic circles, the use of ICTs could be rather dangerous: "many readers…may think of higher education's relationship with information technology as a dance with the devil…many of us in higher education now wish that we could push the information technology genie back into the bottle" (Katz & Associates, 1999). Universities have long produced and disseminated knowledge in an old-fashioned way. Traditionally, universities have functioned in a specific location and cater to mainly a specific age group (late teens — early twenties). In addition, the produced and transmitted knowledge is directed toward a relatively limited local group of students. Nevertheless, the new trend reverses this situation and there is a type of inertia at universities, which is being called on to change a number of their rather strong functioning stereotypes.

What we consider as a major problem in the design and use of ICTs for educational purposes is directly related with the importance of ICTs. As has been stated, integrating ICTs implies a major change for any organization. By their own nature, universities are well-structured institutions, and unavoidably the integration of ICTs leads to a radical change in their function and the balance of "forces" within the system. These changes arise at many different levels: changes in allowing resources for the technological infrastructure and the restructuring of the courses, in order to exploit the new possibilities offered by

ICT, constitute typical examples of profound changes which finally influence the whole structure as well as the function of universities.

Experience shows that the adoption of ICTs, even by the most dynamic institutions of higher education, takes place gradually and at a very slow pace. The internal rivalries of researchers, who have dissenting views, are a common phenomenon. A significant factor in this situation is the fact that the university staff is not always acquainted with ICTs. It is not, in other words, computer literate. Naturally, the use of ICTs and the reorientation of a university's activities require not simply computer literacy but rather a much deeper knowledge of ICTs. This deeper knowledge is many times lacking in the staff members, especially those in fields which are not based on technology, like the Humanities.

At the other end of the spectrum, many obstacles can be found for courses delivered via the Internet. In order to deliver courses via networks, the existence of a fast, robust, reliable, and cheap network (in some places mostly telephone lines) is necessary. Often, for many countries or regions, not even telephone lines are reliable or cheap. It is also necessary that the potential students have the fundamental skills needed in order to be able to follow these courses. The increase in the power and functionality of ICTs, as well as the falling prices, have contributed to ICT adoption and use in developed and newly industrialized countries—but this remains untrue for large sections of the population within these countries that include a large number of other nations.

In some cases another problem arises, that of *institutional recognition* of the courses delivered from a distance. The low cost of these courses, coupled with the increased demand for new ones, has led to a general tendency for the creation of even more new courses. Their institutional status, however, can remain undefined and a large sector of the educational system refuses to accept the total equivalence of these courses to traditional ones delivered only by recognized institutions.

The consideration of institutions of higher education institutions on economic terms is naturally a choice. Viewing universities as a business is contrary to their academic character, not only generally and ideologically, but also in terms of specific strategic choices. A characteristic feature is the example of appropriability. Appropriability is an important factor in the adoption of innovations. If the diffusion of an innovation is too simple, then not only the business that devised the innovation and which was burdened with the costs of this invention will benefit, but also will its competitors. For this reason, there are fewer incentives for the adoption of innovations (Dill & Teixeira, 2000).

However, this principle is in total contrast to academic ideology, which believes in the dissemination of new knowledge without rules and restrictions. Thus, universities will most likely ignore this principle. For example, MIT's recent decision to make its courses available on the Internet is an expression of MIT's choice for openness. Cited in Vest (2001): "We have built a system of higher education that is the envy of all the world, and we have developed the Internet as a universal medium for rapidly distributing and accessing information. These forces must now combine to raise educational opportunity throughout the world."

A second example is the strategic response from universities to the increasing pressure of internationalization, i.e., "the integration of an international dimension into the teaching, research, and service function of higher education" (Van der Wende, 2001). The Anglo-Saxon countries have chosen a categorically stated and at times aggressive — competitive policy, whereas the European countries seem to prefer a more cooperative policy (Van der Wende, 2001).

Universities, therefore, as social institutions must adapt or they will disappear. "Thirty years from now the big university campuses will be relics. Universities will not survive. It is as large a change as when we first got the printed book" (Lenzner & Johnson, 1997). Their readjustment does not mean merely the adoption of ICTs and a few new programs. Universities and institutions of higher education in general must reorganize from their foundations and most importantly redefine their business concept (Jongbloed, 2002).

The views expressed above are most likely exaggerated. However, even if the situation is not as stated, the problem remains open, even on a different scale.

THE STATE OF
INSTRUCTIONAL DESIGN TODAY

Up to this point an attempt has been made to explain that the constant pressures, both internal and external, on the universities to integrate ICTs are accompanied by strong pressure for restructuring, which allow them to keep their initial role, but which make them, most probably, operate on a different basis.

Within this framework, it would seem that the traditional methodologies for instructional design are non-existent because they do not seem to take into account all the new parameters, which must now be included.

Many models have been proposed as a more general consideration of the new factors, such as ACTIONS (Bates, 2000). Khan (1999) proposes a model for the analysis of Web-based courses, which includes many more options than traditional tools. Linguistic themes, cultural considerations and motivations, institutional influences, cost analysis, and so on need to be considered during design. Despite all the proposed analytical tools, none of them seems to be generally accepted. It is, however, very clear that the traditional methods of lesson planning are seriously insufficient at the level of instructional analysis.

The new methods of teaching educational content present many new elements which are not integrated in ADDIE — which presupposes the existence of a class of students with known characteristics, face-to-face teaching, and so on. These basic suppositions, however, do not apply to the new educational frameworks in which distance learning takes place. In fact, the new educational environments are based on a rapidly expanding technology, little researched and little understood (Philson, 1998). Furthermore, up to now, research into the quality of Open and Distance Learning (ODL) has been technology-driven rather than pedagogy-driven (Langlois, 1997).

One important problem arising in Web-based and other technology-based courses is related to their (instructional) efficiency — or inefficiency, as the case may be. Even though potentially ICTs can play a very positive role in teaching, this still remains a strong hypothesis and many researchers have emphasized the absence of a specific pedagogy. To be more precise, the exact conditions necessary to construct a pedagogically efficient course are not known. This seems to be especially true in cases where teaching consists of practical exercises. If one agrees with the constructivist hypothesis, which nowadays is widely accepted, knowledge, either in a procedural or a declarative form, is constructed through a process of interaction between the learner and their environment. In most cases, however, the interaction between them in distance learning courses is very poor, and thus the efficiency of delivered courses is rather questionable in some cases. For example, one of the most promising computing products is that of the so-called open microworlds such as the language LOGO, the physics environments such as Interactive Physics, the Dynamic Geometry environments such as Cabri-Geometer or Geometer Sketchpad. The most contemporary software of this type consists of simple, open environments, but which also integrates possibilities of dynamic variation and direct use of objects. However, to a large extent, nowadays we are not aware of what might be the most successful use of these environments (see, for example, Jonassen, 2000). ICTs are supposed to be able to improve the quality of teaching, but generally we do not know the methodology to achieve this. The ADDIE methodologies, as a rule, are functional in the analysis and creation of lessons in succession and at specific levels of teaching — whereas the possibilities being opened up by the new educational environments allows that lessons be organized on different bases.

In addition, the new educational environments include not only "local" microworlds in which students can conduct experiments, trials, measurements, and generally develop a variety of activities, but they also offer a variety of communication possibilities inside and outside the classroom. Thus, thanks to ICTs, a new type of organization of the classroom is created and often the teacher within this framework is called on to play a new role. Nevertheless, ADDIE methodologies do not have, as a rule, the possibility to integrate and analyze these new didactic situations and remain at that level.

ICTs' strongest influence, however, in institutions of higher education appears to be related to the provision of distance learning lessons and mainly to asynchronous teaching. This is because in essence, these types of lessons will allow the institutions to have a significant cost reduction resulting in a reduced cost of teaching per student.

A difficulty in the design of online lessons is the extreme diversity of the public to whom they are geared. Subjects intended for an international public are especially difficult, requiring a more complex procedure since factors of language, and culture and teaching problems that may arise, all have to be taken into account, as these lessons are available to "anyone."

A second level of difficulty is related to the teaching theory usually implemented with online lessons. Online lessons, in their current form, are most times rather simplistic from the point of view of teaching, and it cannot be sure that they can replace live lessons. As is well known, in a traditional classroom situation, there is a very strong interaction between teacher and students. This interaction is not merely typical; it is not only based on words but on the entire context of the situation. The teacher, for instance, is able to either emphasize or dismiss a student's answer with gestures of the hands, the expression on the face, and in many other ways. This process is neither marginal nor insignificant, but rather it is very important since it consists of a very significant aspect of the teaching process. The lack of this type of communication in distance education is obviously a disadvantage, and it is not known how it can be overcome. It is the same for the very strong interaction between students, which in distance learning is either totally missing or is replaced by communication through the Net. The lack of direct interaction between those taking part, as is the case with those of a traditional classroom, is thus a disadvantage for distance learning, at least in the way that it exists today. This disadvantage naturally increases in the cases when practical application and the learning of practical skills are required on the part of students.

Up to now, online lessons have been designed with low teaching specifications: they are in fact e-books with very little interaction with the student and have closed-type exercises. Especially in the situations where new concepts are introduced — and particularly where these concepts do not conform to the intuition and experience of students — the understanding of these concepts requires, as a rule, rich teaching environments, and the online environment, as has been shown, is relatively insufficient.

From their experience, teachers gain a whole range of knowledge, which enables them to recognize not only the mistakes but also why those mistakes were made, i.e., students' misconceptions. In this way, a mistake made on reasoning, a question apparently without meaning, and generally students' actions are gauges for the teachers who do not intervene in the mistake itself, but rather in the reason for the mistake. If, for example, students insist that a lighter weight body falls slower than a heavy one, the teacher is able to understand that the students have not simply made a mistake, but obviously have not understood the concept of gravity, and thus the teaching involved will not simply be to correct the mistake, but rather to correct the misconception.

Nevertheless, the methods for expressing in a typical manner the teacher's informal and empirical knowledge are still not known (except for commonplace situations such as the above) and thus we are not yet able to "implement" this knowledge within a system of teaching. The teaching systems, which exist at present, do not have the diagnostic abilities an experienced teacher has.

These problems are usually dealt with empirically, according to each case. And in this case, the methodologies of ADDIE are not sufficiently analytical, in order to allow for the creation of successful educational online lessons.

SOME SUGGESTIONS

The problems mentioned above have a common point. They are all related, directly or indirectly, with the profound, radical transformation in the educational process occurring when ICTs are used. In most cases, tools for the design of new educational systems or courses do not take into account the implications of these systems in the organization where the systems must be integrated.

In addition, these tools cannot integrate the new and to a large extent unknown possibilities which are opened up — as well as their limits and any possible weaknesses. ADDIE enables the design of different educational applications, but within an educational system that remains stable and in teaching environments with typical parameters. It is possible that in the current situation, we are not in a position to expand systems like ADDIE in order to include new elements such as the ones mentioned above, because data collected from experience and research are not sufficient to deal with these complex phenomena. However, the elaboration of this expansion is considered a necessity, and research in this area must be encouraged.

Is there, at present, a technology, which enables a very successful design to be created? Possibly not. As Vest (2001, p. 4) states, "There is not one grand solution. Indeed, I believe that it is too early to declare comprehensive positions and strategies. Rather, it is a time for substantial experimentation and calculated risks that will help us to sort out opportunities and find effective paths." Thus, research seems to be the only channel for the accumulated experience to be expressed within the framework of a new methodology.

Along with experimentation, which is an acceptable, although time-consuming scientific procedure, there is a pressing need for the adoption of strategies for ICTs on the part of universities.

The experience up till now allows certain practical rules to be formulated on the use of ICTs (see for example Langlois, 1997):

- Recognition of the systemic variables and conditions affecting the design, development, and implementation of online courses needs to be incorporated into the instructional systems design process.
- A cooperative policy is a basic choice that universities have. It should systematically cultivate the elaboration of subjects at all levels. At an internal level, cooperation among students, faculty, and technical staff should be cultivated, and at an external level, cooperation with related institutions who also adopt ICTs is advisable both to better understand ICTs and their functioning, as well as to facilitate shared decision-making at all relevant levels.
- Promote and support the development of course material using ICTs. That means not only to promote and financially support the research on methods of teaching with ICTs, but also an open collaboration policy with other agents involved, such as computer firms, software developers, and enterprises designing educational delivery systems. Nevertheless, this progress must not be made at the expense of lessons, which must follow the accepted quality standards.
- Develop a systematic training for faculty members in order for them to be able to use more effectively ICTs in teaching. This training must be based not only on formal courses, but also in collaboration with the technical staff.

- Develop an infrastructure that will support new technologies not only within the confines of the university, but also between universities and generally as widely as possible. Within the framework of this infrastructure, a system should also be developed which makes accessing the lessons easy for all students, either on or off campus.
- Simultaneously support the development of library technology, hand-in-hand with instructional technology.

All these rules are obviously not sufficient to determine in an analytical way the strategy of universities toward ICTs. They do, however, consist of a summary of tried directions, and in combination with systematic experimental and related research could be used to formulate a more general policy.

REFERENCES

Bates, W. (2000). *Managing Technological Change.* Jossey-Bass.

Daniel, J.S. (1996). *Mega-Universities & Knowledge Media.* Kogan Page.

Dill, D.D. & Teixeira, P. (2000). Program diversity in higher education: An economic perspective. *Higher Education Policy*, 13(1), 99-117.

Duderstadt, J.J. (1998). Transforming the university to serve the Digital Age. *CAUSE/EFFECT,* 20(4), 21-32.

Evans, T. & Nation, D. (2000). *Changing University Teaching.* Kogan Page.

Hanna, D.E. & Associates. (2000*). Higher Education in an Era of Digital Competition.* Atwood Publishing.

Jonassen, D.H. (2000). *Computers as Mindtools for Schools.* Merrill, Prentice-Hall.

Jongbloed, B. (2002). Lifelong learning: Implications for Institutions. *Higher Education,* 44, 423-431.

Katz, R.N. & Associates. (1999). *Dancing with the Devil, Information Technology and the New Competition in Higher Education.* Jossey-Bass.

Langlois, C. (1997) *Universities and New Information and Communication Technologies: Issues and Strategies.* International Association of Universities.

Lenzner, R. & Johnson, S.S. (1997). Seeing things as they really are. *Forbes*, 10(March).

Marginson, S. & Rhoades, G. (2002) Beyond national sates, markets, and systems of higher education: A Glocanal agency heuristic. *Higher Educa-tion, 43,* 281-309.

Morphew, C.C. (2000). Institutional diversity, program acquisition and faculty members: Examining academic drift at a new level. *Higher Education Policy,* 13(1), 55-77.

Philson, R.M. (1998). Curriculum by bytes—Using technology to enhance international education. In Mestenhauser, J.A. & Ellingboe, B.J. (Eds.), *Reforming the Higher Education Curriculum.* American Council of Education, Oryx Press.

van der Wende, M.C. (2001). Internationalization policies: About new trends and contrasting paradigms. *Higher Education Policy,* 14(3), 249-259.

Vest, C.M. (2001). *Disturbing the Educational Universe: Universities in the Digital Age—Dinosaurs or Prometheans?* Report of the President, MIT, Year 2000-2001.

Chapter XIII

Integrated Training Requires Integrated Design and Business Models

Arthur B. Jeffery
University of South Alabama, USA

Mary F. Bratton-Jeffery
Naval Education and Training Command, USA

ABSTRACT

There are many instructional design models that are based on educational and learning theory. There are also many process-based performance and quality improvement analytic models. When training development is viewed as a design and production process with the training "product" as the outcome, then both traditional ISD models and process improvement models become highly relevant to the goal of developing high-quality, user-focused training. This chapter examines the integration of performance and quality improvement model elements into traditional ISD models with an emphasis on a front-end analysis that uses the Quality Function Deployment Model to insure user-focused and outcome-based results.

INTRODUCTION

Somewhere in the Persian Gulf, Petty Officer Third Class Smith rolls out of his bunk at 05:30. He showers, hits the galley for breakfast, and heads to the hangar bay to be on duty at 06:30. At the duty section brief, he learns his shop will be doing an engine change on an E-2C Hawkeye aircraft that is returning to the aircraft carrier after experiencing an in-flight turbine failure. The Air Boss has made it very clear that the aircraft, which serves as the "Eyes of the Fleet," will be repaired and ready for flight ASAP.

PO3 Smith remembers most of the turbine-related training he received at a Naval Aviation Maintenance Training Group detachment (NAMTRAGRUDET) before he reported to his squadron, but it has been awhile and turbine failures are definitely not a routine evolution. Non-pulsed, he returns to his maintenance shop, sits down at a computer, and searches for the same lessons he sat through at the NAMTRAGRUDET. He downloads the lessons from the local LAN for review, and notes a new engineering change proposal (ECP) has been linked to the turbine-related lessons. After reading the ECP, he is not quite clear on the final step of the overall procedure, which has been modified since he saw it in school.

As his supervisor is assigned to the flight deck recovery of the damaged E-2C aircraft, PO3 Smith sends an email back to the NAMTRAGRUDET instructor who taught the class, with a copy to the stateside manufacturer's technical representative. He then checks out a personal digital assistant (PDA), downloads the turbine maintenance technical specifications from the interactive electronic technical manual files to the large-screen PDA, and heads back to the hangar bay, knowing he will have an answer to his email long before he gets to that step. With the technical specifications at his side, his refreshed knowledge on turbine repairs, and the reliable help from experts stateside, he's confident he'll be done in time to email his girlfriend back home before signing on for his 2100 (9PM) Navy e-learning online class in Electrical Engineering 101.

A Brief History

Since the '50s, the military training systems have embraced the logical and deliberate methodology of the Plan, Analyze, Design, Develop, Implement, and Evaluate (PADDIE) Model in one form or another.

Its inherent linear design structure perpetuates a single input that leads to a single output. Each block or phase has specific tasks associated with it.

Figure 1: Classic PADDIE Model

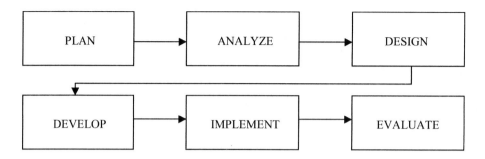

- PLAN: develop organizational structure, tasks, milestones, etc.
- ANALYZE: identify tasks and job performance requirements.
- DESIGN: prepare a detailed plan of instruction including methods, media, and strategies.
- DEVELOP: produce, review, and revise the instructional product.
- IMPLEMENT: integrate the instructional product into the training environment.
- EVALUATE: validate, operationally try-out, and assess tasks or products in the analysis, design, or develop phases (MIL-STND-1379-D).

With the exception of PLAN, notice that each phase is dependent on the phase preceding it. The conceptual model is extremely linear in execution, albeit that ideally EVALUATE should be interwoven within the total process. The model implies terminality. The product is finished and sent to the Fleet. End of story.

The MIL-STND-1379-D was the Department of Defense's corporate cornerstone for building sound instruction. For the Navy, the Instructional Systems or Education Specialist was taught that exhaustive analysis, comprehensive and labored design and development approaches would produce curriculums refined to a level of detail unparalleled by no others.

One cannot refute the efforts or the products, but given the rapid advancement of technology and the complexity of performance systems in battle group deployments, maybe it is time to question the success of time-intensive traditional approaches. If technology advances at a rate of six to nine months, then instructional methodology and development of products must use new technology-based approaches to keep pace.

Quality-Based Instructional Design Model

During the mid-1990s, Quality Improvement processes entered the Navy's instructional design process. Figure 2 represents the new and revised instructional design model (MIL-HNDBK-29612).

The spherical model better illustrates the cyclical nature of the entire process. It also includes the management and support structures that are the underpinnings of any organization, whether engaged in education, training, or business. However, the model continues to present the central phases as independent structures with definite inputs and outputs.

The difference between the original PADDIE and the quality-based model is that evaluation is better portrayed as having impact on the four other phases and that information flows bilaterally between evaluation and the appropriate phase. The position of quality improvement, which encapsulates the process, indicates improvements are made throughout the entire process. The quality-based model for instructional products has matured, but it fails to address the interrelationship between product, process, the system in which the product operates, and the impact of technology.

Figure 2: Quality-Based Instructional Design Model

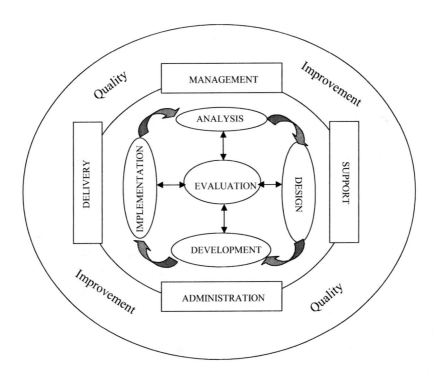

Figure 3: General Systems Model

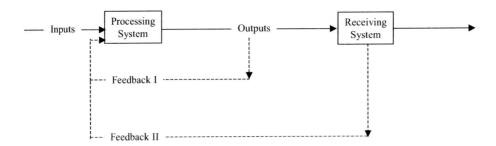

A Systems Approach

Trainees advancing through Navy schoolhouses are reflected in the General Systems Model defined by Brethower and Rummler in the 1960s (see Figure 3).

The General Systems Model identifies, as well, the components and the working relationships between the members of the instructional product development team. The Instructional System Specialist (ISS) working alongside the Subject Matter Expert (SME) identified the content and the skills (inputs) necessary to perform a particular job (outputs). Design and development efforts focused on building a single integrated package of classroom instruction, labs, exercises, job sheets, and of course, tests. Students "classed up" and trained as one unit. The unit moved at the speed and level of the slower students to ensure everyone received equal training and produced similar performance results.

As computers gained acceptance in the training world of the '80s, the personal computer became a glorified and coveted delivery medium. The success of the schoolhouse was measured in tours highlighting how many PCs were at students' fingertips in classrooms and learning resource centers. Technology was not considered a cornerstone of training but merely an electronic sidebar.

Yet, despite technology infusion, what accompanied the sailor to the fleet was the knowledge and procedures that were maintained in the sailor's internal CPU (the sailor's brain). Expectations and performance were no different than sailors predating technology-based training. Instructional strategies which employed rote memorization, repetition, and drill and practice aimed at automaticity and lower level thinking skills. The rise in popularity of self-paced, computer-based training merely reinforced the antiquated strategies; instead of using chalk and talk, the strategies were transferred to the 15" monitor.

Students were required to drill and practice until 100% scores on tests were reached. Remediation feedback in the form of endless loops frustrated learners, drove the price of production up, and still produced the same results.

In the opening scenario, PO3 Smith needs to refresh his memory on turbine failures. Under the previous models, PO3 Smith would be required to fire up the CD-ROM, begin with lesson one, and continue through the program until he reaches the information on turbine failures. Certainly not a very efficient method of using technology.

However, today's Navy requires cross-training in skills, an understanding of the total operational system, and the paramount ability to fix any component within the system no matter what happens. That means that the sailors of the flight deck, the engine room, or the combat information center must be able to problem-solve and generate new solutions when unchartered problems arise. Gone are the days when the enemy sailed into view, neatly lined up its forces, and fired salvos directly at the battle group. Small boat attacks, as in the case of the USS Cole, suicide mass bombers of 9-11, and network-centric warfare (Cebrowski, 1998) are real threats that require multi-faceted and highly orchestrated retaliations.

THE NEED FOR NEW MODELS

The field of instructional design recognizes that no one instructional strategy or approach fits all instructional design situations. Why then would designers accept or advocate that one design model fits all instructional development situations? As we learn more about how people learn, how information is reconstructed in new situations, and how technology-applications can be used to replace outdated instructional strategies, the need for a variety of models becomes readily apparent.

The Systemic Business Model

Michael Porter (1985) posits a conceptual business model that is more closely applicable to the total process of the military training system. The Value Chain (see Figure 4) identifies the strategically important activities and the interrelationships. The model's components are categorized into two major divisions, that of primary activities and support activities.

Primary activities include all stages, which deal with the physical creation of the product, its delivery to customers, and follow-up activities, e.g., customer service. Primary activities are further subdivided into subsystems including:

Figure 4: The Value Chain

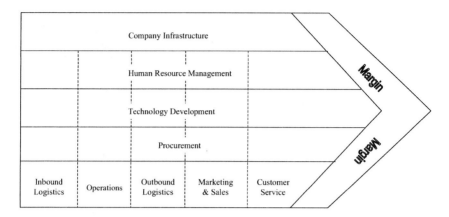

- Inbound Logistics: receiving, storing, scheduling, etc. In other words, this stage houses a variety of inputs.
- Operations: transforming inputs into final products.
- Outbound Logistics: collecting, storing, and physically distributing products.
- Marketing and Sales: providing customers (end users) with information about products.
- Customer Service: enhancing or maintaining the value of the product.

Support activities are the major components of the company, e.g., purchasing, technology, human resources, etc. Margin (value) is the difference between total value and the collective cost of performing value activities (Markland, Vickery, & Davis, 1995). Within the model, the dotted lines indicate associations between components. The value of the model is its ability to portray the associations or linkages between component activities and the identification of the trade-offs that may be made within the company. For example: design vs. cost; delivery vs. operations; human resources vs. customer service.

By using the Value Chain Model, a production team can examine the linkages between company components and make recommendations for strategic or competitive advantages. Quite often teams are asked to study a particular issue and find a solution. Without a model, such as the Value Chain, the impact of a great idea, which may solve a problem in one area, may actually generate a greater problem in another area.

The Systemic Business Process Model is a derivative of the previous model (see Figure 5). It incorporates instructional design guidance from the original PADDIE, recognizes the need for continuous improvement, and addresses the interrelationships needed for product development. Two components set the model apart from the previous discussion. Central to the model's functionality is the concept of data collaboration through the use of the reusability architectures. Unique to the model is the recognition of a continuous search for the definitive departures from the current means of doing business. Continuous process improvement seeks to improve the current process through various iterations. The definitive departure mandates looking away from the current process and using radical methods such as benchmarking or experimentation to improve the process. The model is more akin to business process reengineering than to quality improvement. The repositioning of the vertical lines from the Value Chain reflects the synergistic nature and impact of each identifiable component on the whole.

The Enterprise Infrastructure serves as the foundation to the model. The Navy, as a complete system, determines the way in which the individual commands and activities within the system do business. Those individual commands and activities, then in turn, determine how departments and further subsystems conduct business. Resource Management, either at the Enterprise or local level, impacts product development. Personnel shortages, collateral duties, and individuals in positions without required skills impact the system at three levels: User, System, and Development.

For the User, technology may be readily available. In that case, having interactive courseware products or accessibility to the Web may be important.

Figure 5: The Systemic Business Process Model

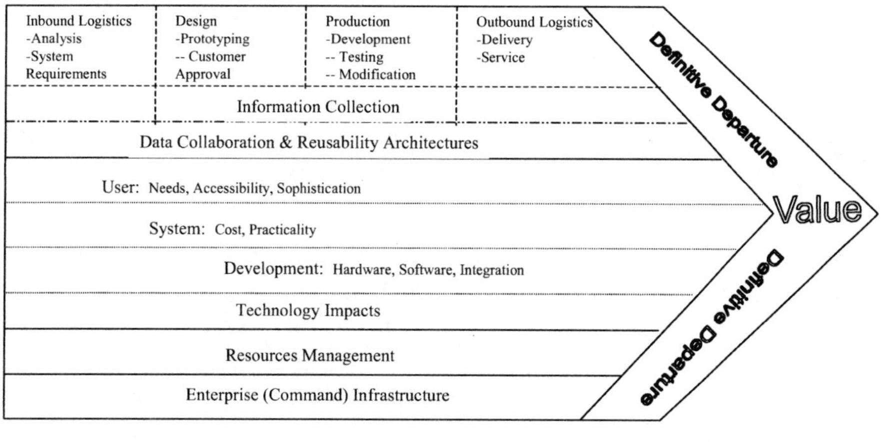

On the other hand, if the User lacks accessibility, then products, which are print-based, are needed. However, print-based products no longer necessarily result in a bound copy of a book. Excerpts, Portable Document Format (PDF) files, chapters, or condensed versions may better address the need of the User more adequately and efficiently than the traditional book. The User's sophistication with computer technology is a major factor as well. Training and experience with technology may impact the effectiveness of the electronic product.

The System, its features, and cost may well determine how technology integrates into the complete infrastructure.

Just in the last year, the Navy has switched to an Integrated Learning Environment and has addressed the need for system-wide support and compatibility of products. However, the dark cloud of cost looms on any one command's horizon. The needs of the Fleet are greater in the areas of mission readiness and capability than in computer accessibility for the individual sailor. Practicality plays upon the system as well. If one thinks in terms of larger carriers, computer rooms should be standard features. However, major players within the Enterprise are small vessels less than 250 feet in length. There's no room for a learning resource center. Laptops, while meeting the needs, are expensive and pose their own problems to the system.

Developments within the science of computer technology, multimedia, and telecommunications probably have the greatest impact on design, development, and distribution of content. Before a production group can create and develop an idea, conduct a prototype, evaluate its effectiveness, and produce a product, Navy warfighting technology, the subject of the content, has changed. The business model must address how a production team can create and produce quality products in fluid environments.

The upper portion of the Systemic Business Model combines the PADDIE and Porter's Value Chain models. The Primary Activities are elaborated by incorporating Porter's practical nature of the business with the traditional instructional design stages. Information, rather than evaluation, is collected throughout the process. That information collection may alter the primary activities at any given stage rather than waiting for specific input or output times.

Data Collaboration is conducted at an Enterprise as well as command-specific level in order to reduce development time and associated costs. Reusability architectures (learning content management systems) capitalize on centrally warehousing data for use by the total Enterprise.

Value, in the Systemic Business Model, is that product or service provided to the Enterprise (the Fleet) which is better, cheaper, faster, or stronger than the competition. In the business of military training, the competition is the training production unit, itself, and its current means of doing business. Again, it is the recognition of the need for definitive departure that brings about value and regenerates the model.

Technology-Based Content Models

During the mid-'90s members of the Department of Defense tackled the problem of lack of interoperability between computer-based systems. Some reading this chapter may recall when Macs and PCs refused to communicate. Software programs built for one did not communicate with the other. Imagine the havoc this created in federal agencies as large as the Department of Defense.

In 1997 the Department of Defense established the Advanced Distributed Learning (ADL) organization. Its primary purpose is to identify and recommend standardization of education and training technologies, and to promote cooperation between government, industry, and academia. The first and foremost contribution ADL has made to the world of technology-based learning has been the definition of the five "-ilities":

- Interoperability — can the system work with other systems?
- Reusability — can the modules of content (learning objects or chunks) be reused in other topics?
- Manageability — can a system track the appropriate information about the learner and the content?
- Accessibility — can a learner access the appropriate content at the appropriate time?
- Durability — will the technology evolve with the standards to avoid obsolescence?

Furthermore, this initiative has led to the design and development model of shareable objects. While heralded by developers as new and innovative, instructional designers have long recognized the value of object-based design. Just as a good paper has a beginning, middle, and end, so should an instructional object, in whatever form it takes, have a well-written beginning, middle, and end. To ensure that training and education content could be shared across the services, the ADL established the Shareable Content Object Reference Model (SCORM). This model serves as the foundation to all content development and delivery. Content built following SCORM guidelines ensures interoperability, reusability, and manageability. By adopting SCORM guidelines, the DOD reduces the dollars spent on repetitive or redundant efforts which were necessary to achieve one or more of these three "-ilities".

SCORM Utilization Model

The instructional product, content, is no longer one comprehensive and single entity. The content of now and of the future is an amalgamation of content pieces taken from a variety of sources and assembled as needed based on the requirements. Figure 6 illustrates how content objects from one development effort may be shared across related fields.

To return to the opening scenario, the impact of SCORM would play-out in the following way. A number of computer-based development contracts have been written: a familiarization program on the E-2C Hawkeye; the manufacturer's training program for its maintenance teams on turbine engine repair and replacement; an interactive electronic training manual on turbine engines; and an interactive manual for aviation maintenance teams. While each development effort has a primary audience and purpose, they all share information in common and all have been developed following the guidance of the ADL and the SCORM. PO3 Smith has access to each of these programs either through the ship's LAN or via the Internet. As noted in the scenario, he relies not just on one body of information, but on several. To effectively utilize the content, he has merely to call up the files on his computer or on his PDA. The software development nuances no longer drive or limit the content usage.

The QFD Product Development Model

Quality Function Deployment has its roots in manufacturing as a design quality tool. Yoji Akao first conceptualized it in 1966 as an approach to new

Figure 6: The Shareable Content Object Reference Model

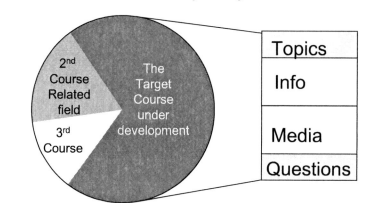

product development and concurrent engineering where customer requirements were integrated into product design (Akao, 1990). John Hauser and Don Clausing of Harvard University brought QFD into the mainstream of the quality movement in the United States in 1988. Hauser and Clausing used the phrase "House of Quality" to describe the modular building process for the QFD matrix in a manner similar to adding features to a house (Hauser & Clausing, 1988). The procedure is extremely well documented in the literature. QFD remains a mainstream quality technique as evidenced by the recent article in the *Quality Management Journal* by Richardson, Murphy, and Ryan (2002). These authors offer a generic QFD methodology for software process improvement.

In competitive market environments, a successful product is one that is perceived by the customer as being of high quality. This quality imperative compels producers to make every effort to make their product possess the attributes desired by the customer. Quality Function Deployment (QFD) is an analytic technique used to insure that products meet customer requirements and preferences. The QFD procedure systematically matches customer requirements and preferences with production requirements, capabilities, and constraints. The result is a product that can be efficiently and cost effectively produced, while fully satisfying the customer.

Training systems developers also strive to produce high-quality products in their product engineering efforts. Their goal is to produce instructional products that are efficient in their implementation, cost effective, and that quickly and fully satisfy the needs of the customer or stakeholders. This means that to produce a high-quality instructional product that supports high performance capabilities, training system developers must fully integrate learner and system needs as well as the needs of the learner's future work environment with instructional design requirements.

Traditional instructional design methodologies provide for the identification of training requirements, address the needs of the learner, and articulate strategies to achieve the required level of training. However, traditional design models tend to be sequential and do not dynamically integrate the different aspects of the training development process from the stakeholder requirement perspective. QFD offers a method that dynamically links and integrates stakeholder needs, training system requirements, and design considerations. QFD also helps designers correlate and identify tradeoffs between the different design elements and insures that all stakeholder needs are met.

The Stakeholder as the Key to Success

A key element of producing a high-quality training product is the ability of the training systems development process to recognize and accommodate stakeholder needs. Stakeholders are described in the Baldridge Award for Education criteria as entities that benefit from quality education. These stakeholders are usually the student, the institution charged with the educational mission, and the future environment of the learner. In the military context, there are three types of stakeholders involved in any training systems development effort.

The first stakeholder is the individual who acquires the skills and capabilities to perform his or her job within the operational system and environment. This stakeholder expects a "doable" and effective training environment, accomplished in a reasonable time frame that equips him or her with skills necessary to achieve success in the "real world." The individual may be concerned with issues beyond the immediate training goals such as his or her ability to perform in the pressures of a real environment, ability to perform with others, and preparation for further skill acquisition and advancement.

The second stakeholder is the future employer or command who relies on the training system to develop the requisite level of competency in the leaner to enable the learner to perform his or her jobs. The needs of this stakeholder can be far ranging and can include skills throughout the environmental spectrum from the individual through various organizational levels to the social context (ISPI, 2002).

The third stakeholder is the training agent of the service. This is the organization charged with the training mission and who is responsible for the efficient and cost-effective operation of the training system. Competency requirements, time to train, training effectiveness, overhead or infrastructure costs, technology, and other considerations are issues of concern for this stakeholder.

Each of these stakeholders has a unique set of needs and expectations that must be addressed in the training systems design effort. The following description of the QFD process will demonstrate how stakeholder needs can be identified, integrated into the design process, and tracked through the development process.

THE QFD PROCESS

The Quality Function Deployment technique is a graphic-based process based on one or more matrices that show the relationships between stakeholder requirements and various design elements. One advantage of the QFD technique is that there is no specific form that must be followed, although the matrix approach is most common. Also, the QFD process is flexible and encourages innovative thinking to tackle the many problems encountered with designing an instructional product that satisfies all the stakeholders. This makes the process adaptable and easy to use for any situation.

Step 1: Identifying Stakeholder Requirements and Instructional Imperatives

The starting point for the QFD process is the identification of the customer or stakeholder needs and requirements. These requirements are stated as simply as possible and represent the stakeholders' desired attributes of the instructional product.

The next task is to identify instructional imperatives (such as strategies, technologies, delivery methods, constraints, or other design considerations) that accommodate the stakeholder requirement.

The stakeholder requirements and instructional imperatives are generated by brainstorming or some similar approach. It is important to maintain a stakeholder focus throughout the process.

The initial matrix will consist of the stakeholder requirements listed down the left-hand side as row labels, and the instructional imperatives listed across the top as column headings (see Figure 7). The cells in the body of the matrix formed by the rows and columns will be used later for a relational analysis in Step 2.

There are some general rules for this step:

1.   For each listed requirement, there should be at least one corresponding instructional imperative that will satisfy the requirement.

Figure 7: Basic Starting QFD Matrix

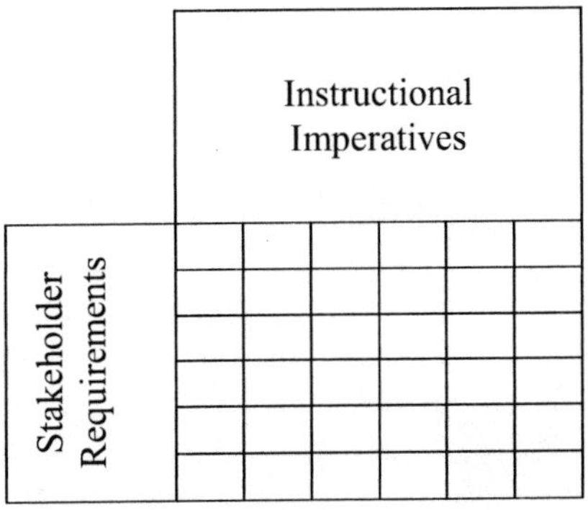

2.   There can be more than one imperative to accommodate a requirement, and a single imperative may accommodate more than one requirement.
3.   There should not be any requirement that is not accommodated by at least one imperative.
4.   An instructional imperative may stand alone as a needed design consideration not related to a specific requirement.

A detailed analysis of the relationships between the stakeholder requirements and instructional imperatives is conducted in Step 2.

Figure 8 depicts the most basic initial matrix. The row and column categories can be further broken down in order to better represent the different needs and requirements for the different stakeholders. For the military training environment, each of the three stakeholders previously mentioned can be represented individually by decomposing the general stakeholder requirements and listing the respective requirements according to the category (see Figure 8). This helps the designer organize and track the specific considerations throughout the design process.

In a similar manner, the instructional imperatives can be further classified (see Figure 9). Since the instructional imperatives are identified in order to accommodate stakeholder requirements, they can be organized according to types of instructional considerations such as instructional strategies, technologies, system capabilities, etc.

The organization shown here is for the purpose of demonstration only. Each circumstance will require a unique organization suited to the situation at

Figure 8: Decomposed Stakeholder Requirements

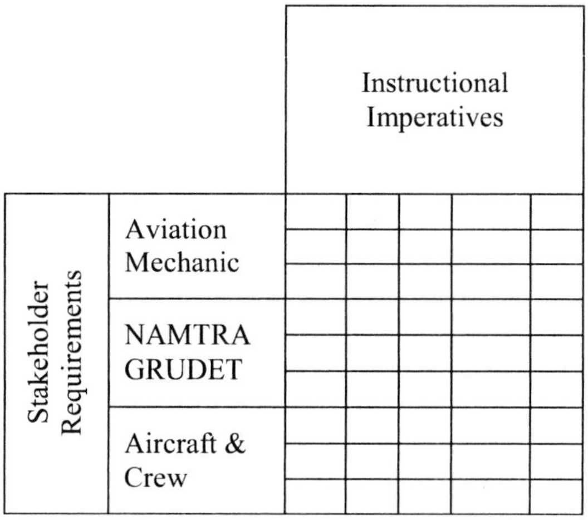

Figure 9: Decomposed Instructional Imperatives

		Instructional Imperatives					
		Strategies			Technology		
Stakeholder Requirements	Individual						
	Command						
	System						

hand. Clearly, these matrices can become extensive and cumbersome. When this occurs, individual starting matrices can be constructed for each stakeholder category.

A Simple Example

Assume a training center, Naval Aviation Maintenance Training Group Detachment (NAMTRAGRUDET), is reengineering an engine repair course. A learner analysis has been conducted, and the top three needs identified by the learners (entry-level mechanics) are computer-facilitated lessons, practical exercises with actual equipment, and a short course duration. The commands (the aviation crews) that will employ the course graduates want skilled technicians that are familiar with the equipment used in the field. Finally, the training center wants to automate the course as much as possible to reduce cost, minimize time to train, and attain higher achieved competency levels. This information might yield the initial matrix shown in Figure 10.

The use of technology is a clear imperative in this case. Instructional strategies designed to provide realistic training, teach team troubleshooting and problem solving, and reduce training time are also indicated. Training consistency is also needed to provide a standard training product.

Step 2: Assessing Relationships Between Stakeholder Requirements and Instructional Imperatives

Once the stakeholder requirements and instructional imperatives are identified, the designer needs to assess the nature and strength of relationships between all requirements and instructional imperatives. The purpose of this step

Figure 10: Sample Matrix

| | | | Instructional Imperatives | | | | |
| | | | Strategies | | | Technology | |
		Requirements	Practical Exercises	Team skills	Fast paced	Current equipment	CBT System
Stakeholder Requirements	Individual	Computer-based					
		Practical training					
		Short course time					
	Cmd	High competency					
		Currency					
	System	Automation					
		Short time to train					
		Increase competency level					

is to identify the specific links between the stakeholder requirements and instructional imperatives and to determine the importance of each instructional imperative to the different requirements. The result of this assessment is useful for prioritizing the instructional imperatives and conducting trade-off analyses later.

This assessment is accomplished by assigning a measure of correlation to each cell formed by the column-row intersection of the stakeholder requirements and instructional imperatives. In the simplest form, the measure of correlation can be indicated by symbols such as a "+" for a positive relationship where the imperative is needed for the requirement, a "0" for no relationship between an imperative and a particular requirement, and a "-" for a negative relationship where an imperative may interfere with satisfying a requirement. There can be any scheme for this assessment. When quantitative data are available, actual correlation values can be calculated and inserted into the cells.

Example Continued

Working through the previous matrix (see Figure 10) might yield the result shown in Figure 11.

The relationship indicators in the matrix cells reveal that there appear to be some imperatives that are needed for some stakeholder requirements, not for others, and might be detrimental for some. Every requirement is supported by at least two imperatives (indicated by the "+"), but every requirement also has

Figure 11: QFD Matrix with Correlations

		Requirements	Strategies			Technology	
			Practical Exercises	Team skills	Fast paced	Current eqpmnt	CBT System
Stakeholder Requirements	Individual	Computer-based	-	-	+	0	+
		Practical training	+	+	-	+	-
		Shorten course time	0	-	+	0	+
	Cmd	High competency	+	+	-	+	+
		Currency	+	0	0	+	+
	System	Automation	-	-	+	+	+
		Reduce time to train	-	-	+	0	+
		Increase competency level	+	+	-	+	+

at least one imperative that might interfere (the "-" indications). Other observations might include that the use of a CBT system as an instructional imperative appears to support the most requirements, teaching team skills might be most problematic in accommodating other requirements, and using current equipment will not negatively effect any requirement. Such a relational analysis helps the designer "see" the big picture, identify conflicts and problems, and point to critical instructional imperatives.

Step 3: Examining Relationships Among Instructional Imperatives

This step and the remaining steps are in a sense optional. Some applications of the QFD involve steps or aspects not addressed here. Additional steps are analytical and employed to achieve specific purposes depending on the situation.

Once instructional imperatives are identified, it is often helpful to examine the relationships, if any, among the imperatives. In the latter stages of a project, decisions to eliminate non-essential imperatives can be better supported when all the relationships between the imperatives are understood. This can preclude eliminating an imperative that is critically linked to an essential imperative and that would diminish the effectiveness of the essential imperative if it is eliminated.

Example Continued

The partial matrix (see Figure 12) provides an example of one approach to a relational analysis among instructional imperatives. The "roof" of the house of quality matrix shows where the designer evaluated the relationships between each pair of imperatives and used the simple method of indicating a positive relationship with a "+", no relationship with a "0", and a negative relationship with a "-." Again, more sophisticated schemes, including quantitative, can be developed to describe the relationships in order to meet the needs of the situation.

In this example, team skills and practical exercises are related. If a decision is made to eliminate practical exercises, then team skills will likely suffer in this situation. Since the designer has identified a negative relationship between practical exercises and fast-paced instruction, if practical exercises are not included in the instruction, this might speed up the time to train in this situation.

At this point, the QFD matrix helps the designer track the accommodation of the stakeholder requirements with various instructional approaches and shows potential trade-off implications in setting the optimal mix of instructional imperatives.

Step 4: Evaluating Stakeholder Needs and Requirements

The fourth step normally involves evaluating how the existing system is accommodating the stakeholder requirements and possibly how competing

Figure 12: Partial QFD Matrix Showing Relationships Between Imperatives

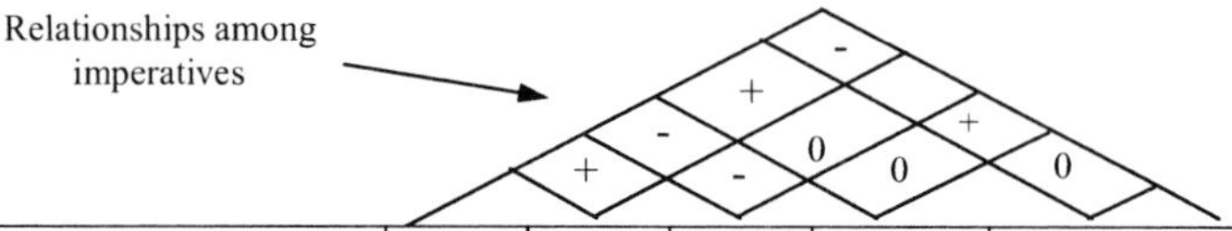

Instructional Imperatives	Practical Exercises	Team Skills	Fast Paced	Current Eqpt.	CBT System
Computer-based	-	-	+	0	+
Practical training	+	+	-	+	-
Short course time	0	-	+	0	+
High competency	+	+	-	+	+
Currency	+	0	0	+	+
Automation	-	-	+	+	+
Short time to train	-	-	+	0	+
Increase competency level	+	+	-	+	+

Figure 13: QFD Matrix with Stakeholder Requirements Evaluation Section

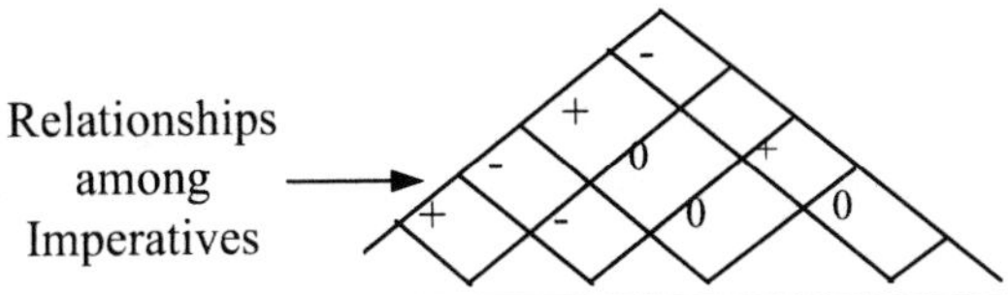

Imperatives / Requirements	Practical Exercises	Team skills	Fast paced	Current Equipment	CBT System	Rating X – Current A – Alt. A B – Alt. B Better →
Computer-based	-	-	+	0	+	X A B
Practical training	+	+	-	+	-	B A X
Short course time	0	-	+	0	+	X A B
High competency	+	+	-	+	+	A X B
Currency	+	0	0	+	+	A X B
Automation	-	-	+	+	+	X A B
Short time to train	-	-	+	0	+	X A B
Increase competency level	+	+	-	+	+	X A B

designs may accommodate the requirements. In terms of the matrix, the designer can create a "porch" that can be used to register a rating scheme that evaluates the existing system or compares the existing system to other alternatives. Figure 13 demonstrates this capability.

In this example, the designer has found a way to evaluate how well each of three alternatives satisfies each requirement. A simple rank-order method is used here to rank each alternative in relation to the others. These comparative evaluations can be very sophisticated based on the nature and extent of data collected for the evaluation. Numerical scales like Likert scales or "snake" diagrams can be used as well if the rating data can be quantified. In this case, it appears that option B best accommodates all the requirements but one. Such evaluations allow decision-makers to compare alternative systems at a glance.

Step 5: Value Analysis of Instructional Imperatives

Each instructional imperative that is included in the training product has a value such as cost, return on investment, time to train impact, etc. A cost figure or some other value or factor representation can be calculated for each

Figure 14: QFD Matrix with Value Analysis for Instructional Imperatives

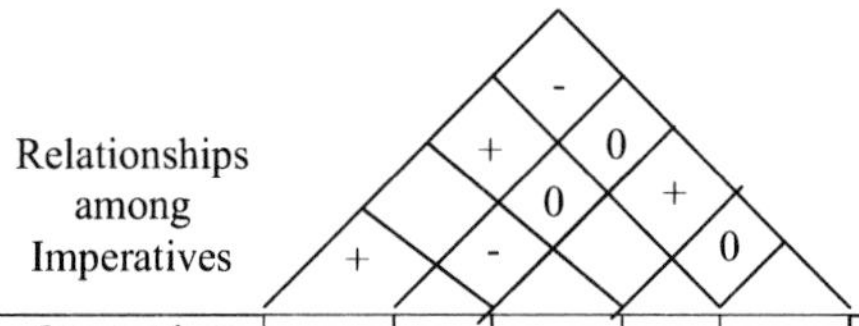

Imperatives / Requirements	Practical Exercises	Team skills	Fast paced	Current equipment	CBT System	Rating X – Current A – Alt. A B – Alt. B Better
Computer-based	-	-	+	0	+	X A B
Practical training	+	+	-	+	-	B A X
Short course time	0	-	+	0	+	X A B
High competency	+	+	-	+	+	A X B
Currency	+	0	0	+	+	A X B
Automation	-	-	+	+	+	X A B
Short time to train	-	-	+	0	+	X A B
Increase competency level	+	+	-	+	+	X A B
Value Analysis ($100K)	4	2	5	3	9	Total 23

imperative. This valuation is normally displayed in the "basement" of the house of quality as shown in Figure 14.

Example Continued

In this example, the designer has developed a dollar figure for the implementation of each instructional imperative for the given situation. The value analysis indicates that if all imperatives are implemented, the total cost would be $2,300,000. Additionally, the relative cost of each imperative can be easily seen. This figure becomes the baseline for efforts to reduce costs while accommodating the stakeholder requirements.

Expanding the Matrix

The QFD Matrix can be tailored to any variety of analytical needs. For more complex situations, a separate matrix can be developed for the different elements being considered in order to keep the matrices manageable. In complex systems a single category of stakeholder requirements may generate a matrix with hundreds of requirement-imperative combinations. Separate matrices can be initiated for each category of stakeholder. Likewise, a separate matrix can be created for each category of instructional imperative. For example, technology issues are usually complex and may be best handled by creating a technology matrix to develop the optimal application of technology characteristics that best accommodate stakeholder requirements related to technology.

Follow-on Matrices

So far, the matrix representing the relationship between stakeholder requirements and instructional imperatives has been examined. Once the instructional imperatives have been selected, a new matrix can be created with the instructional imperatives listed as the rows and specific instructional strategies listed as the columns (see Figure 15).

Figure 15: Instructional Imperative — Strategies Matrix

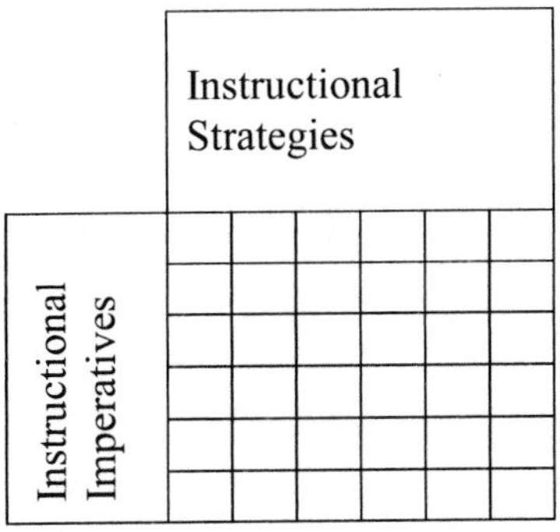

If needed, another matrix can be created with the specific instructional strategies listed as the rows, and the requisite instructional tools and design elements listed as columns (see Figure 16). Yet another matrix might be a set up for examining the relationships between instructional strategies and learner strategies. Each follow-on matrix will be constructed in the form needed to support the analytic goals.

Figure 16: Instructional Strategies — Tools Matrix

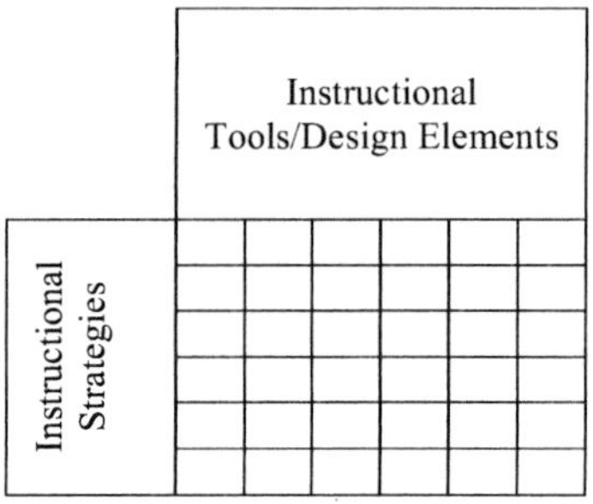

Figure 17 demonstrates yet another variation of the QFD matrix. This matrix is designed to evaluate tradeoffs among technology considerations in the context of comparing three competing systems. The ultimate outcome is a quantified cost factor for each alternative weighted by the importance of the learner requirement and the relative quality score for each alternative.

Figure 17. Technology Allocation Matrix

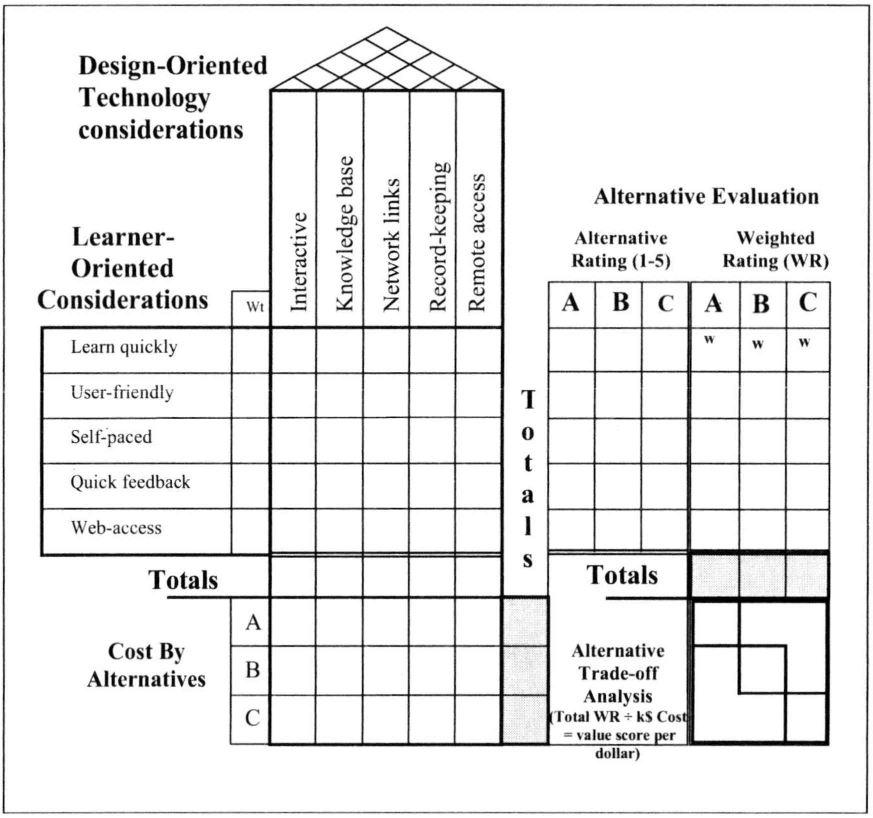

The current methodology for developing instructional products is the tendency to allow design to drive the product rather than the stakeholder needs and requirements. Only by starting with the stakeholder needs and requirements, basing the design on these needs and requirements, and tracking the needs and requirement all the way through the design process, will the instructional product succeed. Quality Function Deployment is a simple, flexible, and easy-to-manage procedure that will allow everyone involved in the project to instantly see the design structure and track the accommodation of the stakeholders' needs and requirements.

Return-on-Investment Model

"Kill Ratios" and "Bombs on Target" do not come to mind when most instructional designers think about Kirkpatrick's four levels, but they are indeed valid metrics within the U.S. Navy. In reality, virtually any metric found within the civilian world is replicated somewhere within the military community, including such domains as production, logistics, education, training, and medicine. Even sales and marketing have military applications, as any Navy recruiter can attest.

Recent Navy efforts are focused on "Human Performance" and associated tasks, training and metrics. Traditional training metrics such as reduced time to train, reduced academic attrition (called "non-graduates" within the Navy, to differentiate between academic and discipline or physical attrite), and reduced travel costs are still an important part of any business case made for a training transformation. Other potential metrics, such as maintenance hours per aircraft, safety incidents, and tracking of potentially hostile submarines, have been measured for years, if not decades. The difficulty in using such metrics as these lies not in obtaining the required data, but in determining how much if any change, either positive or negative, can be attributed to training.

To determine a return on investment (ROI) on training technology investments, a baseline must be established from which future measures of effectiveness (MOEs) can be evaluated. Elements of such a baseline include, but are not limited to:

Quantitative Elements
- Technology (hardware/software/courseware) investments
- Learners
  - Student throughput
  - Student attrition

- Test scores
- Setback rate
- Graduation rate
- Transient account time (dead time in training pipeline)
- Facilities
  - Classrooms/labs/billeting
  - Related overhead
  - Training time (course length)
  - Instructor-to-student ratio (related salaries)

Qualitative Elements
- Technology
  - Student and instructor comfort levels or expertise
- Learners
  - Student evaluations
- Facilities
  - Environmental factors, modernization, lighting, heating, etc.
- Related overhead
  - Lab evaluation marks
  - Surge period, double-shifts, reduced access to technology
  - Remedial training opportunities

Implementation and use of the training MOE elements will rely heavily on the access to and ease of data manipulation. Each of the above quantitative elements can be accessed electronically and is updated as a matter of course within the Navy training communities. The technology baseline information is available via the Office of Training Technology's (OTT SPIDER) website, where each school is required to enter their technology data. With the exception of the instructor-to-student ratios and facility costs, the remaining elements can be gleaned from the Navy's corporate database tracking systems, with cross-checks available from systems such as Bureau of Personnel (BUPERS) officer and enlisted assignment databases (these databases track personnel by time spent at each unit identification code assigned to Navy commands, such as the training organizations).

Planned rather than real instructor-to-student ratios can be determined by comparing instructor (planned), or actual onboard count (real), to the student throughput quotas (planned versus actual) contained in the corporate database. The instructor count is an important factor, as the costs associated with each instructor billet (salary, benefits, moving costs — all available from BUPERS) are a major factor in computing cost savings, with equivalent student data important in computing savings resulting from reduced travel time.

Facility costs can be taken from efficiency review data, unit operating costs, or liaison with the command.

CONCLUSION

This chapter has presented a number of models that currently exist in the military instructional design world or business arenas and proposes new models as well. What is needed in the realm of learning technology for large systems (military and corporate) is an integrated approach which views professional military training from a business perspective as well as a training evolution. By examining the best practices of both worlds and building upon those methodologies, we can improve the business of military training, thereby improving effectiveness for the learner and reducing cost to the taxpayer.

REFERENCES

Akao, Y. (1990). *Quality Function Deployment: Integrating Customer Requirements into Product Design* (translated by Glenn H. Mauser). Productivity Press.

Cebrowski, VADM A.K. (1998). *Network-Centric Warfare: Its Origin and Future.* Available online at: http://www.usni.org/Proceedings/Articles98/PROcebrowski.htm.

Franceschini, F. & Terzago, M. (1998). An application of quality function deployment to industrial training courses. *International Journal of Quality,* 15(7), 753-768.

Hammer, M. & Champy, J. (1993). *Reengineering: The Path to Change.* New York: HarperBusiness.

Hauser, J.R. & Clausing, D. (1988). The house of quality. *Harvard Business Review,* 66(May/June), 63-73.

Hayes, R.H., Wheelwright, S.C., & Clark, K.B. (1988). *Dynamic Manufacturing.* New York: The Free Press.

Markland, R.E., Vickery, S.K., & Davis, R.A. (1995). *Operations Management: Concepts in Manufacturing and Services* (2nd ed). Cincinnati, OH: South-Western.

MIL-HNDBK-1379-D (1996). *Instructional Systems Development Process.* Department of Defense.

Richardson, I., Murphy, E., & Ryan, K. (2002). Development of a generic quality function deployment matrix. *Quality Management Journal,* 9(2), 25-37.

Wallace, G.W. (2001). *T & D Systems View*. Napperville, IL: Caddi Press.

Appendix Section

APPENDIX A
LEARNER ANALYSIS

Part I
Learner Characteristics
    Education:
    Experience Level:
    Affiliations:
    Certifications:

Part II
Pre-Assessment Tests
    Aptitude Tests:
    Learning Style:

Part III
Job Performance Characteristics or Requirements:

		Required	Recommended
Reading Level			
Lifting			
Visual acuity			
Hearing level			
Dexterity			

Part IV
Subject Matter Expert _____

Contact: _____

Expert Users: _____

Novice Users: _____

APPENDIX B
TASK ANALYSIS

Task Description and Name:

Goal:			
Subgoal(s):			
Date:	Time:	Shift:	Shift Length:
Task Length:	Number of Tasks/Hour:	Number of Tasks/Shift:	Interval between Tasks:
Pace of Task: Self-Paced ● Fixed: ● Variable ●			
Peer Interaction:			
Supervisor Interactions:			
Preceding Task:		Succeeding Task:	

Task Demands:

Perceptual Skills: Visual ● Audio ● Tactile ●   Requirements:
Motor Skills: Fine ● Gross ● Discrete ● Continuous ●   Requirements:
Cognitive Skills: Recall ● Compare ● Code/decode ● Analyze ● Estimate ●   Predict ● Evaluate ● Decide ●   Notes:
Background Knowledge Requirements:
Tools Used:
Machines Used:
Manuals, book, and/or documents used:

Task Demands (continued):

Attention Demands: High ● Medium ● Low ●
Criticality: High ● Medium ● Low ●
General Notes:

Job Task/Skills Analysis

Duty: _____

Task: _____

Interview and plant tour with manager, Training Specialist,
Training Manager, and Shop Leads. _____
Date _____

Operation: Actions essential to performing the task and subtasks.
➢ **_Action 1** _____
• sub 1 _____
• sub 2 _____
•
➢ **_Action 2** _____
• sub 1 _____
• sub 2 _____
•
➢ **_Action 3** _____
• sub 1 _____
• sub 2 _____

• Tasks observed performed on the floor:

- _____
- _____
- _____
- _____
- _____
- _____

➢   Available technical manuals, manufacturer publications, position descriptions, job standards, etc.

Note titles: _____

_____

Knowledge: Prerequisite learning necessary before one can perform any of the task elements.

1)Completion of classroom instruction in _____

2)Safety precautions to be enforced on the shop floor _____

3)Required inventories, special activities, etc. _____

4)Documentation and record keeping _____

5)Safety violations and notification of proper authority _____

Sequencing of task(s) _____

_____

_____

Decision points in process _____

_____

Possible safety hazards or issues _____

_____

_____

Common or unintended errors or problems, slips _____

_____

Critical incidents _____

Training need identified by Subject Matter Expert _____

Training need identified by Management _____

Training need identified by operator _____

•Number of personnel requiring training: approximately _____

•The target audience _____

•Identification of existing documentation or courseware _____

- Certifications Needed _____

- Currencies Required _____

Job Demands/Skill Analysis (Alternative Form)

Task:

Goal:			
Subgoal:			
Date:			
Time:			
Shift length:			
Cycle length:			
Interval between cycles:			
Pace:	Self:	Fixed:	Varied:
Micro-breaks	Duration:	Interval:	
Supervisor support	On call:	On Floor:	
Change off position			

Operator:

Perceptual Skills:	Visual:	Audio:	Tactile:	
Motor Skills required:	Discrete:		Continuous:	
Cognitive Skills required	Compare:	Analyze:	Decode:	Recall:
	Predict:	Estimate:	Evaluate:	Decide:
Hard Key Use				
Soft Key Use				
Protocol Use:				
Screens used:	X-Ray		CT Scan	
Attention demands:	Detail:			
Situation Awareness:	Detail:			

APPENDIX C
INTERVIEW/QUESTIONNAIRE

1. What is your educational background?
2. How long have you been doing this job?
3. Where else have you done this work?
4. Do you have any certifications or affiliations?
5. What training programs or courses did you take that prepared you for this job?
6. What parts of the training program prepared you for this job?
7. Was there something that the training program could have done better?
8. What information do you have now that you could have used when you first started working?
9. Are there any special requirements for this position?
10. Are there any safety procedures that need to be followed?
11. What would be the ideal physical conditions for this job?
12. Are there any physical changes that would make your job easier or more effective?
13. What are the usual tasks associated with your position?
14. Where do you go for help when you need it to do your job?
15. What is the hardest part of this job?
16. What is the easiest part of this job?
17. What is your favorite part of this job?
18. What helps you to do a good job?
    Tools:
    Job aids:
    Peers:
    Supervisor:
    Other:

19. Is there anything that interferes with your doing your job?
20. Was there ever a time when you could not do your job? What happened?
21. What is it that makes this job different from other similar jobs or from other shifts?
22. If you could change this job, how would you do it?
23. Is there anything about this job that makes you feel special?
24. Is there another job that you would rather be doing? What is it?

APPENDIX D
ENVIRONMENTAL ANALYSIS

Organization _____

Type of Work Performed _____

Work Schedule(s) _____

Shifts _____

Management by:

    Staff Relationship ❏ Line Relationship ❏ Project Relationship ❏

Quality Control Procedures:

    Physical Conditions, Barriers, or Constraints

    Air quality

    Noise

    Temperature/humidity

    Lighting

    Floor space

Physical or Cognitive Requirements:

Communication Requirements:

    Peers

    Supervisors

    Security

    Departments

    Barriers that might impede, delay, or cause the operation to be halted and/or abandoned as the task(s) are being performed:.

    Visual and oral direction(s) or alerts used for safety, technical, or other reasons:

    Frequency of the task/subtask (weekly, daily, hourly, etc.):

    Teaming, partnering requirements:

    Shift differences:

    Time or coordination requirements:

    Concurrent events:

APPENDIX E
GOAL ANALYSIS

Part I — Performance Needed

What will performer do to complete the task according to:	
Subject Matter Expert?	
Management?	
Operator?	
Other?	

Part II — Performance Gap

What are identified performance improvement needs according to:	
Subject Matter Expert?	
Management?	
Operator?	
Other?	
What is the performance discrepancy according to:	
Subject Matter Expert?	
Management?	
Operator?	
Other?	
How will training improve performance according to:	
Subject Matter Expert?	
Management?	
Operator?	
Other?	

Part III — Other Changes Identified

What environmental changes are needed according to:	
Subject Matter Expert?	
Management?	
Operator?	
Other?	
What motivational changes are needed according to:	
Subject Matter Expert?	
Management?	
Operator?	
Other?	
How information needs to be disseminated according to:	
Subject Matter Expert?	
Management?	
Operator?	
Other?	

APPENDIX F
MATERIALS EVALUATION

Reviewer: Evaluate the instructional materials used in the training session.

Instructional Materials	Yes	No	Comments
Are the objects stated clearly?			
Do the learning activities meet the objectives?			
Is the content organized in a practical sequence?			
Is the course content geared to the level of the intended audience?			
Is there sufficient time to cover the material to meet the course objectives?			
Are the course materials up-to-date?			
Does the material hold the learner's interest?			
Is the material technically and procedurally correct?			
Do reviews measure whether the objectives have been met?			
Does the material use appropriate examples and illustrations?			
Does the material tie in with the OJT activities?			

APPENDIX G
OJT EVALUATION

Reviewer: Evaluate the on-the-job training session.

On-the-Job (OJT) training	Yes	No	Comments or Not Applicable
Was the OJT structured			
Were the complex tasks broken down into smaller chunks or steps for easier practice and learning?			
Were all the action steps included?			
Did the instructor model the task both wholistically and in part steps?			
Did the instructor provide job aids, memory aids, etc. ?			
Did the instructor relate the task to the trainee's prior experiences?			
Did the instructor clearly answer questions?			
Were decision points covered and discussed?			
Was the feedback both positive and negative?			
Was the feedback specific?			
Did the learner understand the feedback?			
Was there sufficient opportunity for hands-on practice?			
Was the practiced task performed under realistic conditions?			
Did the trainee have enough opportunity to practice and perform?			

APPENDIX H
CLASSROOM INSTRUCTION EVALUATION

Reviewer: Evaluate the instruction in the classroom.

Does the instructor . . .	Yes	No	Comments or Not Applicable
Have a good command of the subject matter?			
Have good rapport with the trainees?			
Have good oral communication skills?			
Tailor the content to the audience?			
Did the instructor provide job aids, memory aids, etc. ?			
Use appropriate examples and illustrations?			
Provide clear answers to questions?			
Give trainees opportunity to practice or apply what they are learning?			
Give constructive feedback as needed? Was the feedback specific? Did the learner understand the feedback?			
Tie learning activities back to topic or lesson objectives?			
Hold the trainees' attention?			
Was there sufficient opportunity for hands-on practice?			

APPENDIX I
QA FORM FOR CBT

Program _____

Module _____

Topic _____

Screen # _____

Reviewer: _____

Date: _____

I.   Content — Graphics, Text, Examples

Are the examples, graphics, and text **technically correct**? Yes ❑   No ❑
If No, describe what is needed to make them technically correct:

_____

Are the examples, graphics, and text appropriate for the **learner level**?
Yes ❑   No ❑
Comments _____

Are the examples, graphics, and text **appropriate for the customer**?
Yes ❑   No ❑
Comments _____

Is the text grammatically correct?   Yes ❑   No ❑   NA ❑
If NO, describe what is needed to make it **grammatically correct**:

_____

Is the text **spelled correctly**?   Yes ❑   No ❑   NA ❑
If No, list the misspellings:

_____

II.   Controls and Navigation

Do all the controls (buttons, hotspots, pull-down menus, icons) work?
Yes ❑   No ❑
Comments _____

Are the controls' design style consistent with interface and their functionality?
Yes ❑   No ❑
Comments _____

Do the controls clearly indicate their functionality?
Yes ❑   No ❑
Comments _____

Are the icons based on common, generally understood symbols?
Yes ❑   No ❑
Comments _____

Are the controls available from the keyboard and the mouse?
Yes ❑   No ❑
Comments _____

Is the placement of the controls consistent, logical, and easily located?
Yes ❑   No ❑
Comments _____

Are the user directions clear, logical, and consistent?
Yes ❑   No ❑
Comments _____

Is an Escape provided where needed (e.g., during lengthy segments)?
Yes ❑   No ❑
Comments _____

III.   Aesthetics

Is the screen layout consistent in terms of art style, color scheme, fonts, etc.?
Yes ❑   No ❑
Comments _____

Do the graphics add to the visual design and facilitate the instructions?
Yes ❑   No ❑
Comments _____

Do the graphics provide the appropriate amount of sophistication for the
     learning?
Yes ❑   No ❑
Comments _____

Does the conceptual flow go from top to bottom and left to right?
Yes ❑   No ❑
Comments _____

Is the amount of text sufficient without creating screen clutter?
Yes ❑   No ❑
Comments _____

Is the layout consistent with previous and next screens without abrupt changes?
Yes ❑   No ❑
Comments _____

IV. Learning Objectives

Are the learning objectives apparent?
Yes ❑   No ❑
Comments _____

Is there sufficient instruction to meet the learning objectives?
Yes ❑   No ❑
Comments _____

Are reviews or self-checks provided?
Yes ❑   No ❑
Comments _____

About the Authors

Anne-Marie Armstrong and her husband Terry raised three children before she decided on a career in instructional design. She received her PhD in Instructional Design and Development from the University of South Alabama, Mobile, Alabama, in 1998. She spent several years on the Gulf Coast working on various design projects for the US Navy. Later she switched to Florida's Atlantic Coast and worked on a multimedia supervisor course that is used by the Federal Aviation Agency. Following this she headed north where she was an Instructional Designer and Training Manager for Raytheon and Lucent. After a brief fling in the world of telecomm, Dr. Armstrong now consults for the Government Printing Office in Washington, DC. She likes to draw, garden, and design Web-based presentations and courses. She is presently taking courses in museum studies at George Washington University. At press time, she was hoping to put her new-found knowledge together with her instructional design skills while working for the Smithsonian Institute for the summer of 2003.

*   *   *   *

Bruce Aaron is Chief Evaluator at Accenture, USA, joining the company in 1998 after several years as an Educational Program Evaluator for a large Florida school district. He received his MA in School Psychology and PhD with specialization in Educational Measurement and Evaluation from the University of South Florida. Dr. Aaron has authored and presented numerous papers at state, regional, and international professional conferences on topics including collaborative learning and decision-making systems, criterion-referenced assessment and item analysis, statistical analysis of single-subject data, use of randomization tests, effect sizes indices, multiple regression techniques, identification of giftedness, discrimination of student achievement profiles, and evaluation of drug education programs.

Peter Arashiro is an Instructional Designer with the Michigan Virtual University, USA. His primary responsibilities include evaluating online courses, instructional design consulting, and faculty development training. He is also the Coordinator and an Instructor for MVU's Online Instructor Training program. Prior to coming to Michigan Virtual University, Mr. Arashiro was an Instructional Designer at Lansing Community College, where he assisted in the development of their "Virtual College" and also developed instructional and information management systems. He received his MS in Instructional and Performance Technology and a BA in Music/Business from Boise State University.

Terry R. Armstrong is an Independent Organization Development and Training Consultant living in Washington, DC. For six years he was Director of Organization Development and Training at a Fortune 100 company where he was responsible for all aspects of corporate-wide training and development. Besides being a consultant, he has been a Professor of Management at the University of West Florida in Pensacola and a General Manager in corporations and academia. He loves sailing and "playing" with his ham radio and other electronic technology.

Mary F. (Frankie) Bratton-Jeffery is an Instructional Systems Specialist for the Educational and Training Strategies (ETS) Division of the Naval Education and Training Command. Dr. Bratton-Jeffery's area of expertise lies in the practical application of cognitive learning theories, adult learning and motivation, performance improvement, and large-scale systems design. She received her doctorate from the University of South Alabama in Instructional Design and Development, and is an Adjunct Professor in the College of Education. She holds master's and bachelor's degrees from the University of Kentucky in Secondary Education. She also writes and provides training in the areas of women's issues in business and executive communications.

Neil Carrick is an Independent E-Learning and Knowledge Management Consultant based in Dublin, Ireland. He has designed numerous e-learning solutions for manufacturing industry, corporate business, and for the Irish secondary schools curriculum. Educated in Britain and the United States, he has taught at Trinity College Dublin and the University of Edinburgh. His research interests include learning theory, the work of Vygotsky, and twentieth-century Russian literature, thought, and culture. He can be contacted at carrickn@gofree.indigo.ie.

Geraldine Clarebout graduated in 1998 in Educational Sciences. At present she works as a Research Assistant at the Center for Instructional Psychology and Technology of the University of Leuven, Belgium. Her main research interests are educational technology and instructional design. She has been working on projects dealing with the influence of different support models, the evaluation of computer-based programs, and students' and teachers' instructional conceptions. Currently she is working on her PhD, studying how the (adequate) use of support tools can be encouraged.

John Lew Cox earned a BS in Mechanical Engineering from New Mexico State University and an MSE and PhD in Industrial Engineering from Arizona State University, concentrating in Information Systems. He has industrial experience with companies such as Texas Instruments and Motorola, primarily in information systems within manufacturing operations. In addition, he has academic experience as both Professor and Administrator with the University of West Florida and the University of Arkansas. Dr. Cox is currently Professor and Chairman of Management and Management Information Systems at the University of West Florida, USA, with teaching duties in the MBA program, and research interests in implementation of technology in organizations.

Vassilios Dagdilelis is currently an Assistant Professor in the Department of Educational and Social Policy at the University of Macedonia in Thessaloniki, Greece. Dr. Dagdilelis received a BSc in Mathematics (1976) from Aristotle University of Thessaloniki, a Didactique des disciplines scientifiques (DEA) (1986) from Universite Joseph Fourrier, and a PhD from the Department of Applied Informatics from the University of Macedonia (1996). Dr. Dagdilelis's research interests include: using computers in education and training, and didactics of informatics. He has 15 years of mathematical teaching experience in secondary education and six years of teaching experience at the university level with Introduction to Computer Science, and Using Computers in Education and Training.

David B. Dawson is the Chief Technologist of the College of Professional Studies, University of West Florida, USA, and holds an MA in Communications from the University of Michigan (1990) and a BA in Radio-TV-Film from Florida Atlantic University (1976). Mr. Dawson develops working methods for integrating advanced Web technologies into collaborative instructional design and development processes for online professional development and performance support projects. His research interest and dissertation work is in the area of developing theory-grounded instructional design support tools for integration into reusable learning object database-driven instructional delivery systems. He is also interested in improving the efficiency and effectiveness of expert knowledge elicitation and documentation through the use of database-driven Web interfaces. He is Coordinator of the Division of Engineering and Computer Technology's bachelor's programs. He develops and teaches both online and traditional courses for the Instructional Technology programs. He has worked with institutional support of the Interactive Distributed Learning Laboratory, which includes digital video network teleconferencing facilities for which he has designed and implemented three generations. He provides expertise in network technologies and digital media production, including digital video capture, editing and streaming delivery systems, digital image processing, and manipulation. He served as Director of UWF's Instructional Media Center for 10 years.

Jan Elen first studied to become a secondary school teacher in mathematics, physics, and chemistry. In 1986 he graduated in Educational Sciences. He promoted in 1993 the transition from description to prescription in instructional design. He is currently the Academic Chair of the Educational Support Office of the University of Leuven, Belgium. As a Professor he is linked to the Faculty of Psychology and Educational Sciences. He teaches courses on instructional design and general didactics. In his research in the field of educational technology, he focuses on optimizing the impact of instructional interventions.

Noel Estabrook is currently responsible for the design and instructional integrity of online courses produced by MVU. He has almost 15 years of teaching experience at all levels and has been building and developing online courses, knowledge management systems, and websites for education, industry, and government for almost 10 years. Author of a dozen books on Internet usage and design for Macmillan Publishing, he has spoken at national conferences and consulted on numerous projects designed to implement both technology and education. Mr. Estabrook earned a bachelor's in Secondary Education and a master's in Instructional Design and Technology from Michigan State University, and served on MSU's faculty for almost eight years before joining MVU.

Elizabeth Hanlis is an experienced Instructional Designer with a master's in Instructional Technology and strong technical skills in curriculum design, authoring, and production of multimedia/Web-based courseware for both industry and post-secondary institutions. Her formal education and experience include a Bachelor's in Education and Classroom Instruction, especially in the area of second language learning. She is skilled at providing effective instruction, coordinating training and distributed learning programs, and converting curriculum for online delivery through sound instructional design practices. Ms. Hanlis possesses proven experience and knowledge of learning and communication technologies. She offers solid and diverse skills in project management, research, evaluation, and dissemination of knowledge related to learning technologies.

Arthur B. Jeffery is an Assistant Professor in the Mitchell College of Business at the University of South Alabama, USA. He has a PhD in Instructional Systems Design from the University of South Alabama, an MBA from Kansas University, and an MSSM from the University of Southern California. Dr. Jeffery teaches in the areas of quality management and quantitative business methods. As an Army officer, he served in numerous operational command assignments, and in the latter part of his career served as an operations research and systems analyst in the training and simulation areas. Dr. Jeffery's research interests are quality improvement in training settings, team performance, and human performance technology.

Hee Kap Lee is a Research Associate with the Education and Training Resources Office, School of Education, Indiana University, USA. He has been involved in several performance improvement projects in school and business settings. Prior to his doctoral studies at Indiana University, he was a Manager of the LG-Caltex Oil Company in Korea. Dr. Lee may be contacted at heelee@indiana.edu.

Joost Lowyck is a Professor at the University of Leuven (Belgium) where he teaches courses in educational technology and corporate training design. He is the head of the University Institute for Teachers and Co-Director of the Center for Instructional Psychology and Technology. His main research areas are educational technology, instructional design, and corporate training design. He has been involved in different European research projects.

Pam T. Northrup investigates how technology can be used for teaching and learning. She led the development efforts of STEPS (Support for Teachers Enhancing Performance in Schools), a Web-based performance support tool used to help Florida's teachers plan for school reform. She has also been involved in the development of a standards-based performance support tool: QuickScience. Within this work, she is developing a Web-based EPSS using the SCORM framework that allows teachers to drill down into pre-populated databases aligned to National and State Science Standards, and customize content for Web-based science in the classroom. Her work in Online Professional Development (OPD) has led to the creation of three online in-service workshops for teachers. She was Co-Developer of UWF's first online program, a Master's in Instructional Technology; she wrote the University's strategic plan for distributed learning. She writes frequently of interaction's role in online learning and is currently developing a framework for reusable learning objects for increasing the efficiency of online learning. She consults regularly with school districts, industry, and the Navy. She is an active member of the NW Florida Distributed Learning Consortium. Her primary interests include technology integration, distributed learning, and how EPSS can improve performance.

Over the past 20 years, **Mark Notess** has held a variety of positions in higher education and high-tech industry, including work in software development and user-centered design at Hewlett-Packard and e-learning at both Agilent Technologies and UNext. Mr. Notess holds master's degrees in Education and Computer Science from Virginia Tech, and is pursuing a doctorate in Indiana University's Instructional Systems Technology Program. Currently, he works as a Usability Specialist on a digital music library research grant (Variations2) at Indiana University, USA, where he also teaches human-computer interaction. His main interest is in designing innovative, humane learning technology.

James A. Pershing is an Associate Professor in the School of Education's Department of Instructional Systems Technology, and Director of Education and Training Resources at Indiana University, USA. Currently, he is Editor-in-Chief of ISPI's *Performance Improvement* journal. His research interests are performance improvement in corporate and public agencies, planning and evaluating employee-related education, project management, and cost-benefit analysis. Dr. Pershing may be contacted at pershin@indiana.edu.

Karen L. Rasmussen consults in the design and development of a variety of products, including Webquests for QuickScience, a tool for teachers, supporting science and technology initiatives. She was Co-Designer and Co-Developer of UWF's first online program, a Master's in Instructional Technology, which, in its initial cohort had a retention rate of 96%. She has worked in the creation of technology-rich, authentic learning environments for Florida's PK-12 students. She collaborates extensively in the area of Online Professional Development, including OPDs for Florida's teachers in technology integration, reading, and assessment and curriculum alignment. She has conducted hundreds of training sessions related to technology. Her primary interests lie in the areas of technology integration, online support systems, and the design and development of Web-based learning environments; she publishes in the areas of competencies for instructional designers, assessment and student performance for online expeditions, supporting learners in distance environments through support systems and mentors, design and development of learning communities, and distance learning programs.

Jillian Rickertt has 25 years of IT experience, coupled with 12 years training experience encompassing delivery and design. She has tertiary qualifications in IT and also in Adult Education. She specializes in telecommunications training and designs, and delivers training for both telecommunications Customer Service Representatives and technical software engineers who configure and maintain the system. She travels extensively, designing and delivering training to a large variety of Asian cultures. Ms. Rickertt is an advocate of authenticity in the training field, and firmly believes that skills and knowledge gained in the training environment should accurately reflect the nature of the tasks that the trainee is expected to perform on the job.

Rachael Sheldrick is an Evaluator with Accenture's Performance Measurement team (USA) and joined the company in 2000. She received her MA in Psychology from the University of Chicago and worked at the National Opinion Research Center while earning her degree. She has been responsible for developing course and faculty evaluations, and has presented the results of evaluation analyses at local measurement society meetings. When she's not surfing the rivers in northern Wisconsin or spending hours trapped in cross-country car trips, she is working on a comprehensive testing and evaluation strategy for Accenture's core learning program.

Jef Van den Ende obtained his Medical Degree from the University of Leuven, Belgium. He specialized in Internal Medicine at the same university and in Tropical Medicine at the Institute of Tropical Medicine in Antwerp. In 1996 he wrote his PhD on Imported Malaria at the University of Amsterdam. He worked as a Tropical Doctor in Dungu, Congo, for six years. He became Associate Professor in Tropical Medicine at the Institute of Tropical Medicine, Antwerp, Belgium, in 1998. In 2000 he went on sabbatical leave in Kigali, Rwanda.

Erwin Van den Enden obtained his Medical Degree in 1980 from the University of Antwerp, Belgium. He worked for several years in rural hospitals in Sri Lanka and Zimbabwe, and was a World Health Organization Consultant during the Ebola epidemic in 1995 in Zaire, Congo. He is at present working as a Clinician at the Institute of Tropical Medicine, Antwerp. He is also a Lecturer of Tropical Medicine in Antwerp and Utrecht, The Netherlands.

Tad Waddington is the Director of Performance Measurement at Accenture, USA. After earning his PhD in Measurement, Evaluation, and Statistical Analysis from the University of Chicago's Department of Education in 1995, he worked for the Gallup Organization, where he was a Research Director until joining Accenture in 1997. He also has a BA in Psychology from Arizona State University, and an MA in the History of Chinese Religions from the University of Chicago. He is fluent in Chinese and served as a translator, interpreter, and writer in Taiwan prior to pursuing his doctoral studies. Dr. Waddington has solved the statistical, measurement, sampling, and other quantitative problems of scores of organizations. He has several hundred publications on such topics as sloths, ancient Chinese writing, a mathematical model of understanding, travels in the Soviet Union, the falling price of husbands, the origin of the clock, and how to use meta-analysis to inform policy decisions.

Index

diagnostic reasoning skills 120
discrete skills and knowledge 170

E

e-learning for adults 10
educational goals 120
educational software 75
electronic instruction 105
electronic learning 108
electronic learning object (ELO) 191
end users 185
evaluation model 140
Excel pivot tables 154
expert systems 120
external sources 202

F

felt needs 4
Florida Comprehensive Assessment
    Test (FCAT) 186
flow model 78
flowchart 40

G

general systems model 222
Ghantt chart 57
guerilla evaluation 136
guerilla tactics 137

H

higher education 69
higher education organizations 202
human performance requirements 141
human resource development (HRD)
    138

I

inbound logistics 224
individual compatible 5
individual incompatible 5
information and communication tech-
    nologies (ICTs) 201
instructional design models 33, 218
instructional designers 75

instructional development (ID) 1
instructional message 38
instructional objective 36
instructional strategies 37, 105
instructional system 202
instructional systems design 202
instructional technology 166
instructor-led training 153
integrated design 218
integrated training 218
internal structure 202
Internet 70
intrinsic needs 3
item bank 146
item response theory (IRT) 145
item response theory analysis 153

J

just in time 54

K

knowledge silos 185
knowledge workers 3

L

learner 10
learner analysis 2
learner control 11
learner-centered 11
learning environment 105
learning object 161
learning objects standards committee
    186
learning strategy 202
learning types 106
level of the concerns 5

M

marketing and sales 224
Michigan Virtual University 161

O

objective 108
off-the-shelf courseware 12

International Journal of Distance Education Technologies (JDET)

NEW!   NEW!

The International Source for Technological Advances in Distance Education

ISSN: 1539-3100
eISSN: 1539-3119

Subscription: Annual fee per volume (4 issues):
Individual US $85
Institutional US $185

Editors: Shi Kuo Chang
University of Pittsburgh, USA

Timothy K. Shih
Tamkang University, Taiwan

Mission

The *International Journal of Distance Education Technologies* (**JDET**) publishes original research articles of distance education four issues per year. **JDET** is a primary forum for researchers and practitioners to disseminate practical solutions to the automation of open and distance learning. The journal is targeted to academic researchers and engineers who work with distance learning programs and software systems, as well as general participants of distance education.

Coverage

Discussions of computational methods, algorithms, implemented prototype systems, and applications of open and distance learning are the focuses of this publication. Practical experiences and surveys of using distance learning systems are also welcome. Distance education technologies published in **JDET** will be divided into three categories, **Communication Technologies, Intelligent Technologies, and Educational Technologies**: new network infrastructures, real-time protocols, broadband and wireless communication tools, quality-of services issues, multimedia streaming technology, distributed systems, mobile systems, multimedia synchronization controls, intelligent tutoring, individualized distance learning, neural network or statistical approaches to behavior analysis, automatic FAQ reply methods, copyright protection and authentification mechanisms, practical and new learning models, automatic assessment methods, effective and efficient authoring systems, and other issues of distance education.

For subscription information, contact:

Idea Group Publishing
701 E Chocolate Ave., Suite 200
Hershey PA 17033-1240, USA
cust@idea-group.com
URL: www.idea-group.com

For paper submission information:

Dr. Timothy Shih
Tamkang University, Taiwan
tshih@cs.tku.edu.tw